Spelling and Writing Words

Studies in Writing

VOLUME 39

The series was founded by Gert Rijlaarsdam and Eric Espéret in 1994. It was pursued
by Gert Rijlaarsdam until 2014. Since its inception in 1994 it has become one of the
most influential book series in the field of writing research.

The titles published in this series are listed at *brill.com/siw*

Spelling and Writing Words

Theoretical and Methodological Advances

Edited by

Cyril Perret
Thierry Olive

BRILL

LEIDEN | BOSTON

Library of Congress Cataloging-in-Publication Data

Names: Perret, Cyril, editor. | Olive, Thierry, editor.
Title: Spelling and writing words : theoretical and methodological advances /
    edited by Cyril Perret, Thierry Olive.
Description: Leiden ; Boston : Brill, [2019] | Series: Studies in writing ; Volume 39 |
    Includes bibliographical references and index.
Identifiers: LCCN 2018061471 (print) | LCCN 2019002704 (ebook) |
    ISBN 9789004394988 (ebook) | ISBN 9789004391871 (hardback : alk. paper)
Subjects: LCSH: Language and languages–Orthography and spelling. | Written
    communication.
Classification: LCC P240.2 (ebook) | LCC P240.2 .S69 2019 (print) | DDC 411–dc23
LC record available at https://lccn.loc.gov/2018061471

Typeface for the Latin, Greek, and Cyrillic scripts: "Brill". See and download: brill.com/brill-typeface.

ISSN 1572-6304
ISBN 978-90-04-39187-1 (hardback)
ISBN 978-90-04-39498-8 (e-book)

Printed by Printforce, the Netherlands

Contents

PART 1
Theoretical and Empirical Section

PART 2
Methodological Section

PART 3
Conclusion

Figures and Tables

Figures

Tables

Notes on Contributors

Olivia Afonso
is an Early Career Research Fellow at the Department of Psychology, Health and Professional Development of Oxford Brookes University. She investigates the cognitive processes involved in spelling and handwriting in adults and children, with a special focus on how phonological and orthographic information interact during written production. Her most recent research interests include the nature of spelling difficulties in specific learning disorders, the representation of letter identity and position in writing and the impact of linguistic processes on handwriting movements. E-mail: afonso.o@brookes.ac.uk

Carlos J. Álvarez
is Professor of Psychology at the University of La Laguna. He works in the Cognitive Psychology Department and in the University Institute of Neuroscience (IUNE). His research in experimental psychology and cognitive neuroscience has focused on visual word recognition and written word production, in adults as well as in children with (and without) learning difficulties. Second language acquisition and bilingualism have also been topics of his research. These investigations have been carried out in collaboration with scientists from other American, Australian and European countries. E-mail: calvarez@ull.edu.es

Anna Barnett
is a Professor of Psychology at Oxford Brookes University, UK. Her research on handwriting has included surveys of policy and practice in primary schools and examinations of handwriting in individuals with Developmental Coordination Disorder (DCD) and dyslexia. She has also developed standardised assessment tools to measure handwriting speed (the Detailed Assessment of Speed of Handwriting, DASH), handwriting legibility (the Handwriting Legibility Scale, HLS) and general motor competence (the Movement ABC-2). Another strand of her research focuses more specifically on aspects of DCD—including diagnosis and assessment of children and adults with this condition. E-mail: abarnett@brookes.ac.uk

Patrick Bonin
is full Professor of cognitive psychology at Université de Bourgogne Franche-Comté (LEAD-CNRS UMR5022). He has been nominated at the Institut Universitaire de France (IUF senior member 2010–2015). He is working on written/spoken production, psycholinguistic norms and episodic memory within an evolutionary psychology perspective. E-mail: Patrick.Bonin@u-bourgogne.fr

Vince Connelly

is Professor of Psychology at Oxford Brookes University. His research involves studying children and adults including those diagnosed with dyslexia or specific language disorders. who have difficulty with various aspects of writing such as spelling or handwriting. Working with colleagues at Oxford Brookes, University College London and elsewhere, he has published a wide range of articles contributing to our understanding of struggling writers. He has also worked with teachers and educators in order to investigate the best ways to help struggling writers overcome their difficulties. E-mail: vconnelly@brookes.ac.uk

Markus L. Damian

is a Professor of psychology of language at the University of Bristol, United Kingdom. His research focusses the cognitive and neural basis of spoken as well as written language processing, with a particular emphasis on lexical and phonological/orthographic retrieval. His recent work has focussed on comparisons between Western and non-Western (i.e., Chinese) language production, and involves behavioural, encephalographic and computational approaches. E-mail: m.damian@bristol.ac.uk

Michel Fayol

is Emeritus Professor at the Laboratoire de Psychologie Sociale et Cognitive (LAPSCO CNRS) at Clermont Auvergne University. His research in developmental and educational psychology investigates the learning and use of literacy and numeracy in typical people, children as well as adults. More specifically, he is interested in the way children and adults manage in real time the numerous cognitive processes (handwriting, spelling, translating, planning) involved in composing texts and in problem-solving. E-mail: michel.fayol@uca.fr

Silvain Gerber

works as a statistician at the Centre National de la Recherche Scientifique (CNRS). He works in the GIPSA-lab, which is a joint research unit of the University of Grenoble Alpes and the CNRS. He supervises the design of te experiments and carries out the data analysis. E-mail: silvain.gerber@gipsa-lab .grenoble-inp.fr

Sonia Kandel

is a full Professor in cognitive science at the University of Grenoble Alpes. She carries out her research at the GIPSA-lab (CNRS UMR 5216). Her research focuses on the normal and pathological processes of writing acquisition, both the orthographic and graphomotor aspects. E-mail: Sonia.kandel@univ -grenoble-alpes.fr

Alain Méot

is Assistant Professor in statistics in psychology at Université Clermont Auvergne (LAPSCO-CNRS UMR6024). He is working on written/spoken production, psycholinguistic norms and episodic memory within an evolutionary psychology perspective. E-mail: alain.meot@uca.fr

Marion Nys

PhD, is a neuropsychologist and research engineer at MC2 Lab, at the University Paris Descartes. Her main research investigates memory, spatial cognition, statistical learning and spelling acquisition in children and adults. E-mail: nys.marion@gmail.com

Thierry Olive

is Senior Research Scientist at the Centre National de la Recherche Scientifique (CNRS, France). He works in the Center for Research on Cognition and Learning, a joint unit of the Université de Poitiers and of the CNRS. His research in experimental psychology investigates writing and learning to write in typical writers, as well as in writers with language or learning difficulties. More specifically, he analyses regulation of the cognitive processes involved in writing, their relation with working memory as well as the role of emotions in writing and the impact of writing tools. E-mail: thierry.olive@univ-poitiers.fr

Sébastien Pacton

is Professor of Developmental Cognitive Psychology at the University Paris Descartes. He works in the MC2 Lab in Paris and he is a member of the LABEX EFL (ANR-10-LABX-0083). His main research interests include implicit statistical learning mechanisms and their roles in spelling acquisition, with a particular interest for the role of graphotactic and morphological knowledge. E-mail: sebastien.pacton@parisdescartes.fr

Ronald Peereman

PhD, is Research Scientist for the Centre National de la Recherche Scientifique (CNRS, France). He works at the Psychology and Neurocognition laboratory, Grenoble-Alpes University, France. His main research interests include word recognition processes in the visual and auditory modalities, statistical learning in word segmentation in continuous speech, reading and spelling acquisition, and distributional analyses of the orthographic, phonological, and morphological characteristics of the French writing system. E-mail: ronald.peereman@univ-grenoble-alpes.fr

Cyril Perret

is Assistant Professor in psychology at Université de Poitiers (CeRCA-CNRS). He is working on writing in adult and children, psycholinguistic norms and statistical implementation of written processing. He analyses the cognitive processes involved in word writing and their dynamics with behavioral, neurophysiological (EEG) and statistical implementation methods. E-mail: cyril.perret@univ-poitiers.fr

Qingqing Qu

is full Professor of cognitive psychology at department of Psychology, University of Chinese Academy of Sciences (Beijing, China) and member of the Key Laboratory of Behavioral Science at the Institute of Psychology (Chinese Academy of Sciences). She is working on written/spoken production in Chinese. He analyses the cognitive processes involved in word production and their dynamics with behavioral and neurophysiological (EEG) methods. E-mail: quqq@psych.ac.cn

Brenda Rapp

is a Professor in the Department of Cognitive Science at Johns Hopkins University (Baltimore, USA). She is editor-in-chief of the journal Cognitive Neuropsychology and has served on the boards of various scientific societies including the Academy of Aphasia and the Society for the Neurobiology of Language. Her research focuses on understanding the cognitive and neural processes involved in written language, with a particular emphasis on spelling processes and representations, using methods from cognitive neuropsychology, psycholinguistics, neuroimaging and computational modelling. E-mail: brapp1@jhu.edu

Marie-Josèphe Tainturier

is Senior Lecturer in the School of Psychology at Bangor University, UK. She is also the director of the Bilingualism Research Centre at Bangor University. Her research investigates the cognitive and neural mechanisms that underlie language processing in children and adults with or without neurological conditions, with a particular focus on reading and writing disorders, neuropsychological assessment and rehabilitation, and bilingualism. E-mail: m.j.tainturier@bangor.ac.uk

Laurence Séraphin-Thibon

just finished her PhD at the Grenoble-Alpes University (France) under the supervision of Sonia Kandel. The topic of her thesis in cognitive science investigated the elaboration of motor programs in handwriting for children from ages 6 to 10. More specifically, she studied how the motor programs for letter production develop during handwriting acquisition as well as the specific processes involved in rotation and pointing movements. E-mail: Laurence.thibon@orange.fr

Yannick Wamain
is lecturer at the University of Lille. He works in the Cognitive and Affective Sciences Laboratory (SCALab), a joint unit of the University of Lille and of the Centre National de la Recherche Scientifique (CNRS), where he is a member of the Action, Vision and Learning Team. His research in experimental psychology investigates the relation between Perception and Action with behavioral and neurophysiological paradigm. More specifically, he studies the impact of motor knowledge on visual perception of stimuli implying biological motion: like manipulable objects and/or handwritten letters. E-mail: yannick.wamain@univ-lille.fr

CHAPTER 1

Writing Words: a Brief Introduction

Cyril Perret and Thierry Olive

In modern societies, writing is a fundamental skill for individual, professional and personal development. As a component of literacy, skilled writing is more than merely the ability to produce written language; it is an emancipation tool, a potential for autonomy in society, a substantive freedom that gives the individual power to transform and exercise her or his choices (Nussbaum, 2011; Sen, 1999). In addition, technological changes have led us to reconsider writing in the wider context of the various digital tools that are now available (paper and pen, keyboard, computer monitors, touch keyboard, smartphones, tablets), and the new types of written communication (sms, blogs, chat, etc.). Undoubtedly, the psychological mechanisms that support the development of writing skills deserve to be further understood.

At first glance, it may appear surprising to focus on a language unit, the word, which is rarely produced as such. Why study isolated words, while in the majority of cases writers engage in writing tasks that require the combining of words in sentences and paragraphs in order to compose texts? Actually, the production of isolated words is not so rare: we often write down words when preparing lists of purchases; students and professionals also write down single words when they take notes, prepare for exams, and so on. Furthermore, words are often the support underpinning the teaching of writing; for instance, lexical spelling is learned by producing isolated words. Finally, words are the bricks of language: even a short sentence is made up of words. Knowing how their linguistic characteristics (frequency, length, age of acquisition, orthographic consistency, etc.) affect their processing is fundamental for better understanding the processing that allows words to be combined in larger units of language, as in texts (for an example, see Maggio, Lété, Chenu, Jisa, & Fayol, 2012). In sum, investigating the mental processes that lead to select words with the correct spelling deepens our understanding of one of the basic, lexical writing skills.

Within this framework, this volume aims to present a comprehensive state-of-the art of research on written word production. Each chapter presents a central issue and discusses the latest scientific advances in research on word production and spelling processes. In this introductory chapter, we present a short synopsis of the research on the written production of isolated words. We begin by briefly introducing the psychological processes, structures and levels of rep-

© KONINKLIJKE BRILL NV, LEIDEN, 2019 | DOI:10.1163/9789004394988_002

resentation that the cognitive system engages for producing written words (Section 1). Next, we briefly introduce the main methods and tasks that are used to investigate the writing of isolated words: the picture-naming task, the spelling-to-dictation task and copying tasks (Section 2). We then present two central research questions that are addressed (Section 3): the role of phonological codes for accessing orthographic information (Section 3.1), and the articulation of central and peripheral levels of processing (Section 3.2). Finally, we conclude this chapter by introducing the 12 chapters that make up this volume (Section 4).

1   Psychological Processes Involved in Writing Isolated Words

It is generally accepted that the writing down of an isolated word involves two major stages of processing: central and peripheral processes. This distinction is derived from cognitive neuropsychology work (e.g., Tainturier & Rapp, 2001) and has recently received support from brain imaging work suggesting a neuroanatomical distinction between the central and peripheral levels (e.g., Planton, Jucla, Roux, & Demonet, 2013; Purcell, Turkeltaub, Eden, & Rapp, 2011).

Central processes in written word production refer to cognitive mechanisms for retrieving orthographic information about the word being produced from long-term memory. The orthographic representation that results from these central processes is then stored in the graphemic buffer that keeps orthographic information active during peripheral processing. Next, a set of peripheral processes translates the abstract language codes into a set of motor commands directly usable by the neuromuscular system to perform the graphical trace. Whatever the writing medium (pen or keyboard), it is generally accepted that transcribing a word involves at least two levels of processing (e.g., Ellis, 1988; Rumelhart & Normal, 1982; van Galen, 1991). At first, from the abstract language codes (e.g., the letter, the grapheme, etc.) a motor pattern or engram is recovered in motor memory. Second, the gestures allowing the execution of the different engrams are planned and executed. It is worth noting that some authors posit an intermediate stage, during which allographic information (style: e.g., cursive versus script; size; case: upper or lower case) is encoded (van Galen, 1991).

Access to the orthographic representation can be achieved in two ways. The first, the sub-lexical or Phoneme-Grapheme Conversion (PGC) pathway is designed as a sequential procedure, operating from left to right, and is based on the frequencies of association between phonemes and graphemes. In the second, the lexical pathway retrieves lexical/orthographic representations stored in long-term memory. This lexical pathway can itself be subdivided into two: in the first, the phonological representation is directly applied to an orthographic representation in an orthographic lexicon; the second is an indirect route whereby a semantic representation plays the role of mediator between phonological and orthographic representations. Both these processing pathways operate in parallel but at different speeds. The lexical pathway is dependent on lexical (e.g., word frequency, etc.) while the sub-lexical pathway is influenced by sub-lexical characteristics (e.g., the frequency of phonemic grapheme associations, etc.).

This cognitive architecture makes it possible to account for many results in the literature. For example, it has been shown that the presence of an irregularity / inconsistency slows down the speed of processing a word (e.g., Bonin, Peereman, & Fayol, 2001; Kandel & Perret, 2015a; Roux, McKeef, Grosjacques, Afonso, & Kandel, 2013). This can be explained by the need to manage the conflict between different graphemes for the same phoneme from lexical and sub-lexical pathways. For example, when writing the word chorus (kɔʁys) in French, the lexical way would propose the "ch" grapheme for the (k) phoneme. However, the sub-lexical pathway would propose the "c" grapheme which is the more frequent in French for representing (k). The presence of alternative forms, however, requires time-demanding selection processes. Some studies have examined the dynamics of these different processing pathways. For example, Bonin, Roux, Barry, and Cannell (2012) revealed a different implication of the lexical pathway depending on the task demands: dictation of a word leads participants to prioritise the sub-lexical pathway, whereas a conceptually driven writing task mainly involves the lexical pathway.

2   Methods for Studying Written Word Production

Research on the written production of isolated words can be based on analyses of the written products, and particularly on the errors that are present in *corpora* when produced by typical writers or by patients suffering from brain injuries. Another approach relies on tasks designed to elicit levels of representation engaged in writing and on measures collected as these tasks are performed. This aims to assess the functional characteristics of the cognitive mechanisms involved in writing.

2.1   *The Written Products: Analysing Errors*
The earliest studies of isolated word production were inspired by the error analyses developed in speaking research (e.g., Fromkin, 1971; Shattuck-Hufnagel,

1979). Thus, from the end of the 1970s authors have analysed the spontaneous errors that appear in corpora of texts written by typical writers (e.g., Berg, 2002; Ellis, 1979). These early analyses of patterns of errors have allowed the different levels of representations involved in the written production of isolated words to be described (e.g., Ellis, 1982, 1988; van Galen, 1991). However, such analyses are limited: for instance, the number and nature of the errors that are collected and analysed cannot be controlled and depend on the material collected, which can partly bias the validity of the corpus and therefore any subsequent observations and interpretations (Meyer, 1992).

In parallel, neuropsychologists have focused on the spelling errors of patients with brain damage. The idea is very similar to that previously described for typical writers: an error is not a random phenomenon and is typologically constrained by cognitive functioning. The presence of a particular brain injury has specific repercussions for particular cognitive processes, which should result in errors specific to the damaged neural networks (e.g., Broca, 1861; Exner, 1881; Luria, 1966). Accordingly, knowledge of the anatomical location of the cognitive processing allows assumptions to be made about the cognitive functions affected by an injury. Applying this perspective, Caramazza and Miceli (1990) studied a patient (LB) with impaired graphemic buffer. LB was subsequently enrolled in studies investigating the linguistic structure of representations stored in the graphemic buffer. In this case, and in contrast with corpus analyses, the type and frequency of errors that LB produced resulted from experimental manipulation. It should be noted that, to our knowledge, no study has used experimental methods to create errors in typical participants.[1]

Neuropsychological observations of errors are at the origin of the first theoretical propositions on the cognitive processes and structures involved in the written production of words. They constitute a common base for all current theoretical propositions (e.g., the macroscopic model of Tainturier & Rapp, 2001), although inference from neuropsychological observations may be limited; it is difficult to draw inferences about a non-injured brain from an injured one. The observed errors may in fact be specific to the affected processes and may not appear with typical functioning. In addition, neuropsychological observations tell us nothing about the dynamics of the writing processes. Real-time methods have been developed precisely to go beyond these limitations by allowing researchers to study how information flows in the writing process.

---

1   Nevertheless, this type of approach has been fruitful, for example in investigating the cognitive processes involved in subject-verb agreement (e.g., Fayol, Huppet, & Largy, 1999; Largy & Fayol, 2001).

2.2   *Real Time Analyses of the Preparation and Production of Written*
       Words

Real-time study of the mental processes involved in the written production of isolated words is based on the postulates of mental chronometry: psychological processes have a duration that can be measured, and changes in duration reflect changes in the nature or complexity of the processing required to complete a writing task (Cattell, 1886). Accordingly, the time lapse between presentation of the stimulus triggering word production and the start of writing should provide information on the types of representation that are activated and the time course of their processing.

Mental chronometry relies on three main types of task depending on the nature of the stimulus: oral in spelling-to-dictation, visual with picture naming, and reading in copying tasks. In picture-naming tasks, participants have to write down the name of a pictured object as soon as it is presented. One assumption is that picture naming mobilises the same processes that are involved in conceptually-driven word production (Bock & Levelt, 1994). Certainly, the lexical pathway appears to be emphasised in this task (Bonin, Méot, Lagarrigue, & Roux, 2015). In spelling-to-dictation, single words are dictated to participants which they have to write down as soon as they hear them. During spelling processes, both the lexical and sub-lexical and the lexical pathways are mobilised (Bonin et al., 2015; Rapp, Epstein, & Tainturier, 2002). In copying tasks, writers read words that they have to copy as soon as they are presented. Again, both the lexical and the sub-lexical pathways are mobilised during the spelling processes (Bonin et al., 2015; Kandel, Lassus-Sangosse, Grosjacques, & Perret, 2018). These tasks can also be used to create interference with, or to prime, mental representations (e.g., Bonin & Fayol, 2000). In this case, the target stimulus is combined with a distractor and the participant's task is to name the target stimulus while ignoring the distractor. The distractor may either prime or interfere with naming, respectively creating either a facilitation or an interference effect on the latencies. It is also possible to manipulate the interval between the presentation of the distractor and that of the target stimulus in order to examine when mental representations are activated.

In these tasks, the variable that has received most attention is latency: the time separating the start of the presentation of a word or picture and the first contact of the pen on a tablet (or key press on a keyboard). However, because cognitive processing may also occur during writing (see section 3.2), analyses of latencies have recently been coupled with analyses of writing fluency.

Writing fluency can be assessed by measuring the time between producing each letter (inter-letter interval, ILI) that makes up a word. However, in this case participants must use a particular, unnatural style of handwriting that allows for distinct letter boundaries (e.g., using capital letters, Kandel, Alvarez, & Vallée, 2006). The generalisability of results obtained with such unnatural handwriting is questionable. On the other hand, using natural handwriting, in lowercase for instance creates other difficulties: for example, with cursive handwriting very few or no boundaries appear between the letters. Studies that require typing instead of handwriting are therefore conducive to ILI analyses, although inter-individual variability in typing skills has to be controlled for, whereas handwriting is automatized in adult writers.

The total duration of word writing has also been used (Delattre, Bonin, & Barry, 2006). However, because words differ in length their duration has to be considered, for example by dividing the duration of a word by the number of its letters. This does not completely solve the problem. A letter is defined in terms of the number of gestures or characteristics it takes to produce it and the number of strokes between letters is not constant. Another solution may therefore be to divide word duration by the number of strokes that make up the word (Kandel & Perret, 2015a, 2015b). The problem persists, however, because the number of strokes of a letter remains, at least for the moment, only theoretically defined (e.g., Meulenbroek & van Galen, 1990) and because the number of strokes a participant actually produces varies. Beyond the difficulties of defining the number of strokes, stroke analysis of cursive writing is difficult to perform because it is necessary to define the beginning and the end of a letter in order to measure its duration.

Writing fluency can also be evaluated by measuring the number of micro-accelerations, or velocity peaks, that occur in completing a written trace (e.g., Kandel & Perret, 2015a, 2015b; Roux et al., 2013). However, measuring velocity peaks faces the same pitfalls as writing duration does: counting the number of velocity peaks that occur during the production of a written unit requires its boundaries to be empirically defined.

3   Two Central Issues in the Research on Written Word Production

Within the research that has been carried out in recent years, two questions concerning the written production of isolated words have been and still are widely discussed. The first concerns the role of phonology when accessing orthographic information. The second concerns the articulation between the central and peripheral levels of processing involved in producing a word. Writing an isolated word requires at least two main steps: accessing the spelling codes and planning the motor gestures needed to trace the letters that make up the word. The articulation of these two levels of processing has been the subject of many recent studies in both children and adults.

3.1   *The Role of Phonology*

Whether phonology intervenes during writing—and if it does, how and when it does—has received considerable attention during more than a century of research. The subjective experience of writing suggests that retrieving the spelling of a word necessitates the preliminary activation of the spoken word. How else to explain that inner voice when writing? It seems, however, that the situation is not so simple. Two main conceptions of the role of phonology in writing can be distinguished.

The *obligatory phonological mediation* posits that writing requires the activation of phonological codes before accessing orthographical codes. Compared with speaking, writing is an evolutionarily recent cultural capacity of humankind. Additionally, children acquire the ability to speak before learning to write. This suggests that writing may depend on speaking, as indicated by experimental findings showing that the pre-activation of phonological codes facilitates writing.

This conception has been challenged by both neuropsychological data and other experimental results. For instance, Rapp Benzing and Caramazza (1997) described a patient who presented with a speaking deficit but no systematic or related orthographic difficulties. This patient had great difficulty naming objects but was able—though not in all cases—to correctly write down their name. Similarly, Roux and Bonin (2012) failed to find phonological priming effects. A second view has therefore been proposed to account for these results, known as *orthographic autonomy*, which suggests that word spelling is activated directly from the semantic system without any phonological activation.

The *orthographic autonomy view* is based on the idea of direct access to lexical orthographic representation from semantic codes without intermediate passage through phonological codes. However, from the results of the literature it is difficult to support a completely autonomous conception, i.e., a conception in which the phonological codes have no influence on retrieval of the orthographic representation. For example, the inconsistency/irregularity effects observed on both latencies (e.g., Bonin et al., 2001) and handwriting duration (e.g., Kandel & Perret, 2015a; Roux et al., 2013) are explained by a conflict between two alternative routes for the graphemic transcription of the same phoneme. An intermediate position is thus currently privileged with autonomous recovery of the orthographic codes by the lexical pathway and influence of the phonology by means of the sub-lexical pathway. Nevertheless, recent studies of non-alphabetic languages such as Chinese highlight difficulties with this conception. If the impact of phonology bypasses the lexical route, how then to account for the fact that these codes influence writing in languages for which the hypothesis of a sub-lexical pathway seems more difficult to sustain? More generally, this raises the question of the universality of written production models.

3.2   Articulating the Central Lexical and Sub-lexical Processes in Handwriting or Typing

A more recent domain of writing research deals with how information flows between levels of processing. Several findings suggest that information cascades in the writing system and, as a consequence, several levels of processing may overlap at a given time (for a review, see Olive, 2014). Information is described as *cascading* because it continuously flows or spreads from central to peripheral processes. In full-cascading models, information automatically flows between levels of processing as soon as a concept is activated (e.g., Dell, 1986; Humphreys, Riddoch, & Quinlan, 1988). In limited-cascading systems, information flows only within a level of representation, as in Levelt, Roelofs, and Meyer (1999)'s model in which information flows only at the lexical level for a single active concept. One advantage of cascading processes is that they allow for flexible overlap of the levels of processing to adapt to the task demands (e.g., Sausset, Lambert, Olive, & Laroque, 2012).

How information cascades from higher- to lower-order writing processes has received particular attention in recent years. For example, Roux and Bonin (2012) showed that two superimposed pictures that shared orthographic and/or phonological characteristics facilitated writing. They concluded that both pictures activated their corresponding concepts at the semantic level and that information cascaded to the orthographical level (see also Bonin et al., 2012). Delattre et al. (2006) showed that spelling processes begin before writing down a word, but that while they are completed prior to execution in the case of regular words they continue during handwriting in the case of irregular words as though they occurred sequentially for each grapheme. Roux et al. (2013) observed interactions between spelling and handwriting suggesting that higher levels of processing are still active during lower level processing. Interestingly, these studies confirm that both latencies and measures of handwriting (or typing) are needed to offer a more complete picture of the dynamics of writing.

Further empirical studies will be required to better understand whether information spreads in limited vs. full cascading in the writing system. At least three issues will need to be addressed. First, at a given level of processing does information cascade within the different processes involved at that level? Second, does information cascade between levels of processing? Finally, how flexible are the writing systems, and which task demands affect the extent of processing overlap? Some answers have already been provided, but more extensive research is still warranted.

4   Presentation of the Volume

Within this framework, the present volume brings together chapters that explore various aspects of written word production. Following this Introduction, the volume opens with a first part that focuses on the main theoretical issues around word production: the relation between written word production and the production of larger units of language; the role of phonology; the implicit learning of spelling through graphotactic regularities; word production in bilingual writers and children with language disorders; and, the role of peripheral handwriting processes in the perception and recognition of letters when reading.

After this introduction, *Markus Damian* provides a comprehensive review of the existing literature on the role of phonology in word production. Adopting a historical and comparative approach, he reviews data ranging from early to modern neuropsychology as well as experimental studies of healthy individuals (e.g., Bonin et al., 2001). While reviewing how different conceptions of the role of phonology contribute to word production, *Markus Damian* also explores the commonalities and differences in handwriting between languages with alphabetic script (with sub-lexical correspondence between print and sound) and those with non-alphabetic scripts (in which such spelling-to-sound correspondence is limited). It is clear from this chapter that phonological processes are involved in writing, but the two questions that remain unanswered are in what condition and when, during the course of writing, is phonology activated?

How do we learn to spell? Although we learn to spell through formal instruction, and a phoneme-to-grapheme conversion procedure is required to correctly spell new and less familiar words, *Sébastien Pacton, Michel Fayol, Marion Nys and Ronald Peereman* remind us that we implicitly acquire knowledge of the graphotactic regularities of our first language, as proven by the typical forms children use for spelling pseudo-words. Of course, such implicit learning takes more importance in opaque languages that do not present univocal phoneme-grapheme relations.

In Chapter 4, *Marie-Josèphe Tainturier* presents a theory of bilingual spelling in alphabetic systems. Multilingualism is common, with more than half of the world's population able to speak more than one language (Grosjean, 2010).

Research on word production must therefore also describe how the characteristics of different languages constrain word spelling. The theory she proposes relies on dual-process models of monolingual spelling and integrates key representational and processing assumptions from research on bilingual spoken word production. Mechanisms are proposed for spelling both familiar and unfamiliar words. In addition, the theory makes specific predictions about spelling performance in bilingual individuals, in particular about the way it may be influenced by interactions between the two languages, by word characteristics and by the degree and type of bilingualism. Experimental evidence supporting this theory, from the spelling performance of healthy and neurologically impaired bilingual adults, is presented.

In the next chapter, *Olivia Afonso, Vincent Connelly and Anna L. Barnett* examine the writing difficulties of children who present with language disorders, particularly Specific Language Impairment, Developmental Dyslexia and Developmental Coordination Disorder. Children with writing difficulties typically have less fluent writing; they introduce more pauses and produce fewer words than healthy writers do. To better understand these difficulties, the authors examined the pattern of writing difficulties experienced by these children and analysed whether or not the difficulties they face come from difficulties with peripheral processes. It is interesting to note that research on young writers with language disorders has rarely been conducted by researchers of word production. Rather, a considerable majority of the research the authors use comes from studies of text composition. Obviously, composing text is a much more cognitively elaborate task than producing an isolated word is, and therefore in such situations the difficulties will be exacerbated. Nevertheless, models of word production should also be able to explain lexical processes in children (and adults) with language disorders.

The role of peripheral processes of handwriting on reading is addressed by *Yannick Wamain*, who investigates how the way in which a person writes a letter affects how he/she reads it. As Wamain stresses, in a society in which numerical tools are ubiquitous the question of changing writing methods from handwriting to numerical is legitimate in order to evaluate the potential risks of such change, in particular on reading decoding skills (see also Longcamp et al., 2008). Grounding his approach in embodied cognition theories (Barsalou, Simmons, Barbey, & Wilson, 2003), he reviews behavioural and neurophysiological studies showing interactions between motor and perceptual processes during the perception of stimuli inducing motion. The findings he presents remind us that writing is a component of literacy, and that research should investigate more deeply how learning to read contributes to learning to write, and vice versa.

Although theoretical considerations are important for a better understanding of word production, advances in knowledge are made through the correct use of experimental and observational methods for gathering data. The second part of this volume therefore focuses on methodological and statistical aspects of research on word production. The four chapters that comprise this section examine individual differences, task differences, and measures of handwriting fluency, stroke segmentation and the use of electroencephalography. Interestingly, all four chapters draw a strong link between theoretical questions and methodological issues.

Patrick Bonin and Alain Méot open this second section by addressing a theoretical and methodological issue: how to investigate individual differences in word production? They focus on findings obtained with picture-naming and spelling-to-dictation tasks, before presenting two studies examining individual differences and task differences in skilled spelling. Overall, the findings of their review support the idea that in order to gain a better understanding of skilled spelling, researchers interested in adult spelling should take individual differences into account. In addition, they highlight that certain tasks may be more relevant than others, as certain psycholinguistic effects are reliably found in some and not others.

Next, *Olivia Afonso and Carlos Alvarez* question the variables that are usually measured in experimental studies of word production. In particular, they examine the interactions between central and peripheral processes and suggest that this is not just a theoretical issue but a methodological one too. Online measures of handwritten responses do indeed support the idea that central processes have an impact on the dynamics of motor performance. Based on this evidence, the number of studies investigating spelling using measures of writing duration is growing considerably. However, it is still unclear how exactly this influence of central processing over motor processing takes place, or even what factors have a significant impact on writing duration. The authors therefore summarise the factors that may have a significant impact and discuss their theoretical and methodological relevance.

As highlighted earlier in this Introduction, measuring writing duration requires letters to be broken down into strokes in order to control for differences in word length that directly influence their duration. *Laurence Séraphin-Thibon, Silvain Gerber and Sonia Kandel* present a study in which they attempt to quantify the variability of handwriting in adults. For this purpose, they asked writers to write out the alphabet and measured the strokes of each letter either according to a model presented on the computer screen or 'spontaneously' as the writers normally wrote them. They showed that individual styles of handwriting affect the number of strokes used to compose certain letters. Interestingly, they further demonstrated that writing using a model of the letter produced less variability than doing so without a model. As they conclude, it would appear that the 'grammar of action' that is learned continues to prevail in adulthood for many letters.

As we have already indicated, latency measurement has proved useful in exploring written word production. Latencies cannot, however, be divided into time windows corresponding to different levels of processing. As a result, research questions that require levels of processing to be isolated in order to test hypotheses require comparisons of situations which either do or do not involve the targeted level of processing. Neuroscientific methods provide investigations techniques that allow the levels of processing elicited during latencies to be better understood. Neurophysiological recording methods such as EEG, fMRI and PET scans rely on the recording of brain activity. The changes detected in these activities are related to the experimental conditions for testing hypotheses, as in mental chronometry experiments, but these differences can be temporally localised during preparation of the written response. *Perret and Qu* show how electroencephalographic recordings can be an interesting solution when looking for the locus of an effect. They describe two studies whose objectives were to specify the time windows of the effects of age of acquisition and lexical frequency (Perret, Bonin, & Laganaro, 2014; Qu, Zhang, & Damian, 2016). Recording electrophysiological activity therefore allows questions to be answered that mental chronometry can only tackle using experimental manipulation and indirect variables.

The volume ends with two concluding chapters. *Michel Fayol* considers the place of word production research in research on writing, as well as how lexical processes are used in tasks that require the production of sentences and texts. Fayol stresses that words contain sub-lexical units, and therefore that understanding word production also requires investigating how these units are combined to compose words. Throughout his chapter, he sets out the issues that constitute the main scientific challenges in research on written word production.

The final chapter, written by *Brenda Rapp*, explores the research questions that writing research should further consider. She begins by reminding us of the place and role of writing in modern societies, highlighting in particular the fact that writing is becoming more and more common to the point of overtaking reading (Brandt, 2014) in this age of *e*-communication. Next, as a neuropsychologist, she reminds us that the complexity of writing provides an opportunity to explore how multiple cognitive systems interact in the brain. The final part of her chapter tackles themes relating to the cognitive neurosciences of writing, and reviews recent findings obtained with neuroimaging. There is no need to say that psycholinguistics and neuroscientists will have to work hand in hand to develop understanding of the basic skills of writing and detailed theoretical and computational models of the writing process.

References

Barsalou, L.W., Simmons, W.K., Barbey, A.K., & Wilson, C.D. (2003). Grounding conceptual knowledge in modality-specific systems. *TRENDS in Cognitive Sciences*, *7*, 84–91.

Berg, T. (2002). Slips of the typewriter key. *Applied Psycholinguistics*, *23*, 185–207.

Bonin, P., & Fayol, M. (2000). Writing words from pictures: What representations are activated, and when? *Memory & Cognition*, *28*, 677–689.

Bonin, P., Peereman, R., & Fayol, M. (2001). Do phonological codes constrain the selection of orthographic codes in written picture naming. *Journal of Memory and Language*, *45*, 688–720.

Bonin, P., Méot, A., Lagarrigue, A., & Roux, S. (2015). Written object naming, spelling to dictation, and immediate copying: different tasks, different pathways? *The Quarterly Journal of Experimental Psychology*, *68*, 1268–1294.

Bonin, P., Roux, S., Barry, C., & Canell, L. (2012). Evidence for a limited-cascading account of written word naming. *Journal of Experimental Psychology: Learning, Memory, and Cognition*, *6*, 1741–1758.

Bock, K., & Levelt, W.J.M. (1994). *Language production: Grammatical encoding.* In M.A. Gernsbacher (Ed.), Handbook of Psycholinguistics (pp. 945–984). London: Academic Press.

Brandt, D. (2014). *The rise of Writing*. Cambridge: Cambridge University Press.

Broca, P. (1861). Perte de la parole, ramollissement chronique et destruction partielle du lobe antérieur gauche du cerveau. [Loss of speech, chronic softening and partial destruction of the left anterior lobe of the brain]. *Bulletins de la Société d'Anthropologie de Paris*, *2*, 235–238.

Caramazza, A., & Miceli, G. (1990). The structure of graphemic representations. *Cognition*, *37*, 243–297.

Cattell, J.M. (1886). The time it takes to see and name objects. *Mind*, *11*, 63–65.

Delattre, M., Bonin, P., & Barry, C. (2006). Written spelling to dictation: Sound-to-spelling regularity affects both writing latencies and durations. *Journal of Experimental Psychology: Learning, Memory, and Language*, *32*, 1330–1140.

Dell, G.S. (1986). A spreading-activation theory of retrieval in sentence production. *Psychological Review*, *93*, 283–321.

Ellis, A.W. (1979). Slips of the pen. *Visible Language*, *13*, 265–282.

Ellis, A.W. (1982). Spelling and writing (and reading and speaking). In A. Ellis (Ed.). *Normality and Pathology in Cognitive Functions*. (pp. 60–85) London: Academic Press.

Ellis, A.W. (1988). Normal writing processes and peripheral acquired dysgraphias. *Language and Cognitive Processes, 3,* 99–127.

Exner, S. (1881). *Untersuchungen über die Localisation der Functionen in der Grosshirnrinde des Menschen.* Braumüller.

Fayol, M., Hupet, M., & Largy, P. (1999). The acquisition of subject-verb agreement in written French: From novices to experts' errors. *Reading and Writing: An Interdisciplinary Journal, 11,* 153–174.

Fromkin, V.A. (1971). The non-anomalous nature of anomalous utterances. *Language, 47,* 29–52.

Grosjean, F. (2010). *Bilingual: Life and Reality.* Harvard: Harvard University Press.

Humphreys, G.W., Riddoch, M.J., & Quinlan, P.T. (1988). Cascade processes in picture naming identification. *Cognitive Neuropsychology, 5,* 67–104.

Kandel, S., & Perret, C. (2015a). How does the interaction between spelling and motor processes build up during writing acquisition? *Cognition, 136,* 325–336.

Kandel, S. & Perret, C. (2015b). How do movements to produce letters become automatic during writing acquisition? Investigating the development of motor anticipation. *International Journal of Behavioral Development, 39,* 113–120.

Kandel, S., Alvarez, C.J., & Vallée, N. (2006). Syllables as processing units in handwriting production. *Journal of Experimental Psychology: Human Perception and Performance, 32,* 19–31.

Kandel, S., Lassus-Sangosse, D., Grosjacques, G., & Perret, C. (2018). How does dyslexia/dysgraphia affect movement production during word writing? *Cognitive Neuropsychology, 34,* 219–251.

Largy, P., & Fayol, M. (2001). Oral cues improve subject-verb agreement in written French. *International Journal of Psychology, 36,* 121–132.

Levelt, W.J.M., Roelofs, A. & Meyer, A.S. (1999). A theory of lexical access in speech production. *Behavioral and Brain Sciences, 22,* 1–75.

Longcamp, M., Boucard, C., Gilhodes, J.-C., Anton, J.-L., Roth, M., Nazarian, B., & Velay, J.-L. (2008). Learning through hand- or typewriting influences visual recognition of new graphic shapes: behavioral and functional imaging evidence. *Journal of Cognitive Neuroscience, 20,* 802–815.

Luria, A.R. (1966). *Higher cortical functions in man.* New York: Basic Books.

Maggio, S., Lété, B., Chenu, F., Jisa, H., & Fayol, M. (2012). Tracking the mind during writing: immediacy, delayed, and anticipatory effects on pauses and writing rate. *Reading and Writing: An Interdisciplinary Journal, 25,* 2131–2151.

Meulenbroek, R.G.J., & van Galen, G.P. (1990). Perceptual-motor complexity of printed and cursive letters. *Journal of Experimental Education, 58,* 95–110.

Nussbaum, M. (2011). *Creating capabilities: the human development approach.* Cambridge, Massachusetts: The Belknap Press of Harvard University Press.

Meyer, A.S. (1992). Investigation of phonological encoding through speech error analyses: Achievements, limitations, and alternatives. *Cognition, 42,* 181–211.

Olive, T. (2014). Toward a parallel and cascading model of the writing system: A review of research on writing processes coordination. *Journal of Writing Research, 6,* 173–194.

Perret, C., Bonin, P., & Laganaro, M. (2014). Exploring the multiple-level hypothesis of AoA effects in spoken and written picture naming using a topographic ERP analysis. *Brain and Language, 135,* 20–31.

Planton, S., Jucla, M., Roux, F.-E., & Démonet, J.-F. (2013). The "handwriting brain": A meta-analysis of neuroimaging studies of motor versus orthographic processes. *Cortex, 49,* 2772–2787.

Purcell, J.J., Turkeltaub, P.E., Eden, G.F., & Rapp, B. (2011). Examining the central and peripheral processes of written word production through meta-analysis. *Frontiers in psychology, 2:1, doi:10.3389/fpsyg.2011.00239.*

Qu, Q., Zhang, Q., & Damian, M. (2016). Tracking the time course of lexical access in orthographic production: An event-related potential study of word frequency effects in written picture naming. *Brain and Language, 159,* 118–126.

Rapp, B., Benzing, L., & Caramazza, A. (1997). The autonomy of lexical orthography. *Cognitive Neuropsychology, 14,* 71–104.

Rapp, B., Epstein, C., & Tainturier, M.-J. (2002). The integration of information across lexical and sub-lexical processes in spelling. *Cognitive Neuropsychology, 19,* 1–29.

Roux, S., & Bonin, P. (2012). Cascaded processing in written naming: Evidence from the picture-picture interference paradigm. *Language and Cognitive Processes, 27,* 734–769

Roux, S., McKeeff, T.J., Grosjacques, G., Afonso, O., & Kandel, S. (2013). The interaction between central and peripherial processes in handwriting production. *Cognition, 127,* 235–241.

Rumelhart, D.E., & Norman, D.A. (1982). Simulating skilled typists: A study of skilled cognitive-motor performance. *Cognitive Science, 6,* 1–36.

Sausset, S., Lambert, E., Olive, T., & Larocque, D. (2012). Processing of syllables during handwriting: Effects of graphomotor constraints. *The Quarterly Journal of Experimental Psychology, 65,* 1872–1879.

Sen, A. (1999). *Development as Freedom.* Oxford: Oxford University Press.

Shattuck-Hufnagel, S. (1979). Evidence for a serial-ordering mechanism in sentence production. In W.E. Cooper & E.C. Walker (Eds.) *Sentence Processing: Psycholinguistic Studies Presented to Merrill Garrett.* (pp. 295–342) Hillsdale, New York: Erlbaum.

Tainturier, M.-J., & Rapp, B. (2001). The spelling process. In B. Rapp (Ed.), *The Handbook of Cognitive Neuropsychology: what deficits reveal about the Human Mind.* (pp. 263–289) Philadelphia: Psychology Press.

Van Galen, G.P. (1991). Handwriting: Issues for a psychomotor theory. *Human Movement Science, 10,* 165–191.

PART 1

Theoretical and Empirical Section

∵

A Role of Phonology in Orthographic Production? A Historical Perspective and Some Recent New Evidence

Markus F. Damian

Most of us share the intuition that handwriting (or typing, or texting) is based on "inner speech": we formulate what we intend to write as some sort of speech-based code in our head, and then transfer this code into orthographic output. This intuition is so powerful that ostensibly, empirical research is not needed— if introspection provides such a clear (and positive) answer, what is the point in pursuing the issue? However, as it turns out, identifying the role (if any) of speech-based mental codes in the preparation of orthographic output is more complex than it seems, and there is a substantial history to the underlying question. In this chapter, I intend to analyse the issue in some detail, first by providing a historical perspective mainly based on neuropsychological work, and then by summarising more recent studies, conducted on neurotypical individuals.

1   The Issue—Does Phonology Contribute to Orthographic Production?

For this chapter, orthographic production will be defined as being "conceptually driven", i.e., involving the conversion of thought into orthographic output. Other forms of orthographic production, such as written spelling (conversion of spoken input into orthographic output) or written copying (conversion of orthographic input to output) are not conceptually driven and therefore have their own processing characteristics (e.g., Bonin, Méot, Lagarrigue, & Roux, 2015; Delattre, Bonin, & Barry, 2006). However, when orthographic production is based on meaning, introspection tells us that it involves "inner speech", an intuition which seems to indicate a strong involvement of phonology in handwriting. However, even if this intuition is true this does not shed light on whether phonological codes are *causally* involved in orthographic production, or whether phonology simply is co-activated as a result of a life-long history of association between sound and spelling. Interestingly, a case study of a brain-

impaired individual by Levine, Calvanio and Popovics (1982) suggested that
the absence of inner speech might not imply impaired written production.
This suggests that indeed, inner speech might not causally be involved in writing.

Potentially relevant evidence comes from the fact that most of us frequently
make writing/typing errors ("slips of the pen") which result in homophones:
we sometimes write THERE instead of THEIR, YOUR for YOU'RE, etc. Further, a
good number of form-related ("structural") writing errors result in pseudohomophones (RIDGID instead of RIGID; QUES instead of CUES; examples from
Hotopf, 1980). Errors of this type appear more difficult to "explain away" via
the argument that in handwriting, phonological codes are concomitantly activated but do not play a causal role. However, an argument for phonology based
on structurally similar slips of the pen is rather difficult to construct. Hotopf
(1983) analysed structural slips of the pen in some detail, with the aim of determining whether the basis for such errors is phonological or graphemic, but did
not arrive at clear-cut results, partly due to the limited size of the sample of
errors but also because homophone errors, the most instructive source of evidence, are exclusive to the written domain, so a comparison between written
and spoken structural errors is not possible.

In the following two sections, I shall summarise the surrounding debate from
a neuropsychological angle, first outlining the contributions of the pioneers of
19th Century neuropsychology, and then moving on to relevant case studies
from the last few decades.

2   The Historical Perspective: the 19th Century "Diagram Makers"

The pioneers of 19th Century neuropsychology developed models of language
which mapped onto underlying brain regions, based on case studies of individuals with acquired brain lesions. These models maintain high relevance for
present-day neuroscience (Poeppel & Hickok, 2004). Perhaps less well known
is the fact that these pioneers also generated detailed hypothesis about *written*
language. In a historical perspective, de Bleser and Luzzatti (1989) highlighted
"the lack of interest in subtotal written language disorders (dyslexias and dysgraphias) in modern aphasiology until recently" (p. 502). Below I shall briefly
summarise thought on the issue in the 19th Century, and how these map onto
more recent theoretical frameworks in aphasiology.

In the late 19th Century, a model of spoken language (Figure 2.1) crystallised
which consists of a stream for auditory input feeding into a centre for "auditory word representations", a stream for motor output which is fed by a centre

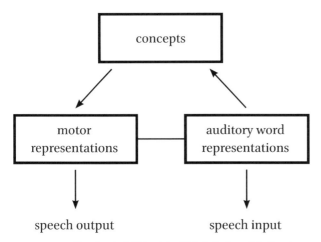

FIGURE 2.1 The classical "Wernicke-Lichtheim" model of spoken
            language

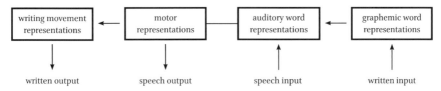

FIGURE 2.2 Wernicke's (1874) model of spoken and written language processing

for "motor speech output", and a centre for "object concepts". Furthermore, auditory and motor word representations are directly linked. Via the assumption that each centre, as well as each link, can be independently damaged, the model predicts separate types of aphasias (e.g., cortical motor aphasia, transcortical motor aphasia). Even though this framework was roundly criticised over the next 150 or so years (e.g., it makes few assumptions about syntax), the division into input and output streams is echoed in many modern models of language in the brain (e.g., Hickok, Houde & Rong, 2011).

Literate individuals represent knowledge about language not only in spoken but also in written format, and hence components and pathways for orthographic processing need to be added to a model of language in the mind and brain. In his landmark work, Wernicke (1874) proposed a solution (still without a centre for "concepts", which was only added by Lichtheim in 1885) in which written language was "parasitic" upon spoken language (Figure 2.2). Reading activates a sort of visual lexicon, which itself is connected to the "auditory word" centre. On the output side, handwriting is supported by "writing movement representations" (essentially, an orthographic output lexicon)

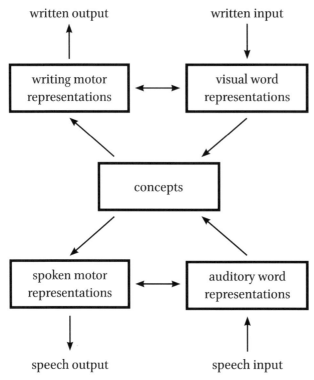

written output   written input

| writing motor representations | ←→ | visual word representations |

concepts

| spoken motor representations | ←→ | auditory word representations |

speech output   speech input

FIGURE 2.3 A fully parallel, independent model of spoken and
                    written language processing

which itself is driven by the "motor representations" centre for spoken language. Critically, according to this model, orthographic access, both in input
and output activities, always requires access to corresponding spoken codes
("phonological mediation").

An alternative idea, considered but ultimately rejected by Wernicke (1886), is
a "parallel" model in which auditory input and motor output streams are mir-
rored by orthographic input and output channels (Figure 2.3). However, the
model championed by Lichtheim (1885) was a "symmetrical, dependent" model
(Figure 2.4) in which, as in Wernicke's (1874) original framework, written language (with the exception of direct copying of written words) was fully dependent on spoken codes. This model was ultimately also discounted by Lichtheim,
as it seemingly made incorrect clinical predictions: for instance, Wernicke's
aphasia, conceptualised as an impairment to "auditory word representations",
should according to this view leave spontaneous writing intact, which was not
believed to be the case. Lichtheim's final solution therefore consisted of an
"asymmetrical, dependent" model (Figure 2.5). Key features are that access to

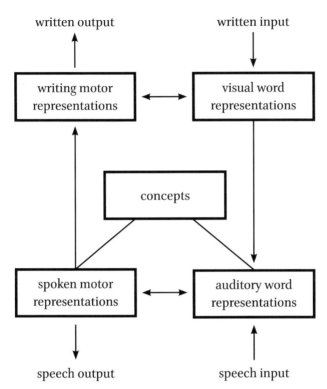

FIGURE 2.4 A parallel, dependent model of spoken and written
            language processing
            AFTER LICHTHEIM, 1885

the meaning of printed words mandatorily proceeds via activation of spoken codes, and that there is no direct link from concepts to written motor representations; handwriting takes place via activation of spoken codes. However, even the asymmetrical model made predictions which appeared incompatible with the available evidence (such as the often-observed conjunction of Broca's aphasia with a reading impairment).

In subsequent work, Wernicke (1886) radically departed from these earlier views, inspired by an article by Grashey from the previous year (1885). The notion of visual and written motor lexical representations was abandoned altogether; instead, both reading and writing took place entirely based on sublexical codes (letters) rather than words (Figure 2.6). To the spoken language system, he added the notion of γ, a phoneme-like representations with sensory (for comprehension) and motor (for production) aspects. Reading interfaced with this spoken system via a sublexical spelling-to-sound (and vice versa) conversion route. Hence, within this framework both orthographic input, and

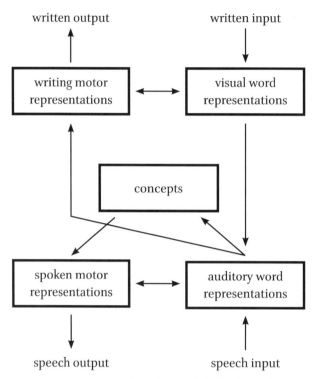

FIGURE 2.5 Asymmetric, dependent model of spoken and writ-
               ten language processing
               AFTER LICHTHEIM, 1885

output, processing (reading and writing) take place fully sublexically. Broadly then, reading and writing are entirely parasitic upon spoken language not only in the sense that both require obligatory access to spoken representations; even the notion of separate lexical (visual or motoric) codes is repudiated.

3   Modern-Day Neuropsychology

The general notion of assigning secondary status to orthographic language, and the idea that written language is largely "parasitic upon" spoken codes, remained popular for much of the 20th Century. For instance, Luria (1966) described orthographic production thus: "... both writing from dictation and spontaneous writing begin with the analysis of the phonetic complex that goes to form the pronounced word. [...] The phonemes identified as a result of such activity must be arranged in a certain order and recoded into the corresponding optic structure—graphemes [...] in the final stage, the graphemes must

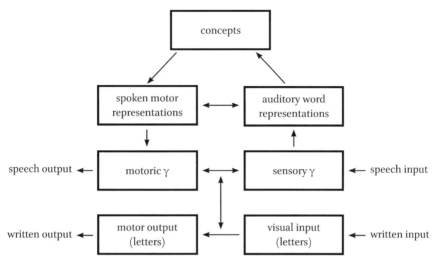

FIGURE 2.6 Wernicke's (1886) model of spoken and written language

again be recoded into a system of motor acts" (pp. 528–529). Hence, Luria advocated a strong version of obligatory "phonological mediation"—orthographic production is strongly based on prior retrieval of phonological codes. Similarly, Geschwind (1974) wrote: "How does one write the name of a seen object? Some of the classical authors were inclined to feel that the sight of the object could directly arouse the written production, just as they felt that the production of the spoken name could take place over a direct pathway from the visual region to Broca's area. But what makes this supposition unlikely is that writing is *invariably* abnormal in patients with the *speech* pattern of Wernicke's aphasia, while one might expect it to be spared at least occasionally if this were the case. Hence it appears that to write the word, the spoken form must be aroused first" (p. 439).

In a seminal paper, Rapp, Benzing and Caramazza (1997) pointed out that although impairments in spoken and written language often go together (e.g., Alajouanine & Lhermitte, 1960; Basso, Taborelli & Vignolo, 1978) this does not imply obligatory phonological mediation of written output, for the following reason. *Association* of errors in the two modalities might arise from impairment to a shared higher-level mental representation, such as a lexical-semantic store, or perhaps written and spoken lexical stores are independently but jointly impaired in these individuals. Hence, the empirical association between the two types of impairment is less informative. More instructive would be a *dissociation* between the two types of impairment, with the critical test case an individual which shows spared knowledge of orthographic forms yet impairment to phonological forms—a constellation which should be impossible to find if obligatory phonological mediation were to hold. More specifically, Rapp et al. pointed out that the most informative evidence would come from individuals in which the spoken impairment can be attributed to a *lexical* (as opposed to a post-lexical) impairment. This constellation—lexical impairment in the spoken domain, but relatively preserved orthographic production— would constitute the ultimate test case for the "obligatory phonological mediation" hypothesis. And furthermore, empirically the most diagnostic case would for an individual to attempt to produce a written and a spoken response for the same item on the same trial.

Rapp et al. (1997) documented such an individual, named PW. PW exhibited difficulties both in spoken and written output which could be localised to the lexical level, an additional post-lexical disturbance in the written modality only, and a possible slight semantic deficit. In the critical experimental test, PW was asked to first write, and then pronounce, each of a series of simple line drawings. PW was instructed to write blindly (i.e., not to look at his written output) in order to prevent him from reading his response. The critical test cases were potential responses in which semantic errors and/or "don't know" spoken responses were preceded by the *correct* written production of the same word, a constellation which should never occur if written production is phonologically mediated. On 18% of trials on which PW generated a spoken error, he generated the correct written response, or at least a recognisable orthographic form (picture: raccoon; written response: "RACOONA"; spoken response: "sheep"). PW was also assessed on a number of variations of the described procedure, and across all tasks, PW generated spoken errors on 20% of all trials, and among these error trials, the correct written response was generated on 19%. In addition, observed error patterns were at odds with the phonological mediation claim, such as different semantic errors on a spoken and written response; and correct spoken responses in association with a semantic error in writing. The authors concluded that "given that under the obligatory phonological mediation hypothesis this conjunction of events should never occur, the hypothesis would seem to be invalidated" (p. 99).

This inference has to date not been earnestly challenged, and "orthographic autonomy" is at present the dominant view, with the general assumption that orthographic output codes can be directly accessed from semantics. Interestingly, while this view discounts models without such a direct access route (e.g., those in Figures 2.4–6) it does not imply full symmetry between spoken and written output, as schematised in Figure 2.2. Even assuming direct links from semantics to both spoken, and written, output lexical codes, the process dynamics could be rather different between the two modalities. As regards spoken production, the typically tacit view is that it does not involve co-activation

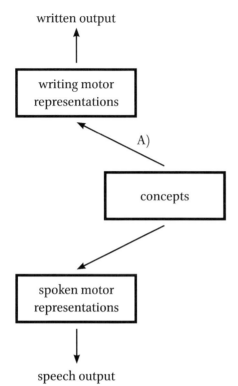

written output

writing motor
representations

A)

concepts

spoken motor
representations

speech output

FIGURE 2.7
The assumption of "orthographic autonomy". Orthographic output codes can be
directly accessed from conceptual representations.

of orthographic codes. Whether or not this is the case (i.e., speaking involves
cross-talk with spelling) is an unresolved and controversial issue (e.g., Damian
& Bowers, 2003; Gaskell, Cox, Foley, Grieve, & O'Brien, 2003). The answer to the
reverse issue—does orthographic production involve co-activation of phonological codes?—is even less obvious. Given that most individuals have the
intuition that writing is based on "inner speech", a contribution from phonology, even if not "obligatory", is certainly possible. In other words, despite the
assumption that spoken and written codes can both be independently accessed
from meaning, processing could be asymmetrical such that written production
is influenced by spoken codes, whereas spoken production is perhaps not. In
the following section I shall summarise the experimental evidence which is
available at present to speak to this issue.

4   **Experimental Evidence from Neurotypical Orthographic
         Production**

Research on handwriting has a long-standing tradition in psychology (e.g.,
Thomassen & van Galen, 1992; van Galen, 1991), but only recently has the availability of digital graphic tablets made research on orthographic production
more accessible. As a consequence, many experimental tasks from the spoken production literature have now been adapted to written production. These
studies focus on neurotypical individuals, and have mostly explored writing
of single words, or short phrases. Below, I will summarise the work which has
emerged over the last two or so decades, regarding the potential contribution
of phonological codes to written production. Broadly, the aim is to identify a
potential contribution from phonology to writing, by varying orthographic and
phonological properties of to-be-written target words and hoping to observe
"priming" effects (in- or decreased latencies, and/or effects on accuracy). In
alphabetic languages, spelling and sound are strongly confounded, and so a
"pure" manipulation of phonological properties while orthography is held constant, or vice versa, is difficult. For this reason, a number of recent studies have
therefore targeted written production in non-alphabetic languages. In the following, I will outline the tasks used so far alongside relevant evidence, roughly
sorted by popularity of the task.

4.1   *Picture-Word Interference*
In the so-called "picture-word interference" (PWI) task, participants name
objects while instructed to ignore "distractor" words presented simultaneously
or in close temporal vicinity to the target. In this task, form-related distractors
(picture: *cat*; distractor: *cap*) lead to faster object naming times than unrelated
distractors (picture: *cat*; distractor: *top*, e.g., Schriefers, Meyer, & Levelt, 1990;
Starreveld & La Heij, 1995), suggesting that target preparation and distractor
processing engage in "cross-talk" (see Roelofs, 1997, for detailed computational
modeling). The PWI paradigm can also be used with written word production.
Rather than orally naming the target pictures, participants write down object
names on a graphic tablet (in many studies, participants write with an inking digitiser on a response sheet placed on top of the tablet, which allows
paper-based recording of written responses, as well as digital measurement
of response properties). As in studies of spoken production, the relatedness
between target and distractor is varied, and its potential effects on latencies
and accuracies is measured. A further variable which can be manipulated is the
stimulus onset asynchrony (SOA) between onset of picture and distractor. This
allows distractors to tap into successive processing stages of target preparation
(e.g., Schriefers et al., 1990).

The earliest study of this type was reported by Bonin, Fayol and Gombert (1997). In an effort to dissociate phonological from orthographic priming, objects were paired with distractor letters (rather than words) which were either orthographically identical to the silent initial letter of the target (object: "harpe", distractor "h"), phonologically but not orthographically related (object: "citron", distractor "s"), phonologically and orthographically related (object: "taupe", distractor "t"), or unrelated. Results exhibited a complex pattern, with the largest priming emerging in the "graphemically related" condition, but surprisingly no significant priming from orthographically and phonologically related distractors in both spoken and written picture naming. In a second experiment, distractors were spoken (i.e., the target letter/phoneme followed by a neutral vowel) and relatedness was restricted to phonological overlap. Again, results were complex, with some priming obtained with spoken responses, but less reliably so with written responses.

The idea of combining PWI with written responses was revisited by Zhang and Damian (2010), who tested English participants and used words as distractors. They showed larger priming from phonologically related distractors (object: "hand"; distractor: "sand") than from orthographically equally related, but phonologically less related (object: "hand"; distractor: "wand") distractors, relative to an unrelated condition. This effect of phonology appeared restricted to the "earliest" SOA (i.e., picture and distractor appeared simultaneously), but at "later" SOAs (distractor lagged picture onset by 100 or 200 ms), priming was largely based on orthography only. These findings suggest that phonology affects written word production, particularly so in earlier stages of written word preparation.

The most informative case for present purposes would be a picture-target pair in a PWI task which is phonologically related, but orthographically unrelated—if priming was found for such a combination, this would provide unequivocal evidence for a role of phonology. In languages with alphabetic scripts, it is problematic to fully dissociate sound from spelling. Hence, a number of recent studies have used non-alphabetic response languages (mainly Chinese Mandarin). Qu, Damian, Zhang and Zhu (2011) reported results conducted with Chinese writers in which distractors and pictures were phonologically *and* orthographically related, only phonologically related, or unrelated. Relative to the unrelated condition, facilitation was found for both types of form overlap; critically, phonological overlap in the absence of any orthographic overlap still resulted in priming. Furthermore, results showed a similar time course to the one reported by Zhang and Damian (2010): priming from phonologically and orthographically related distractors was found at SOAs of 0 ms and 100 ms, but priming from phonologically related but orthographically unrelated distractors was restricted to the SOA = o ms. This might suggest that phonological codes of target words are activated rapidly (perhaps more rapidly so than orthographic properties), and hence impact early stages of orthographic encoding. At a later stage, the impact of the phonological route becomes less relevant, and priming is mainly orthographically based.

Conflicting results, however, were recently reported in another PWI study with Chinese participants and written and spoken responses (Zhang & Wang, 2015; for current purposes I shall focus on written responses). In these experiments, orthographic and phonological overlap were factorially crossed. Orthographically based priming was found under all SOAs (–100 ms, o ms, +100 ms) but phonological priming was found only under the latest SOA (+100 ms). This pattern might suggest that orthographic encoding takes place based on a rapid and efficient link between meaning and orthography, whereas a slow and indirect link from meaning to phonological representations to orthographic codes, influences a later stage of orthographic preparation. In a similar study in which a PWI task was combined with measurement of electroencephalography (EEG), Zhang and Wang (2016) also factorially crossed orthographic and phonological overlap, but used only a single SOA (o ms). EEG indicated onset latencies of 370 ms and 464 ms for orthographic and phonological relatedness, respectively. Hence, in agreement with Zhang and Wang (2015), the results suggest that a direct link from meaning to orthography might be more rapid than the indirect route via phonology. Needless to say, this inference conflicts with the one drawn by Zhang and Damian (2011) and Qu et al. (2011), and the reasons for this discrepancy are not clear at present.

4.2   *Implicit Priming*
In this procedure, wildly popular in research on spoken production, participants carry out a series of relatively short experimental blocks. In each block, they repeat multiple times and in random order a small set of response words, typically elicited by memorised "prompt" words (fruit-melon). The critical manipulation is that within a block, all responses either share a particular form property such as the initial sound(s) ("homogeneous"), or they don't ("heterogeneous"). Numerous studies have shown that word-initial overlap in terms of phonological segments facilitates responses whereas non-initial overlap does not yield a benefit, and that the size of this effect grows with increasing overlap (Meyer, 1990, 1991). The effect is accounted for in terms of partial planning (e.g., Roelofs, 1997): information about word-initial segments, available in homogeneous blocks, allows speakers to partially plan their utterances compared to heterogeneous blocks, resulting in a response time benefit. This paradigm

can also be used with handwritten rather than spoken responses. Afonso and Álvarez (2011) reported results from Spanish writers. In Spanish, some speech sounds are expressed in multiple spellings, e.g., "banana" and "vacuna" are both pronounced with an initial /b/. The authors obtained implicit priming even when words with identical word-initial sound but different graphemes were mixed, which suggests a role of phonology in writing. By contrast, Shen, Damian, and Stadthagen-Gonzalez (2013) tested English native speakers on a very similar procedure and found substantial graphemic priming, but they failed to obtain any phonologically based priming. The discrepancy between the two sets of findings awaits explanation.

4.3   *Masked Priming*

Presenting prime words (or nonwords) very briefly, such that participants find it difficult to perceive them, and then measuring a potential impact on subsequent processing of a target stimulus, is a commonly used technique in cognitive psychology (Kinoshita & Luper, 2003). Bonin, Fayol and Peereman (1998) pioneered the use of masked priming in conjunction with written responses. Participants wrote down the names of objects on a digitiser, and objects were preceded by briefly presented and masked nonwords. Nonwords were either pseudohomophones of the target name (e.g., a picture of a tooth—DENT in French—preceded by the nonword DANT), orthographically related nonwords (e.g., the prime DUNT), or control primes (e.g., DISE). Hence, pseudohomophones were more phonologically related than orthographically related primes (both were matched on orthographic overlap). Compared to the control condition, pseudohomophones and orthographically related primes generated similar-sized priming, a pattern which suggests that priming was based on orthographic overlap, with little involvement of phonology. Two further experiments replicated this pattern with slightly modified masking conditions, suggesting that with masked nonword primes, phonology does not appear to affect written object naming.

   More recently, Qu, Damian and Li (2016) reported a similar masked priming study, but conducted with native writers of Chinese. As in Bonin et al. (1998) participants wrote down names of objects on a digitiser. Objects were preceded by masked prime words which were either phonologically and orthographically related (PO) to the picture label, phonologically related but orthographically unrelated (P), or unrelated. For both types of overlap, priming effects were found relative to the control condition in two experiments in two experiments. In a third experiment, a manual semantic judgment task replaced written object naming, and here priming effects disappeared, suggesting that facilitation in the earlier experiments originated at the orthographic level. Overall, and in contrast to the earlier findings by Bonin et al., these results add support to the claim that written word production is supported by phonological codes. However, the exact reason for the discrepancy in findings is at present unclear.

4.4   *Bare Picture Naming*

Bonin, Peereman, and Fayol (2001) investigated with French participants whether sound-to-print consistency of picture names affects written latencies. When inconsistency was defined at the lexical level, writing latencies for heterographic homophones (e.g., "verre" and "vert") did not differ from non-homophone controls. When inconsistency was defined sublexically, results showed again no difference between consistent and inconsistent response words. A further experiment demonstrated that the position of the inconsistency within the target word was critical, with only word-initial, but not medial or final positions, affecting latencies. Two further experiments showed that in a spelling-to-dictation task, middle or final inconsistencies also affected latencies. These results suggest that in picture naming, phonology affects orthographic encoding mainly via a sublexical sound-to-print conversion routine which operates sequentially. However, Bonin et al. (2015) more recently compared three orthographic output tasks (written picture naming; copying of written words; and spelling-to-dictation), and in multiple regression analyses found effects of inconsistency only in spelling-to-dictation, but neither in copying, nor (crucially) in picture naming. This lead them to conclude that only spelling-to-dictation involves a nonlexical, phonologically based, pathway.

4.5   *Picture-Picture Priming*

In spoken word production, Morsella and Miozzo (2002) pioneered the "picture-picture priming" (PPP) technique in which two coloured line drawings are superimposed on each other, and participants name one (cued by colour) and ignore the other. If the names corresponding to the two objects are form-related (e.g., bell-bed), naming times are faster than when they are unrelated. Hence, speakers apparently retrieve phonological codes associated with both objects. Roux and Bonin (2011) adopted this technique to written word production, and with French participants demonstrated similar form-related priming effect as previously found with spoken responses. This priming effect was still found when object and distractor names began with the same letter, but with a different sound (cigar-camion), but no priming was found when both names had different initial letters but shared the same sound (singe-ceinture). This pattern of results suggests that activation from the distractor picture "cascades" to the orthographic level, but evidently it does not do so via an indirect route to phonology.

4.6   Cross-Modal Long-Lasting Repetition Priming

Some forms of priming in psychological research are surprisingly persistent. One such instance is repetition priming, i.e., a processing benefit (faster response times, and/or increased accuracy) when a particular stimulus had been processed before. For instance, a picture is named faster and/or more accurately when it had been previously named, and this benefit might survive delays of several weeks (e.g., Cave, 1997; Mitchell & Brown, 1988). And indeed, even when on the prime trial, the response word is spoken in response to a definition ("What is the largest animal swimming in the sea"?), priming is obtained onto subsequent naming of a target ("whale"), implying that repetition of the visual image is not necessary (Wheeldon & Monsell, 1992). Damian, Dorjee and Stadthagen-Gonzalez (2011) reported persistent repetition priming not only in spoken but also in written word production. Two further experiments found priming from spoken to written responses and vice versa. Such a "cross-modal" priming effect suggests that phonology is involved in orthographic encoding, and supports the view that access to orthography codes is accomplished both via the autonomous link between meaning and spelling, and an indirect route via phonology.

4.7   Stroop Task

The Stroop colour naming task (Stroop, 1935) is perhaps the most popular cognitive procedure. Colour naming constitutes a specific instance of the broader domain of spoken word production, and an account of the Stroop effect can plausibly be embedded in a general model of spoken production (e.g., Roelofs, 2003). A Stroop task can also be used to involve written responses, and Damian and Qu (2013) recently conducted a study in which Chinese participants wrote the colour of Chinese characters on a digitiser. Spoken Mandarin is characterised by homophony, with relatively few spoken syllables mapping onto thousands of written characters. In Damian and Qu, characters were homophonic to the target (congruent), homophonic to an alternative colour word (incongruent), or unrelated. In addition, for the two homophonic condition, tone of the syllable could be either matching or mismatching. Relative to the unrelated condition, interference which was independent of tone match or mismatch, was found from the incongruent condition, which most likely reflects the fact that writers co-activated an incongruent colour name via shared phonology. More importantly, facilitation was found from congruent homophonic distractors, but only when the homophone shared the same tone with the target.

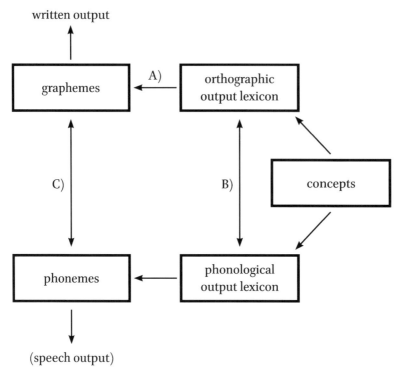

written output

FIGURE 2.8 A model of orthographic production. "Orthographic autonomy" is
established via link (A), co-activated phonological codes may affect
orthographic encoding via a lexical (B) or sublexical (C) route.

Given that the task required an orthographically based response, and distractor and written response never shared graphemic properties, priming from homophone distractors constitutes further evidence for the claim that written production is supported by phonological codes.

5   Outlook—Where to Go from Here?

5.1   Accounting for the Extant Evidence

Although overall, the empirical evidence suggests a role of phonology in orthographic production, there are a number of null or inconsistent findings which deserve discussion. In psychological tasks, it is always possible that effects arise only in response to specific task demands, hence it is worth analysing negative findings in greater detail. In some instances, null findings might reflect insufficient power to manipulate the variable of interest, e.g., in Bonin et al.'s (1998) masked priming study, it was perhaps difficult to achieve a sufficient separation between orthographic and phonological overlap. By contrast, Qu et al.'s (2016) parallel experiments used Chinese as a target language in which spelling and sound are more clearly separated, and this might account for their positive finding. In the "implicit priming" task Shen et al. (2013) reported a null finding, and argued that if priming in this task reflects "partial preparation" (e.g., Roelofs, 1997) then this pattern is expected because writers cannot partially plan written output based on phonological codes. However, Afonso and Álvarez (2011) reported rather sizeable effects of phonology with Spanish writers in—on the face of it—quite similar experiments. An explanation in terms of different target languages (English vs. Spanish) seems on the face of it unlikely (although not impossible), and the discrepancy awaits further explanation. Perhaps most striking is Roux and Bonin's (2011) failure to find phonological priming in the "picture-picture priming" task. Here, a possible but currently untested possibility is that this null finding is due to the specific timing characteristics of the target and to-be-ignored dimension: perhaps a systematic manipulation of the time interval between onset of the two pictures will at some point render phonologically based priming.

5.2   *Writing across Different Scripts*

As outlined above, a number of studies have used Chinese as the target language, mainly because in non-alphabetic languages it is easier to disentangle the phonological from the orthographic dimension. The very few number of studies conducted on Chinese writers (e.g., Damian & Qu, 2013; Qu et al., 2011; Qu et al., 2016; Zhang & Wang, 2015) have suggested an effect of phonology on handwritten production. In non-alphabetic languages, the link between sound and spelling is much more indirect than in alphabetic languages (e.g., in Chinese the most obvious link is between spoken syllables and written characters, most of which are morphemes). For this reason it is in a way more surprising that an indirect route via phonology nevertheless impacts on orthographic encoding. Indeed, in both reading (e.g., Spinks, Liu, Perfetti & Tan, 2000) and writing (see above) of Chinese words, an impact of phonology is now well documented. Hence, despite the absence of sublexical correspondences between spelling and sound, the two domains appear strongly interrelated.

5.3   *Writing of Single vs Multiple Words* (*Laboratory vs Real Life*)

The available empirical evidence mainly comes from tasks in which participants write, type or spell single words in an experimental setting. The processing dynamics might fundamentally differ from those involved in writing in real life, which typically requires the coordination of multiple constituents. Specifically, writing of multiple words necessitates buffering of lexical constituents due to the slow speed of execution, which is presumably done via phonological codes. Therefore, the role of phonology in writing could be particularly pronounced in multi-word writing, since rehearsal in short-term memory is generally assumed to involve phonological codes. This possibility, raised by Tainturier and Rapp (2001), is currently untested, but it is supported by evidence from patients with preserved writing yet impaired access to phonology which tend to produce short written utterances, often with omission or substitution of function words (e.g., Bub & Kertesz, 1982). Future research with neurotypical individuals should explore the possibility that phonological effects are more pronounced in longer compared to shorter written utterances.

5.4   *Individual Differences in the Role of Phonology in Handwriting*
It is likely that considerable individual differences exist in orthographic processing. For instance, Perfetti's "lexical quality" hypothesis (see Perfetti & Hart, 2002, for a summary) postulates that readers vary strongly on how well-integrated their orthographic, phonological, and semantic codes are. Typical participants in psychological experiments tend to be rather highly skilled in reading, which could limit the range of observable individual differences. Likewise as regards writing, perhaps the available evidence overestimates a role of phonology because "typical" writers have well-integrated linguistic representations. Future research ought to take this possibility seriously, via an explicit consideration of individual differences (see Bonin, Méot, Millotte, & Barry, 2013), as well as the inclusion of a more diverse range of participants.

5.5   *Time Course of Form Encoding*
Assuming that orthographic encoding is supported not only via a direct route from meaning, but also via an indirect, phonologically based, stream, then one ought to explore the relative processing speed of the two pathways. Chronometric studies render only limited information on this question, but as described in section 4, SOA manipulations in PWI tasks render some information, although the evidence is somewhat inconclusive. The time course of orthographic and phonological encoding can be more directly assessment via measurement of EEG. Zhang and Wang's (2015) study in which a PWI procedure was combined with EEG measurement was already summarised above. Qu, Li and Damian (2014) recently reported a study in which native speakers of Chinese Mandarin were presented with coloured pictures and wrote down colour and picture names as adjective-noun phrases. Colour and picture names were either phonologically related (i.e., they shared a rhyme), orthographically related (they shared a radical), or unrelated. EEG revealed phonological effects in the 200–500 ms time window, and orthographic effects in the 300–400 ms

time window. This could imply that activation of phonological codes takes place approximately 100 ms earlier than access to orthographic codes, which in turn would highlight the "primacy" of phonological codes in production tasks, even in written ones. Even though the two highlighted studies arrived at contradictory inferences, they highlight the importance for future research to consider EEG in order to make progress on temporal issues.

References

Afonso, O., & Álvarez, C.J. (2011). Phonological effects in handwriting production: Evidence from the implicit priming paradigm. *Journal of Experimental Psychology: Learning, Memory, and Cognition, 37,* 1474–1483.

Alajouanine, T., & Lhermitte, F. (1960). Les troubles des activités expressives du langage dans l'aphasie. Leurs relations avec les apraxies. *Revue Neurologique, 102,* 604–629.

De Bleser, R.D., & Luzzatti, C. (1989). Models of reading and writing and their disorders in classical German aphasiology. *Cognitive Neuropsychology, 6,* 501–513.

Basso, A., Taborelli, A., & Vignolo, L.A. (1978). Dissociated disorders of speaking and writing in aphasia. *Journal of Neurology, Neurosurgery and Psychiatry, 41,* 556–563.

Bonin, P., Fayol, M., & Gombert, J. (1997). Role of phonological and orthographic codes in picture naming and writing: An interference paradigm study. *Cahiers de Psychologie Cognitive, 16,* 299–324.

Bonin, P., Fayol, M., & Peereman, R. (1998). Masked form priming in writing words from pictures: Evidence for direct retrieval of orthographic codes. *Acta Psychologica, 99,* 311–328.

Bonin, P., Méot, A., Lagarrigue, A., & Roux, S. (2015). Written object naming, spelling to dictation, and immediate copying: Different tasks, different pathways? *The Quarterly Journal of Experimental Psychology, 68,* 1268–1294.

Bonin, P., Méot, A., Millotte, S., & Barry, C. (2013). Individual differences in adult handwritten spelling-to-dictation. *Frontiers in Psychology, 4, 402, doi: 10,3389/fpsyg.2013 .00402.*

Bonin, P., Peereman, R., & Fayol, M. (2001). Do phonological codes constrain the selection of orthographic codes in written picture naming? *Journal of Memory and Language, 45,* 688–720.

Bub, D., & Kertesz, A. (1982). Evidence for lexicographic processing in a patient with preserved written over oral single word naming. *Brain, 105,* 697–717.

Cave, C.B. (1997). Very long-lasting priming in picture naming. *Psychological Science, 8,* 322–325.

Damian, M.F., & Bowers, J.S. (2003). Effects of orthography on speech production in a form-preparation paradigm. *Journal of Memory and Language, 49*, 119–132.

Damian, M.F., Dorjee, D., & Stadthagen-Gonzalez, H. (2011). Long-term repetition priming in spoken and written word production: Evidence for a contribution of phonology to handwriting. *Journal of Experimental Psychology: Learning, Memory, and Cognition, 37*, 813–826.

Damian, M.F., Qu, Q. (2013). Is handwriting constrained by phonology? Evidence from Stroop tasks with written responses and Chinese characters. *Frontiers in Psychology, 4:765. doi: 10.3389/fpsyg.2013.00765.*

Delattre, M., Bonin, P., & Barry, C. (2006). Written spelling to dictation: Sound-to-spelling regularity affects both writing latencies and durations. *Journal of Experimental Psychology: Learning, Memory, and Cognition, 32*, 1330–1340.

Gaskell, M.G., Cox, H., Foley, K., Grieve, H., & O'Brien, R. (2003). Constraints on definite article alternation in speech production: To "thee" or not to "thee"? *Memory & Cognition, 31*, 715–727.

Geschwind, N. (1974). *Selected papers on language and the brain.* Boston Studies in the Philosophy of Science, Vol. XVI. Dordrecht, NL: Reidel.

von Grashey, H. (1885). Archiv fur Psychiatrie und Nervenkrankheiten—*Archiv fur Psychiatrie und Nervenkrankheiten.*

Hickok, G., Houde, J., & Rong, F. (2011). Sensorimotor integration in speech processing: computational basis and neural organization. *Neuron, 69*, 407–422.

Hotopf, W.H.N. (1980). Slips of the pen. In U. Frith (Ed.), *Cognitive processes in spelling.* (pp. 287–307) London: Academic Press.

Hotopf, W.H.N. (1983). Lexical slips of the pen and tongue: What they tell us about language production. In B. Butterworth (Ed.), *Language production, Vol. 2.* London: Academic Press.

Kinoshita, S., & Lupker, S.J. (Eds.). (2004). *Masked priming: The state of the art.* New York: Psychology Press.

Levine, D.N., Calvanio, R., & Popovics, A. (1982). Language in the absence of inner speech. *Neuropsychologia, 20*, 391–409.

Lichtheim, L. (1885). Über Aphasie. *Deutsches Archiv für klinische Medizin, 36*, 204–268. (English version: On aphasia. *Brain, 7*, 433–485).

Luria, A.R. (1966). *Higher cortical functions in man.* New York: Basic Books.

Meyer, A.S. (1990). The time course of phonological encoding in language production: The encoding of successive syllables of a word. *Journal of Memory and Language, 29*, 524–545.

Meyer, A.S. (1991). The time course of phonological encoding in language production: Phonological encoding inside a syllable. *Journal of Memory and Language, 30*, 69–89.

Mitchell, D.B., & Brown, A.S. (1988). Persistent repetition priming in picture naming and its dissociation from recognition memory. *Journal of Experimental Psychology: Learning, Memory, and Cognition, 14*, 213–222.

Morsella, E., & Miozzo, M. (2002). Evidence for a cascade model of lexical access in speech production. *Journal of Experimental Psychology: Learning, Memory, and Cognition, 28*, 555–563.

Perfetti, C.A., & Hart, L. (2002). The lexical quality hypothesis. In L. Verhoeven. C. Elbro, & P. Reitsma (Eds.), *Precursors of functional literacy* (pp. 189–213). Philadelphia, PA: Benjamins.

Poeppel, D., & Hickok, G. (2004). Towards a new functional anatomy of language. *Cognition, 92*, 1–12.

Spinks, J.A., Liu, Y., Perfetti, C.A., & Tan, L.H. (2000). Reading Chinese characters for meaning: The role of phonological information. *Cognition, 76*, B1–B11.

Qu, Q., Damian, M.F., Zhang, Q., & Zhu, X.B. (2011). Phonology contributes to writing: Evidence from written word production in a nonalphabetic script. *Psychological Science, 22*, 1107–1112.

Qu, Q., Li, X., & Damian, M.F. (2014). *An electrophysiological analysis of the time course of phonological and orthographic encoding in written word production*. Poster presented at the International Workshop on Language Production, Geneva, July 2014.

Qu, Q., Damian, M.F., & Li, X. (2016). Phonology contributes to writing: evidence from a masked priming task. *Language, Cognition and Neuroscience, 31*, 251–264.

Rapp, B., Benzing, L., & Caramazza, A. (1997). The autonomy of lexical orthography. *Cognitive Neuropsychology, 14*, 71–104.

Roelofs, A. (1997). The WEAVER model of word-form encoding in speech production. *Cognition, 64*, 249–284.

Roelofs, A. (2003). Goal-referenced selection of verbal action: modelling attentional control in the Stroop task. *Psychological Review, 110*, 88–125.

Roux, S., & Bonin, P. (2011). Cascaded processing in written naming: Evidence from the picture-picture interference paradigm. *Language and Cognitive Processes, 27*, 734–769.

Schriefers, H., Meyer, A.S., & Levelt, W.J. (1990). Exploring the time course of lexical access in language production: Picture-word interference studies. *Journal of Memory and Language, 29*, 86–102.

Shen, X.R., Damian, M.F., & Stadthagen-Gonzalez, H. (2013). Abstract graphemic representations support preparation of handwritten responses. *Journal of Memory and Language, 68*, 69–84.

Starreveld, P.A., & La Heij, W. (1995). Semantic interference, orthographic facilitation, and their interaction in naming tasks. *Journal of Experimental Psychology: Learning, Memory, and Cognition, 21*, 686–698.

Stroop, J.R. (1935). Studies of interference in serial verbal reactions. *Journal of Experimental Psychology, 18*, 643–662.

Tainturier, M., & Rapp, B. (2001). The spelling process. In B. Rapp (Ed.), *The handbook of cognitive neuropsychology: What deficits reveal about the human mind.* (pp. 263–289) Psychology Press.

Thomassen, A.J., & van Galen, G.P. (1992). Handwriting as a motor task: Experimentation, modelling, and simulation. *Advances in Psychology, 84,* 113–144.

Van Galen, G.P. (1991). Handwriting: Issues for a psychomotor theory. *Human Movement Science, 10,* 165–191.

Grashey, H. (1989). Über Aphasie und ihre Beziehungen zur Wahrnehmung (On aphasia and its relations to perception). *Archiv für Psychatrie und Nervenkrankheiten, 16,* 654–688.

Wernicke, C. (1874). *Der aphasische Symptomencomplex.* Breslau: Max Cohn & Weigert.

Wernicke, C. (1886). Nervenheilkunde. Die neueren Arbeiten über Aphasie (Review of Lichtheim 1885). *Fortschritte der Medicin, 4,* 371–377.

Wheeldon, L.R., & Monsell, S. (1992). The locus of repetition priming of spoken word production. *The Quarterly Journal of Experimental Psychology, 44,* 723–761.

Zhang, Q., & Damian, M. (2010). Impact of phonology on the generation of handwritten responses: Evidence from picture-word interference tasks. *Memory & Cognition, 38,* 519–528.

Zhang, Q., & Wang, C. (2015). Phonology is not accessed earlier than orthography in Chinese written production: Evidence for the orthography autonomy hypothesis. *Frontiers in Psychology, 6:448. doi: 10.3389/fpsyg.2015.00448*

Zhang, Q., & Wang, C. (2016). The temporal courses of phonological and orthographic encoding in handwritten production in Chinese: An ERP study. *Frontiers in Human Neuroscience, 10:417. doi: 10.3389/fnhum.2016.00417*

CHAPTER 3

Implicit Statistical Learning of Graphotactic Knowledge and Lexical Orthographic Acquisition

Sébastien Pacton, Michel Fayol, Marion Nys and Ronald Peereman

In order to attain literacy, children must learn the relations between the written (alphabetical) symbols and the spoken language. This is an especially challenging task for learners given that orthographies such as English or French adhere to several complex regularities at different levels: grapho-phonological, morphological and graphotactic. In this chapter, we focus on graphotactic regularities. Graphotactic regularities refer to patterns involving the order and arrangement of letters in written words, for instance that certain letters or letter sequences are most likely to occur in specific positions in the words of a specific language (Chetail, 2017; Mano, 2016; Treiman, 2017; Treiman & Boland, 2017). We first review studies examining children's knowledge about various types of graphotactic regularities. Then, we show that sensitivity to these graphotactic regularities influences people when they learn/produce the spelling of a specific word.

1   Sensitivity to Graphotactic/Orthographic Regularities

Most of the time, determining whether correct spellings result from the use of word-specific knowledge and/or graphotactic knowledge turns out to be difficult. For example, misspellings such as MMIS for *miss* clearly indicate a lack of reliance on a rule specifying that doublets never occur in word-initial position in English. However, correct spellings could reflect word-specific knowledge alone, independently of any knowledge about graphotactic regularities. For this reason, graphotactic knowledge has often been assessed with nonwords spelling (Section 1.1) and judgment (Section 1.2) tasks.

1.1   *Investigating Graphotactic Knowledge with Nonwords Spelling Tasks*
Pacton, Fayol and Perruchet (2002) investigated whether French-speaking children spelled the vowel /o/ differently according to its position and its consonant context. They asked second- to fifth-grade children to spell three-syllable nonwords such as /obidar/, /ribore/, and /bylevo/. In French, the phoneme /o/

can be spelled *o, au, eau, ot, aud aut*, but the distribution of these spellings varies as a function of the position and the context. For example, the grapheme *eau* is frequent in final position, very uncommon in medial position, and nonexistent in initial position. From the second grade, the spellings of /o/ differed according to the position and the consonantal environment. For instance, *eau* was more often used in final position than at the beginning and the middle of words. Moreover, in final position, *eau* was more often used after a *v* (where its appearance is frequent) than an *f* (where it is rare). These results show that children have learned statistical regularities related to word position and letter sequences within words.

In English, Treiman and Kessler (2006) compared how children spell two kinds of nonwords. In experimental nonwords, consideration of the context may result in a spelling of a phoneme that is not necessarily typical overall (e.g., /glɛd/ with /ɛ/ spelled *ea* before the coda /d/ on the basis of real words such as *head* and *dead*). In control nonwords, consideration of the context leads to the most common spelling of a phoneme (e.g., /glɛp/ with /ɛ/ before the coda /p/ which does not favor *ea* spelling). Children were more likely to produce the critical context-conditioned vowel spellings (*ea* in the example) for the experimental nonwords than for the control nonwords. Treiman, Kessler and Bick (2002) reported similar results with adults.

Sensitivity to graphotactic regularities has also been investigated in transparent writing systems like Spanish (Carrillo & Alegría, 2014) and Finnish (Lehtonen & Bryant, 2005). In Spanish, the sound /b/ is inconsistently spelled *b* or *v* and the frequency of these two graphemes depends on the following vowel. Carrillo and Alegría (2014) asked 2nd to 6th grade Spanish-speaking children to spell infrequent words and nonwords that began with /b/ followed by a vowel. Children's spelling of both words and nonwords strongly depended on the relative frequency of bigrams from grade 2 onward, and this effect increased with schooling. For example, *v* was preferred to *b* before *i* and *e* while *b* was preferred to *v* before *u*. According to Carrillo and Alegría (2014), children would use graphotactic knowledge even in consistent writing systems in which simple sound-to-spelling rules would seem to be all that is needed for success.

The above-mentioned studies clearly show that, from an early age, children do not rely on phonemes and graphemes independently of context. We attributed these effects to graphotactics but alternative explanations may be possible. First, some of these effects may reflect the influence of lexical neighborhood. Individuals could spell by analogy with specific words or could use sound-to-spelling correspondences that are larger than the phoneme-grapheme (e.g., Houghton & Zorzi, 2003; Nation, 1997; Nation & Hulme, 1996). Second, the context effects were observed by comparing contexts that differ both in graphotactic and in phonological regularities. Therefore, as we suggested above, context effects may reflect sensitivity to graphotactic regularities, for instance, that *eau* is more common after *v* than after *f in* French, independently of any regularity at a phonological level. However, context effects may also reflect sensitivity to the association between *eau* and certain sounds, for instance that *eau* is more common after /v/ than after /f/.

With regard to the influence of lexical neighborhood and spelling by analogy, there is evidence that orthographic knowledge about known words influence individuals' choice among spelling options. Nonword spelling appears to be influenced by the spelling patterns of previously heard words in "lexical priming" experiments in both children and adults (e. g., Angelelli et al., 2017; Barry & Seymour, 1988; Campbell, 1983, 1985; Patterson & Folk, 2014). For example, the same nonword is often spelled as FREAT after having heard the word *cheat* and as FREET after the word *greet* (Campbell, 1985). This influence of lexical knowledge has also been observed in free-spelling tasks that do not involve a priming paradigm. In spelling tasks, words and nonwords having many orthographic neighbors cause fewer errors (e.g. Laxon, Coltheart, & Keating, 1988; Lété, Peereman, & Fayol, 2008; Nation, 1997), lexical neighbours being defined as words that differ by only one letter from the item to be spelled or that share a common rime unit with the item to be spelled (e.g., BEEN-BEEP, Laxon et al., 1988; FILE-TILE; Nation, 1997).

The similarity with a specific word also influences spelling performance. For example, in Angelelli, Notarnicola, Marcolinbi and Burani's (2014) study, Italian-speaking children in grade 3 and 5 made fewer errors on 7–9 letters-long nonwords derived from high-frequency words (e.g., *fambino* derived from *bambino*) than on nonwords derived from low-frequency words (e.g., *zornice* derived from *cornice*). In French, Bosse, Valdois and Tainturier (2003) asked French children to spell nonwords to dictation, some of which were phonological neighbors of words with uncommon endings. As early as in Grade 1, children used low-probability phoneme/grapheme mappings (e.g., /y/ -> ut in French) significantly more often in spelling nonwords with a close phonological lexical neighbor with that spelling (e.g., /daby/ derived from "début," /deby/) than in spelling nonwords with no close neighbors (e.g., faby/ or /laSy/). Similar evidence for spelling by analogy was reported after only three months of reading instruction in a study that strictly controlled for the lexical database to which children had been exposed (Martinet, Vadois & Fayol, 2004) and with adults (Tainturier, Bosse, Roberts, Valdois & Rapp, 2013). Although one cannot rule out that the characteristics of the lexical neighbor could have impacted the results of certain experiments examining the influence of graphotactic knowledge, these characteristics are nevertheless unlikely to account for findings with long nonwords that differ from real words by several phonemes (e.g., /vitaro/ and /vitafo/ used by Pacton et al., 2002).

With regard to the issue of whether individuals' spelling can be influenced by their sensitivity to graphotactic regularities independently of any regularity at a phonological level, a few studies have examined how a target phoneme is transcribed when the influence of phonological and graphotactic contexts can be dissociated (e.g., Hayes, Treiman, & Kessler, 2006; Treiman & Boland, 2017; Treiman & Kessler, 2016). Hayes et al. (2006) examined whether spellers rely on graphotactic regularities to decide to use a simple spelling or an extended spelling that contains an additional letter, for example to decide between *f* and *ff* for /f/ or between *k* and *ck* for /k/. Spellers may select between simple and extended spellings on a phonological basis: Extended spelling are more common after a short vowel whereas simple spellings are more common after a long vowel. However, spellers may also select between simple and extended spellings on a graphotactic basis: Extended spellings are more common after a vowel spelled with a single letter whereas simple spellings are more common after a vowel spelled with more than one letter. Hayes et al. (2006) found that the use of simple or extended spellings in second-grade children was better explained by the number of letters that children used to spell the vowel than by whether the vowel was phonologically short or long. Treiman and Kessler (2016) confirmed this result with a group of adults and concluded that "people select a spelling of the final consonant in a way that allows them to avoid rimes such as *aick* and *uk* that are graphotactically odd" (p. 1157).

Convergent results come from a study by Treiman and Boland (2017) investigating whether adults rely on the rule specifying that a single medial consonant phoneme placed between a stressed vowel and an unstressed vowel is spelled with a doublet if the preceding vowel is phonologically short and with a singleton if the preceding vowel is long or diphthongized. This phonological doubling rule, like the one used by Hayes et al. (2006) works well most of the time but it is not foolproof (i.e., words such as *canon* or *manic* do not adhere to this principle). This is why it has been suggested that children should be taught the phonological doubling rule and should individually memorize the spellings of words that do not conform to it (e.g., Carreker, 2005). Treiman and Boland asked participants to spell disyllabic nonwords with short stressed vowels in the first syllable, a context in which the phonological doubling rule specifies that the medial consonant has to be doubled. Participants exhibited an effect of preceding graphotactic context, with less doubling when they spelled the vowel that came before the critical consonant with more than one letter than when they spelled it with one letter. Their doubling of medial consonants was also affected by the letters that follow, an effect that would reflect their sensitivity to the fact that doubling is less common before certain letter sequences than before others (Berg, 2016). Taken together these findings suggest that people take the surrounding orthographic context into account when selecting between singleton and doublet spellings of medial consonants and that how they spell final consonant is constrained by how they spell the preceding vowel.

1.2 Investigating Graphotactic Knowledge with Nonwords Judgment Tasks

In nonword judgment tasks, people are asked to make a choice between two alternatives that would not necessarily appear in their orthographic productions (e.g., Cassar and Treiman, 1997; Pacton, Perruchet, Fayol & Cleeremans, 2001; Sanchez, Magnan, & Ecalle, 2012). Cassar and Treiman (1997) used pairs such as {*wabb—wakk*}, with the two doublets in each nonword pair matched for height, to assess children's knowledge about which letters can or cannot be doubled in English. Children were asked to choose which items within each pair looked more like a real word. First and second graders judged that *wabb*, with a legal doublet, looks more like real words than *wakk*, with and illegal doublet. Danjon and Pacton (2009) assessed children's knowledge that, among consonants that can be doubled in French, certain are more frequently doubled than others. They exploited the fact that some consonants occur frequently in both single and double formats (e.g., *m* or *l*) and others occur frequently only in single formats (e.g., *c* or *d*). Children were presented with nonword pairs in which the two nonwords are pronounced similarly but spelled with the target consonant in the single format in one nonword (e.g., *imose*) versus in the double format in the other (e.g., *immose*). From the first grade, children more often chose nonwords including double letters for pairs like {*imose—immose*}, with the target consonant *m* frequent in both single and double formats, than for pairs like {*idose—iddose*}, with the target consonant *d* frequent only in the single format. This sensitivity to the frequency of double consonants increased with schooling (see also Pacton et al., 2001).

While the identity of the letters that may or may not be doubled constitutes an idiosyncratic property of each letter, other properties can be described with a rule. For instance, in English, French, and Finnish, doublets are illegal in word-initial position. Cassar and Treiman (1997) presented pairs such as {*nuss—nnus*} to test whether children know that consonants cannot double in the beginning of words. Even kindergarteners judged *nuss* as more word-like than *nnus*. Sensitivity to the illegality of doublets in word-initial position has also been reported from the first grade onward both in French (Pacton et al., 2001) and Finnish (Lehtonen & Bryant, 2005).

Some graphotactic regularities would be harder to learn than others. For example, in Danjon and Pacton's (2009) study, as early as in Grade 1, French-speaking children were sensitive to the illegality of doublets in word-initial position and to the fact that some consonants are more often doubled than others. However, only older children were sensitive to the fact that allowable doublets are more frequent in certain contexts than in others and to the fact that, within a consonant cluster, a double consonant can occur before, but not after, a single consonant. Sensitivity to this last graphotactic property was assessed with pairs such as {*apprulir—aprrulir*} and {*ippraler—iprraler*} in which *ppr* is legal and *prr* is illegal. The legal cluster followed a vowel after which it is frequent in French in some pairs (e.g., the cluster *ppr* after the vowel *a* in the pair {*apprulir—aprrulir*}) versus a vowel after which it rarely or even never occurs in others (e.g., the cluster *ppr* after the vowel *i* in the pair {*ippraler—iprraler*}). A preference for nonwords including a legal cluster emerged in Grade 3. However, performances remained significantly lower for legal clusters that followed vowels after which they rarely or never occur in French; and the difference between the two types of items was stable across grades. This result suggests that, even after as long as five years of exposure to print, children do not seem to rely on general rules such as "doublets are impermissible after single consonants". Indeed, if this was the case, their performance should not have varied as a function of the vowel preceding the consonant cluster (see Pacton et al., 2001 for similar findings with regard to the impermissibility of doublets in word-initial position).

To sum up, knowledge of certain graphotactic regularities develops as early as the first school year, but sensitivity to more complex regularities emerges later. How quickly graphotactic regularities can be learned has also been illustrated by Samora and Caravolas (2014) who investigated statistical learning of novel graphotactic constraints in 7-year-old children and adults. They showed that a few minutes of incidental exposure is sufficient to induce learning of novel graphotactic constraints on the position (a set of consonants appeared only in word-initial position whereas another set appeared only in final position) or on letter distributions (a set of consonants always followed by a given vowel whereas another set was always followed by another vowel).

2   The Influence of Sensitivity to Graphotactic Regularities on the
        Spelling of Real Words

In this section, we first review studies suggesting that, even early spellings, produced by children who have not begun to spell phonologically, preserve certain patterns in the writing to which the child has been exposed. Next, we review studies examining the spelling of real words and studies assessing the learning of new spellings which show that conformity to the graphotactic patterns of the system influence how children and adults spell specific words. Finally, we show that graphotactic knowledge evaluated with judgment tasks like those described in section 1.2 predict variance in orthographic learning of new spellings.

2.1   *The Influence of Knowledge about Certain Formal or Graphic Properties of Writing in Pre-phonological Spellings*

In their early life, young children see the spelling of their own name quite often, and this appears to impact their spellings. Even children whose spellings are far from being phonologically plausible because they are not yet able to connect sounds to letters overuse letters of their own names when trying to spell other words (Bloodgood, 1999, Pollo, Kessler, & Treiman, 2009; Treiman Kessler, & Bourassa, 2001for English; Gombert & Fayol, 1992, for French; Pollo, Kessler, & Treiman, 2005 for Portuguese). This effect reflects the disproportionate frequency with which they encounter those letters. As children are exposed to a greater number of printed words, they are increasingly influenced by more general patterns of the writing system, and the effects of exposure to their own names decrease. For example, the phonologically inappropriate letters used by the 6 years old children studied by Treiman et al., (2001) tended to be letters that are frequent in their reading materials.

Pollo et al. (2009) showed that the invented spellings produced by English-speaking children in the United States and Portuguese-speaking children from Brazil (mean age 4 years 9 months), who did not yet spell phonologically, were influenced by various statistical regularities: (1) Portuguese and English use the same Latin alphabet but the frequency distributions of those letters differ. For example, *a* is more frequent in Portuguese than English whereas the opposite holds for *e*. The frequency distribution of letters in children's spellings correlated with the distribution of letters in their own textual environment; (2) There was also a link between the distribution of bigrams in children's textual environment and how often they write bigrams; (3) The percentage of vowel letters is higher in Portuguese than English, and Brazilian children used a higher proportion of vowel letters than the American ones (see also Pollo,

Kessler & Treiman, 2005); (4) Geminates are more frequent in English (4% to 5%) than Portuguese (1% to 2%), and American prephonological spellers used geminates at about three times the rate of Portuguese spellers; (5) Portuguese has more consonant-vowel-alternations than English, and Brazilian children were more likely than American children to alternate consonants with vowels in their spellings.

Thus, very early, even when they are not yet able to connect sounds to letters, children are able to pick up certain formal or graphic properties of writing, such as the frequency with which different letters are used and juxtaposed. This is an example, among many others, that people learn about more or less subtle statistical regularities in the environment (e.g., Deacon, Conrad, & Pacton, 2008).

2.2   The Influence of Graphotactic Knowledge on the Spelling of Real Words

A few studies have explored whether children's misspellings tended to match the graphotactic regularities of their written language. Treiman (1993) has shown that incorrectly spelled words by first grade American children who did not receive any explicit spelling teaching, were compatible most of the time with the graphotactic regularities of the English written system. For instance, /k/ was sometimes erroneously written *ck*, but *ck* was used only rarely at the beginning of the words, a position where it never appears in English.

In French, Sénéchal, Gingras, and L'Heureux (2016) explored how children in grades 1, 2 and 3 spelled 14 monomorphemic words that end with a silent letter, 7 with the frequent silent *t*, and 7 with the less frequent silent *d*. In grades 2 and 3, children accurately marked the frequent silent *t* more often than they marked the less frequent silent *d*. Omission errors, the most common error, were as common in *t*-words as in *d*-words. The distribution of substitution errors (e.g., spelling a *t*-word with a final silent *e*, *d*, or *s*) suggests that children took into account the preceding orthographic context in trying to determine plausible silent-letter endings for words. The phonological and orthographic contexts of *t*- and *d*-words differed in this study. For instance, the final rime /ar/ appeared in four of the seven *d*-words but did not appear in any of the *t*-words.

Also in French, Pacton, Nys, Fayol and Peereman (in preparation) explored whether the spellings produced by children in grades 2 and 3 were influenced by their sensitivity to the frequency of final silent letters for a given rime. For example, French words ending in /ar/ are more often spelled *ard* than *art* and French words ending in /ã/ are more often spelled *ant* than *and*. Furthermore, whereas Sénéchal et al. (2016) used only words including final silent letters, we

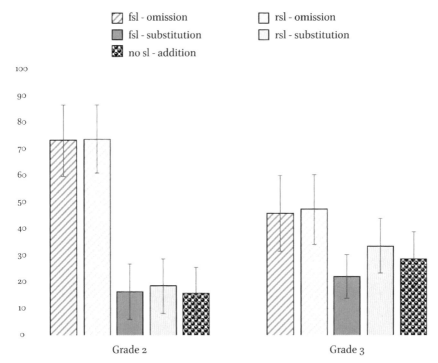

FIGURE 3.1   Mean percentages (and standard deviation of the mean) of omissions and substitution errors as a function of item type and grade. 'No SL' words do not include a silent letter, 'FSL' words include a silent letter that is frequent in the target context; 'RSL' words words include a silent letter that is less frequent in the target context.

also used words without silent letters in order to investigate whether and to what extent children include silent letters in their spellings when this is inappropriate. Children had to spell 16 words that do not include a silent letter ('No SL'), 16 words that include a silent letter that is frequent in the target context ('FSL') and 16 words that include a silent letter that is less frequent in the target context ('RSL'), all matched on the final phonological rime. For example, six words ended with the phonological rime /ar/, the 'no SL' words *nénuphar* and *radar*, the 'FSL' words *regard* and *foulard*, and the 'RSL' words *départ* and *rempart*.

In grade 2, 'no SL' words were spelled more accurately than both 'FSL' and 'RSL' words. As shown in Figure 3.1, omission of the final silent letters (e.g., *rempar* instead of *rempart*) was by far the most common error in grade 2. Substitution errors (e.g., *rempard* or *rempare* instead of *rempart*) and addition errors (e.g., *radare* or *radard* instead of *radar*) were very rare. Omission and substitution errors were as common for 'FSL' and 'RSL' words. In Grade 3, 'no

SL' words were also spelled more accurately than both 'FSL' and 'RSL' words, although to a lesser extent than in Grade 2. Omission errors were less common in Grade 3 than in Grade 2 and their rate was similar for 'FSL' and 'RSL' words. In contrast, both substitution and addition errors increased form Grade 2 to Grade 3. Substitution errors became more common for 'RSL' than 'FSL' words in Grade 3. We further took into account the substitution errors that involve only the target final silent letters of the words selected in this study, for instance only the spellings *ard* and *art* for 'FSL' and 'RSL' words ending in /ar/. Third graders spelled 'RSL' words with the silent letter of the matched 'FSL' words (*rempard* instead of *rempart*) more often than they spelled 'FSL' words with the silent letter of the matched 'RSL' words (*foulart* instead of *foulard*). This confirms Sénéchal et al.'s (2016) finding that children use their graphotactic knowledge to choose among plausible silent-letter endings even when the comparison involves items matched on the phonological rime and the frequency is defined for a specific context. The finding that correct spellings, but also substitution errors on 'FSL' and 'RSL' words and addition errors on 'no SL' words, increased from grade 2 to grade 3 suggests that children become increasingly sensitive to the fact that many French words include a final silent letter, to the point of including silent letters when this is not required.

2.3   *The Influence of Graphotactic Knowledge on the Learning of New Spellings*

The studies reported in this section have investigated whether and how people's knowledge of graphotactic regularities impacts their ability to learn and remember spellings of new words. The impact of graphotactic knowledge on the learning of new spellings has been evaluated as a function of the type of graphotactic patterns (e.g., patterns located in internal versus edge positions), the learning conditions (e.g., new spellings embedded within texts or presented in isolation; new spellings presented with or without instruction to memorize these spellings), spellers' level of graphotactic knowledge, and the delay between the learning phase and orthographic learning assessment.

Pacton, Sobaco, Fayol and Treiman (2013, Experiment 2) exposed French 9-year-olds to novel spellings in meaningful texts that they read without any instruction to remember the spellings. Such a task has often been used to investigate orthographic learning, and it allows strict control over how often participants see each novel item (e.g., Nation, Angell, & Castles, 2007; Share, 2004). The texts included three types of novel spellings. AB spellings such as *guprane* did not contain any doublets. AAB items, such as *gupprane*, contained a doublet in a position that is legal in French. ABB items such as *guprrane* contained a doublet after a single consonant letter, a position in which doublets are illegal in French. In a later spelling task, children recalled AB items better than AAB and ABB items. Among items with doublets, they performed better on legal AAB items than on illegal ABB items. Omission of the doublet was the most frequent error on both AAB and ABB items. However, children also made some errors in which they doubled the wrong consonant. Such transposition errors occurred on ABB items when the illegal *guprrane* was misspelled as the legal *gupprane*. Children almost never misspelled a legal AAB item such as *gupprane* as *guprrane*. This pattern of transposition errors, together with the fact that AAB spellings were rarely used for AB items, suggests that children sometimes remembered the presence of doubling but not the specific letter that was doubled. To account for the observation that illegal ABB items were more often misspelled with a legal doublet, Pacton, et al. (2013) suggested that children sometimes reconstructed a spelling based on their knowledge of the position in which letters are most likely to double. This reconstruction yielded correct spellings for AAB items but transposition errors for ABB items.

The idea that the children tested by Pacton et al. (2013, Experiment 2) had some knowledge of the position in which letters are most likely to double was supported by their performance in a graphotactic judgment task in which they preferred spellings such as *apprulir* over spellings such as *aprrulir* and spellings such as *nummar* over spellings such as *nnumar*. Although children scored above chance on the two types of pairs, they were far from perfect on the items testing the illegitimacy of doublets after a singleton whereas they were almost perfect on the items testing the illegitimacy of doublets in word-initial position (respectively 76% and 95% of correct choices). Pacton, et al. (2013) hypothesized that a different pattern of results might be found among participants who showed stronger knowledge that doublets cannot occur after single consonants. When these participants read texts, if their attention is drawn to unusual items such as *guprrane* they might remember these spellings with illegal doublets well. These children recalled nonwords containing a doublet in illegal word-initial position (e.g., *mmupile*) *better* than nonwords containing a doublet in legal word-internal position (e.g., *muppile*). The children almost never committed transposition errors, either from the initial position to the medial position or the reverse. The children's good memory for illegal spellings such as *mmupile* is consistent with the idea that people who are highly knowledgeable that a certain pattern is illegal pay special attention to spellings that deviate from the pattern and remember them well. This is also consistent with Wright and Ehri's (2007) finding that 6-year-olds who were less knowledgeable about this graphotactic property than the children studied Pacton et al. (2013) showed poor learning of spellings containing initial doublets such as *rrug* and sometimes made a transposition error when they recall this type of spellings (spelling *rugg* instead of *rrug*).

Another possibility is that even people who have a strong knowledge that ABB items like *guprrane* are highly unusual nevertheless show poor memory for illegal items such as *guprrane* and make transposition errors such as *guprrane* because *prr*, the illegal part of *guprrane*, is in the middle, not at the beginning as with items like *mmupile*. There is indeed evidence that adults and children often remember the initial letters of words better than the subsequent letters (e.g., Jensen, 1962; Kooi, Schutz, & Baker, 1965; Treiman, Berch, & Weatherston, 1993) and that letters at the edges of words, especially the initial letter, play a special role in reading for both children and adults (e.g., Ehri & Saltmarsh, 1995; Rayner, White, Johnson, & Liversedge, 2006). Sobaco, Treiman, Peereman, Borchardt and Pacton (2015, Experiment 1) addressed this issue. They used the same material and procedure as in Pacton et al.'s (2013) study with university students who almost always chose the graphotactically correct item when they were presented with pairs like *apprulir—aprrulir* in the graphotactic judgment task. Despite this strong knowledge that doublets cannot occur after single consonant letters, their participants showed the same pattern of results in the nonword learning task as the 9-year-olds. In particular, like the children, they better recalled AAB than ABB items; their omission errors, the most frequent errors, were as common for AAB and ABB items; and their transposition errors were almost restricted to ABB items. Thus, even though the students were very knowledgeable that ABB spellings are illegal, they produced transposition errors such as *guprrane* probably because illegal patterns occurring in word internal position did not capture their attention when they read items like *guprrane*.

In another experiment (Sobaco et al. 2015, Experiment 2) using the same nonwords presented in isolation, the authors explored whether explicit instructions to learn the items' spellings lead participants to perform an exhaustive analysis of the letters in the nonwords, and therefore improve spelling performance on illegal ABB consonant clusters. Some participants were asked to read aloud the nonwords and memorize their spellings (explicit learning condition) and others were instructed to read aloud the nonwords but were not asked to memorize their spellings (implicit learning condition). Instruction type did affect the pattern of results. Participants who received explicit instructions to remember the spellings recalled more correct spellings than participants who did not, confirming previous findings (e.g., Ormrod, 1986). The analyses of the misspellings revealed fewer omission errors in the explicit learning condition than in the implicit learning condition, but no fewer transposition errors. For both instruction types, AAB items were better recalled than ABB items, omission errors were as common for AAB items as for ABB items, but transposition errors were almost restricted to ABB items. This suggests that the participants of the explicit learning condition have paid more attention to the presence of doublets in specific items than the participants in the implicit condition but sometimes failed to remember which letter was doubled.

Finally, Sobaco et al. (2015, Experiment 3) used a copy task in which the nonwords of Experiments 1 and 2 were presented in isolation on a computer screen for one second and participants had to write down the spelling of each nonword after it vanished from the screen. Orthographic learning was subsequently assessed as in Experiment 2. They considered the rendition of the spellings in both the copy phase and the final recall test in order to investigate when graphotactic knowledge influences orthographic learning. On the one hand, if participants expect novel words to contain familiar patterns, when presented with an item like *guprrane*, they may encode it as *gupprane*, making a transposition error during the initial encoding of the items. On the other hand, if participants correctly encode the presence and the position of a doublet, but loose positional information somewhere between item's exposure and the final recall test, transposition errors should occur only in the final recall test. In the final recall task of Experiment 3, as in Experiments 1 and 2, participants committed transposition errors and they did so only for ABB items. This shows that copying, even though it forces attention to every letter, did not eliminate transposition errors. Copying did benefit memory, however. Indeed, level of orthographic learning in Experiment 3 was higher than in Experiment 1 and in the implicit learning condition of Experiment 2, and was as good as in the explicit learning condition of Experiment 2. This is consistent with previous studies showing that writing words leads to better memory for their spellings than does reading them (e.g., Bosman & van Orden, 1997; Bosse, Chaves, & Valdois, 2014; Shahar-Yames & Share, 2008). With regard to the issue of when knowledge about the legal position of doublets influences orthographic learning, transposition errors in the copy task were more common than transposition errors occurring in the recall test on items correctly spelled in the copy task. This result suggests that most transposition errors reflect processes that occur soon after the presentation of an item. Cases of ABB spellings correctly produced in the copy task but reconstructed as AAB spellings in the recall test did exist but were rather rare. These findings suggest that most transposition errors do not result from belated reconstructive processes of memory. Further researches are required to determine whether these errors resulted from inefficient coding or early reconstructive processes.

Although the mode of presentation of the nonwords and the instructions given to participants differed greatly across the three experiments, the pattern of results in the final recall test was strikingly similar, with ABB items recalled less well than AAB items, and transposition errors almost restricted to ABB items. These results strongly differed from those of Pacton et al.'s (2013, Experiment 1) in which 9-year-olds showed good memory for spellings such as *mmupile* and almost never committed transposition errors like *muppile*. Taken together, the studies just reviewed suggest that good memory for unusual patterns depends on both the degree of knowledge that participants have about the unusual nature of the pattern and the orthographic context in which it occurs. In Wright and Ehri's (2007) study, children's attention may not have been captured by the presence of a doublet, even in a salient position, because they were not very knowledgeable that doublets are illegal in this position. In Sobaco et al.'s study, despite their strong graphotactic knowledge, participants' attention may not have been captured by items that contained illegal patterns like *prr* because these patterns were located in the less salient word-internal position.

In the above studies, conformity to graphotactic patterns was manipulated by contrasting legal and illegal patterns. Convergent results have been reported with probabilistic graphotactic regularites. For example, Pacton, Borchardt, Treiman, Lété and Fayol (2014) used patterns that are frequent and patterns that are less frequent, but still legal. They asked university students to read texts that included no-doublet items that contained only single consonants (e.g., *tidunar*), frequent-doublet items that contained one frequent consonant doublet (e.g., *tidunnar*), and rare-doublet items that contained one rare consonant doublet (e.g., *tiddunar*). The three types of nonword spellings had the same pronunciations. In the test phase, participants were explicitly instructed to spell the item as it was written in the story, as in Pacton et al. (2013) and Sobaco et al. (2015). Accuracy was higher for spellings that contained only singletons than for spellings that contained a doublet, and for spellings that contained a frequent doublet than for spellings that contained a less common but still legal doublet. Transposition errors were far more frequent on rare-doublet items (e.g., *tiddunar* misspelled as *tidunnar*) than on frequent-doublet items (e.g., *tidunnar* misspelled as *tiddunar*) and spellings including a doublet (frequent or rare) were used far less often for no-doublet items than for frequent- and rare-doublet items. These findings suggest that participants sometimes remembered the presence of doubling but not the specific letter that was doubled. They fit well with studies showing that certain brain-damaged patients remember that a particular word contains a doublet but not which letter is doubled (e.g., Caramazza & Miceli, 1990; McCloskey, Badecker, Goodman-Shulman, & Aliminosa, 1994; Tainturier & Caramazza, 1996). When the participants of our studies remembered the presence of doubling but not the specific letter that was doubled, they would rely on their graphotactic knowledge about which letters are most likely to double and in which positions. Thus, participants sometimes mistakenly doubled a letter that by virtue of its identity and position often doubles: a frequently doubled medial consonant. Only very occasionally did they double a letter in a position that permits doubling but that does not often double: a rarely doubled medial consonant. Similar findings were found when orthographic learning was assessed with a recognition task in which participants were asked to indicate which of the three spellings (e.g., *tidunar*, *tidunnar* and *tiddunar*) was in the text that they read.

Borchardt (2012) used the same material and procedure as did Pacton et al. (2014) in a study that involved third and fifth graders. Orthographic learning was assessed by asking certain children to spell the nonwords as written in the stories and by asking other children to indicate which of three phonologically plausible spellings corresponded to the spelling in the stories. The results, and more specifically, the fact that omission errors were as common for frequent- and rare-doublet items whereas transposition errors were far more common on rare-doublet items (e.g., *tiddunar* misspelled as *tidunnar*) than on frequent-doublet items (e.g., *tidunnar* misspelled as *tiddunar*), were very similar to those reported by Pacton et al. (2014) whether orthographic learning was assessed with a recall or a recognition task in grade 5 and when orthographic learning was assessed with a recognition task in grade 3. In the recall task, children in grade 3 almost never included a doublet in their spellings for the three types of items. Thus, correct spellings and transposition errors were very low, and in similar proportions, for frequent- and rare-doublet items in grade 3.

In all the preceding studies, the test took place soon after the learning phase, around 10/15 minutes. Recently, Peereman and Pacton (in preparation) used the same material and procedure as in Pacton et al. (2014) and Borchardt (2012) in the learning phase and they investigated orthographic learning one week later with a forced-choice recognition task. Children were Swiss French-speaking in grade 5. Some of them were asked to read the nonwords and memorize their spellings (explicit learning condition) and others were asked to read the nonwords but were not asked to memorize their spellings (implicit learning condition). As shown in Table 3.1, children were less accurate for spellings that contained rare doublets than for spellings that contained only singletons or frequent doublets, without significant difference between these two latter. The analysis of the errors revealed that transposition errors were more common for rare- than frequent-doublet items whereas omission errors were as common for rare- and frequent-doublet items. Neither instruction type, nor the interaction between instruction type and item type were significant, whether the dependent variable was the choice of the correct spelling, the transposi-

TABLE 3.1   Percentage of different types of spellings chosen as a function of learning conditions for the three types of items presented d

	Implicit condition			Explicit condition		
Type of spelling chosen	No-doublet item presented	Frequent-doublet item presented	Rare-doublet item presented	No-doublet item presented	Frequent-doublet item presented	Rare-doublet item presented
No doublet	**55.6 (34.9)**	42.6 (43.2)	46.3 (41.4)	**55.6 (37.6)**	40.7 (36.8)	42.6 (38.5)
Frequent doublet	37.0 (35.6)	**44.4 (40.0)**	*27.8 (37.6)*	33.3 (36.7)	**51.9 (37.9)**	*27.8 (32.0)*
Rare doublet	7.4 (18.1)	*13.0 (22.3)*	**25.9 (40.1)**	11.1 (25.3)	*7.4 (18.1)*	**29.6 (31.8)**

Note. Correct spellings are in bold and transposition errors in italics; standard deviations in parentheses

tion of the doublet or its omission. As in previous studies, the prevalence of transposition errors on rare-doublet items could not be explained by a general trend to choose spellings containing frequent doublets because these spellings were more often chosen for frequent- than rare- and no-doublet items. The similarity of the pattern of transposition errors according to whether orthographic learning is assessed soon after the learning phase (Borchardt, 2012) or after a prolonged delay (Peereman & Pacton, in preparation) is in accordance with Sobaco et al.'s (2015, Experiment 3) results with a copy task suggesting that the influence of graphotactic regularities resulted from inefficient coding or early reconstructive processes rather than from belated reconstructive processes of memory. However, at this delay, children made more addition errors (i.e., choosing a frequent- or a rare-doublet spelling) for items presented with only singletons than in previous studies. For example, in the recognition task, Borchardt (2012) found 16.7 % of addition errors (10.4 % with a frequent doublet and 6.3 % with a rare doublet) when the children of Peereman and Pacton's (in preparation) study made 44.4 % of addition errors (33.3 % with a frequent doublet and 11.1 % with a rare doublet).

To sum up, children and adults' memory for spellings, like memory for other things, is influenced by experience with specific items and by general knowledge built up from experience with sets of items. This phenomenon appears to be robust given that it is observed with children and adults, with graphotactic properties that can be described with general rules and with probabilistic regularities, whether nonwords are presented in isolation or embedded in texts, and whether participants are asked to learn spellings, copy them, or read them aloud. In spelling, as in other domains, reliance on statistical regularities can yield systematic errors when that event includes less common patterns. More often, however, it yields correct responses.

2.4   *The Contribution of Children's Prior Word-Specific Knowledge and Graphotactic Knowledge to Their Learning of Novel Spellings*

The studies reviewed in section 2.3 compared the learning of new spellings depending on whether they contain graphotactic patterns that are frequent, less frequent but still legal, or even illegal. The studies reported in this section have explored whether children's graphotactic knowledge, assessed with non-word judgment tasks such as those described in section 1.2, predicts variance in the learning of new spellings.

There is large evidence that the degree of orthographic learning is closely tied to overall levels of decoding success (e.g., Share, 2008). Although statistically significant, most of the time these correlations are modest, suggesting that there is considerable variance associated with orthographic learning that is not captured by initial phonological decoding. Furthermore, Nation et al., (2007) suggested that, even when a strong relation between phonological decoding and orthographic learning is observed, this effect does not hold at an item-by-item level of analysis. The variance in orthographic learning unexplained by the ability to phonologically decode the stimulus correctly has sometimes been accounted for under the general rubric of "orthographic processing skills" (Berninger, 1994, 1995). Although it has been difficult to pin down precisely what is meant by this term (Castles & Nation, 2006; Nation et al., 2007), two facets of orthographic knowledge have often been distinguished. One is lexical and word-specific. For example, that the word /rɛn/ is spelled *rain* rather than *rane*. The second is sub-lexical; it is about the statistical patterns in the arrangement of letters in words and, as we have seen from the beginning of this chapter, it is often called graphotactic knowledge. A few studies have explored the contribution of children's prior graphotactic knowledge to their learning of novel spellings (Cunningham, 2006; Pacton, Borchardt, & Bosse, 2017).

In English, Cunningham (2006) reported regression analyses showing that individual differences in orthographic learning were related to prior orthographic knowledge and predicted first graders' degree of orthographic learning after controlling for general decoding ability. Prior orthographic knowledge corresponded to both word-specific knowledge, assessed with two forced-choice tasks (choosing the correct spelling between two phonologically similar letter strings such as *rain* and *rane* and indicating the spelling corresponding to a flower between *rows* and *rose*) and graphotactic knowledge, assessed with a nonword judgment task (choosing the spelling that looks most like a real word between which *boap* and *bowp*). Unfortunately, in the regression analyses on orthographic learning, a composite orthographic knowledge score was used for the three orthographic tasks that did not differentiate between the contributions of general and word-specific orthographic knowledge.

In French, Pacton et al. (2017) investigated the role of knowledge about word-specific spelling and graphotactic regularities during orthographic learning via self-teaching in fourth graders. Children read 12 novel words embedded within texts. Each novel word included phonemes for which several spellings are possible (e.g., the final /ã/ of loufant that can be spelled *an, ant, and* or *ent*). After a delay of about 20 minutes, their orthographic learning was assessed with a task of spelling to dictation. Previous word-specific orthographic learning was assessed with the dictation task of the Corbeau standardized spelling subtest (Chevrier-Muller et al., 1997) and a recognition task in which children had to choose the correct spelling among three phonologically plausible spellings (e.g., *meson—maison—maizon*). Graphotactic knowledge was assessed with Pacton et al.'s (2013) nonword judgment task. Regression analyses show that both types of orthographic knowledge make separate and unique contributions to orthographic learning, over and above the contributions of phonological skills. Thus, this study suggests that these two facets of orthographic knowledge are important in orthographic learning.

The above-mentioned studies have examined the implicit learning of novel spellings embedded in texts that participants read for meaning. In a recent study with French-speaking children from second to sixth grades, Binamé and Poncelet (2016) have investigated the contribution of graphotactic knowledge to the acquisition of new spellings in an explicit learning situation, beyond that of the level of phonological recoding, indexed by a nonword reading task, and word-specific orthographic knowledge. Graphotactic sensitivity was assessed with a nonword judgment task with pairs such as {capurne—quapurne} to test sensitivity to the frequency of Phoneme-Grapheme mappings and pairs such as {rimmuche—ridduche} to test sensitivity to the frequency of medial double consonants. In the orthographic learning phase, children first read nonwords containing orthographic inconsistencies (e.g., /drinɔp/ spelled drynoppe, with /i/ and /p/ that are less often spelled *y* and *pp* than *i* and *p* in French). Then, children had to spell under dictation each nonword 10 times, as they had been presented during the previous reading. Finally, orthographic learning was assessed 1 week and 1 month after the learning phase with a dictation task. Graphotactic sensitivity accounted for a portion of variance in the retention of the representations at 1 week, but not at 1 month, probably because of a substantial drop-off in the retention of the orthographic information in the absence of refreshment. According to the authors, the contribution of graphotactic knowledge at 1 week delay suggests that orthographic sensitivity would be particularly involved in the retrieval of newly learned orthographic representations.

Thus, several studies have found that graphotactic knowledge contributes unique variance in learning the spelling of novel words above that contributed by word specific orthographic knowledge. This finding is well in accordance with Conrad, Harris and Williams (2013) who found that word specific and general orthographic knowledge make separate and unique contributions to both reading and spelling, assessed with standardized tests, over and above the contributions of phonological skills (see also Conners, Loveall, Moore, Hume, & Maddox, 2011). According to Conrad et al. (2013), graphotactic knowledge may contribute to reading and spelling because, as readers learn about spelling patterns that recur, they can use these larger units to form connections between a word's spelling, its pronunciation and its meaning in memory (Ehri, 2005). Furthermore, children could use their graphotactic knowledge to determine the pronunciation or the spelling of an item that is not yet lexically acquired.

3   Conclusion

There has been ongoing interest in whether and how people learn about more or less subtle statistical regularities in the environment (e.g., Saffran, Aslin, & Newport, 1996; Perruchet & Pacton, 2006). In this chapter, we focus on the statistical learning of graphotactic regularities and on what spellers do with what they learn about graphotactic regularities. We first reviewed studies showing that children are sensitive to graphotatic regularities from a young age. For instance, pre-phonological invented spellings produced by children even before 5 years reflects their sensitivity to the frequency with which different letters are used and juxtaposed in their language (Pollo et al., 2009). As early as the first grade, and sometimes even in kindergarten, children are sensitive to salient graphotactic regularities such as the illegality of doublets in word-initial position or the fact that some letters can be doubled whereas others cannot (e.g., Casar & Treiman, 1997). However, other graphotactic regularities, such as the illegality of doublets after single letters, appear to be more difficult to detect. Sensitivity to these kinds of regularities might emerge later and remain less developed, even at the end of the elementary school (Danjon & Pacton, 2009; Pacton et al., 2013).

Sensitivity to graphotactic regularities has been documented in isolation, mainly with nonword judgment and spelling tasks (e.g., Cassar & Treiman, 1997; Pacton et al., 2001, 2002). These tasks have been used because it is difficult to determine whether someone has spelled a real word correctly using his/her word-specific knowledge and/or general orthographic knowledge. However, studies examining misspellings have revealed an influence of graphotactic knowledge on the orthographic production of words among children of different ages and different spelling abilities, as well as among adults (e.g., Pacton et al., in preparation; Treiman, 1993; Treiman et al., 2002). For example, when French-speaking children spell words such as *foulard*, with a final silent *d* that is frequent after *ar*, and *rempart*, with a final silent *t* that is less frequent after *ar*, they are less likely to misspell the first word as *foulart*, with the less frequent silent *t* instead of the frequent *d*, than to spell the second word as *rempard*, with *d* instead of *t* (Pacton et al., in preparation). When children and adults use regularities that are probabilistic, for instance that a given vowel is very often, but not always, spelled with a specific grapheme in a specific consonantal context, this leads to misspellings for words including letter combinations that do not match the more frequent patterns (Treiman et al. 2002). Importantly, although these studies have primarily focused on misspellings, most of the time, reliance on statistical regularities yields correct responses. Similar findings have been reported with other sources of information. For instance, most of the time, use of morphologically related words yields to correct spellings, as when the morphologically simple word *music* is used to spell the morphologically complex word *musician*. However, because some words do not follow this principle of morphological constancy, this can lead to misspellings, as when the use of the morphologically simple word *explain* leads to spell the morphologically complex word *explanation* as *explaination* (Bourassa & Treiman, 2008; Pacton & Deacon, 2008).

The idea that conformity to graphotactic patterns may explain, in part, the difficulties of acquisition of lexical knowledge also comes from studies examining the learning of new words (Pacton et al., 2014; Sobaco et al., 2015). The influence of graphotactic regularities on the memory for specific words exhibited in these studies appears to be robust given that it has been found with various graphotactic patterns, in different learning conditions, with different types of orthographic learning assessment, and with spellers of different ages and different levels of graphotactic knowledge. Further studies are nevertheless required to determine more precisely whether the influence of graphotactic knowledge comes from inefficient coding, or from more or less early reconstructive processes.

The influence of graphotactics on the acquisition of word-specific knowledge aligns with other suggestions that people use their knowledge of graphotactic patterns even when other sources of information, *a priori* more relevant, are available to produce correct spellings. In this chapter, we reported studies showing that children and adults' choice between simple and extended spellings, such as *f* and *ff*, was better explained by the number of letters that children used to spell the vowel than by whether the vowel was phonologically short or long (Hayes et al., 2006; Treiman & Kessler, 2016). Even when the rules on which spellers can rely have few or even no exceptions, children and adults appear to be influenced by their graphotactic knowledge (e.g., Deacon & Pacton, 2007; Kemp & Bryant, 2003; Pacton, Fayol, & Perruchet, 2005). In English, for example, both children and adults are more likely to correctly spell the noun plural marker /z/ with *s* after a consonant, as in *dogs*, than after a long vowel, as in *fleas*. Such a difference should not be observed if spellers rely on a rule specifying that plurals are marked with *s* whether they are pronounced with final /s/ or /z/. The difference appears to reflect spellers' knowledge that at the end of words *eaz* is graphotactically legal whereas *bz* is not.

The finding that children and adults rely on graphotactic regularities even when they can rely on phonographemic or morphological rules suggests that the use of graphotactic knowledge is irrepressible. Future studies should further investigate the interactions between graphotactic knowledge and other sources of information and the irrepressible nature of the use of graphotactic knowledge with children and adults of varying reading and spelling abilities and of varying capacity for statistical learning (Arciuli & Simpson, 2011). Future studies should also determine how knowledge about graphotactic regularities may be represented/implemented in the overall cognitive spelling system. Although this issue has rarely been addressed, Treiman and Boland (2017, see also Treiman, 2017) recently argued that existing models of the spelling process require modification in order to explain their finding that the letters that are selected for one phoneme can influence the choice of spellings for another phoneme.

Acknowledgements

This study was supported by the LABEX EFL (ANR-10-LABX-0083). We wish to thank Elise Boos and Laura Wider for their help in conducting the Swiss study described in Section 2.2.

References

Arciuli, J., & Simpson, I.C. (2011). Statistical Learning Is Related to Reading Ability in Children and Adults. *Cognitive Science, 36*, 286–304.

Angelelli, P., Marinelli, C.V., Putzolu, A., Notarnicola, A., Iaia, M., & Burani, C. (2017). Learning to spell in a language with transparent orthography: Distributional properties of orthography and whole-word lexical processing. *The Quarterly Journal of Experimental Psychology, 7*, 1–14.

Angelelli, P., Notarnicola, A., Marcolini, S., & Burani, C. (2014). Interaction between the lexical and sublexical spelling procedures: A study on Italian primary school children. In Special issue M.A. Pinto, & S. D'Amico (Eds.), Lexical access: Studies on monolingual and plurilingual subjects at different developmental stages, *Journal of Applied Psycholinguistics*, XIV, 2.

Barry, C., & Seymour, P.H.K. (1988). Lexical priming and sound-to-spelling contingency effects in nonword spelling. *The Quarterly Journal of Experimental Psychology*, 40A, 5–40.

Berg, K. (2016). Double consonants in English: Graphemic, morphological, prosodic and etymological determinants. *Reading and Writing: An Interdisciplinary Journal*, 29, 453–474.

Berninger, V.W. (1994). *The varieties of orthographic knowledge. I: Theoretical and developmental issues*. Dordrecht, The Netherlands: Kluwer.

Berninger, V.W. (1995). *The varieties of orthographic knowledge. II: Relationships to phonology, reading and writing*. Dordrecht, The Netherlands: Kluwer.

Binamé, F., & Poncelet, M. (2016). The development of the abilities to acquire novel detailed orthographic representations and maintain them in long-term memory. *Journal of Experimental Child Psychology*, 143, 14–33.

Bloodgood, J.W. (1999). What's in a name? Children's name writing and literacy acquisition. *Reading Research Quarterly*, 34, 342–367.

Borchardt, G. (2012). *L'influence des connaissances graphotactiques sur l'acquisition de l'orthographe lexicale: étude chez l'enfant de l'école élémentaire*. (Unpublished doctoral dissertation). Université Paris Descartes, Boulogne-Billancourt, France.

Bosman, A.M.T., & Van Orden, G.C. (1997). Why spelling is more difficult than reading. In C.A. Perfetti, M. Fayol, & L. Rieben (Eds.), *Learning to spell: Research, theory, and practice across languages* (pp. 173–194). Hillsdale, NJ: Erlbaum.

Bosse, M.-L., Chaves, N., & Valdois, S. (2014). Lexical orthography acquisition: Is handwriting better than spelling aloud? *Frontiers in Psychology*, 5.

Bosse, M.-L., Valdois, S., & Tainturier, M.-J.P. (2003). Analogy without priming in early spelling development. *Reading and Writing: An Interdisciplinary Journal*, 16, 693–716.

Bourassa, D.C., & Treminan, R. (2008). Morphological constancy in spelling: a comparison of children with dyslexia and typically developing children. *Dyslexia*, 14, 155–169.

Campbell, R. (1983). Writing nonwords to dictation. *Brain and Language*, 19, 153–178.

Campbell, R. (1985). When children write nonwords to dictation. *Journal of Experimental Child Psychology*, 40, 133–151.

Caramazza, A., & Miceli, G. (1990). The structure of graphemic representations. *Cognition*, 37, 243–297.

Carreker, S. (2005). Teaching spelling. In J.R. Birsh (Ed.), *Multisensory teaching of basic language skills* (2nd ed., pp. 257–295). Baltimore, MD: Paul H. Brookes.

Carrillo, M.S., & Alegría, J. (2014). The development of children's sensitivity to bigram frequencies when spelling in Spanish, a transparent writing system. *Reading and Writing: An Interdisciplinary Journal, 27*, 571–590.

Cassar, M., & Treiman, R. (1997). The beginnings of orthographic knowledge: Children's knowledge of double letters in words. *Journal of Educational Psychology, 89*, 631–644.

Castles, A., & Nation, K. (2006). How does orthographic learning happen? In S. Andrews (Ed.), *From inkmarks to ideas: Challenges and controversies about word recognition and reading.* (pp. 151–179). Hove, East Sussex: Psychology Press.

Chetail, F. (2017) What do we do with what we learn? Statistical learning of orthographic regularities impacts written word processing. *Cognition, 163*, 103–120.

Chevrier-Muller, C., Simon, A.M., & Fournier, S. (1997). *Batterie Langage Oral-Langage Ecrit, Mémoire, Attention. L2MA* [*Oral and Written Language Battery. Memory. Attention. L2MA*]. Paris: Editions du Centre de Psychologie Appliquée.

Conners, F., Loveall, S.J., Moore, M.S., Hume, L.E., & Maddox, C.D. (2011). An individual differences analysis of the self-teaching hypothesis. *Journal of Experimental Child Psychology, 108*, 402–410.

Conrad, N.J., Harris, N., & Williams, J. (2013). Individual differences in children's literacy development: the contribution of orthographic knowledge. *An Interdisciplinary Journal: Reading and Writing, 26*, 1223–1239.

Cunningham, A. (2006). Accounting for children's orthographic learning while reading text: Do children self-teach? *Journal of Experimental Child Psychology, 95*, 56–77.

Danjon, J., & Pacton, S. (2009). Children's Learning about properties of double letters: The case of French. *The 16th European Society for Cognitive Psychology Conference (ESCOP)*, Cracow, Poland, September 2–5.

Deacon, S.H., Conrad, N., & Pacton, S. (2008). A statistical learning perspective on children's learning about graphotactic and morphological regularities in spelling. *Canadian Psychology/ Psychologie Canadienne, 49*, 118–124.

Deacon, S.H., & Pacton, S. (2007). Using spelling as an empirical test of rules versus statistics. *Society for the Scientific Study of Reading*, Prague, CZ, July 12–15.

Ehri, L. (2005). Learning to read words: Theory, findings, and issues. *Scientific Studies of Reading, 9*, 167–188.

Ehri, L.C., & Saltmarsh, J. (1995). Beginning readers outperform older disabled readers in learning to read words by sight. *Reading and Writing: An Interdisciplinary Journal, 7*, 295–326.

Gombert, J.E., & Fayol, M. (1992). Writing in preliterate children. *Language and Instruction, 2*, 23–41.

Hayes, H., Treiman, R., & Kessler, B. (2006). Children use vowels to help them spell consonants. *Journal of Experimental Child Psychology, 94*, 27–42.

Houghton, G., & Zorzi, M. (2003). Normal and impaired spelling in a connectionist dual-route architecture. *Cognitive Neuropsychology, 20*, 115–162.

Jensen, A.R. (1962). Spelling errors and the serial-position effect. *Journal of Educational Psychology, 53*, 105–109.

Kemp, N., & Bryant, P.E. (2003). Do Beez Buzz? Rule-Based and Frequency-Based Knowledge in Learning to Spell Plural –s. *Child Development, 74*, 63–74.

Kessler, B., & Treiman, R. (2001). Relationships between Sounds and Letters in English Monosyllables. *Journal of Memory and Language, 44*, 592–617.

Kooi, B.Y., Schutz, R.E., & Baker, R.L. (1965). Spelling errors and the serial-position effect. *Journal of Educational Psychology, 56*, 334–336.

Laxon, V.J., Coltheart, V., & Keating, C. (1988). Children find friendly words friendly too: Words with many orthographic neighbors are easier to read and spell. *British Journal of Educational Psychology, 58*, 103–119.

Lehtonen, A., & Bryant, P.E. (2005). Doublet challenge: form comes before function in children's understanding of their orthography. *Developmental Science, 8*, 211–217.

Lété, B., Peereman, R., & Fayol, M. (2008). Consistency and word-frequency effects on spelling among first- to fifth-grade French children: A regression-based study. *Journal of Memory and Language, 58*, 952–977.

Mano, Q.R. (2016). Developing sensitivity to subword combinatorial orthographic regularity (SCORe): A two-process framework. *Scientific Studies of Reading, 20*, 231–247.

Martinet, C., Valdois, S., & Fayol, M. (2004). Lexical orthographic knowledge develops from the beginning of literacy acquisition. *Cognition, 91*, B11–B22.

McCloskey, M., Badecker, W., Goodman-Shulman, R.A., & Aliminosa, D. (1994). The structure of graphemic representations in spelling: Evidence from a case of acquired dysgraphia. *Cognitive Neuropsychology, 2*, 341–392.

Nation, K. (1997). Children's sensitivity to rime unit frequency when spelling words and nonwords. *Reading and Writing: An Interdisciplinary Journal, 9*, 321–338.

Nation, K., Angell, P., & Castles, A. (2007). Orthographic learning via self-teaching in children learning to read English: Effects of exposure, durability, and context. *Journal of Experimental Child Psychology, 96*, 71–84.

Nation, K., & Hulme, C. (1996). The Automatic Activation of Sound-Letter Knowledge: An Alternative Interpretation of Analogy and Priming Effects in Early Spelling Development. *Journal of Experimental Child Psychology, 63*, 416–435.

Ormrod, J.E. (1986). Learning to spell while reading: A follow-up study. *Perceptual and Motor Skills, 63*, 652–654.

Pacton, S., Borchardt, S. & Bosse, M.L. (2017). Orthographic learning via self-teaching in children learning to read French: Effects of previous knowledge about word-specific spelling and graphotactic regularities. *Society for the Scientific Study of Reading*, Halifax, Canada, July 12–15.

Pacton, S., Borchardt, G., Treiman, R., Lété, B., & Fayol, M. (2014). Learning to spell from reading: General knowledge about spelling patterns influences memory for specific words. *Quarterly Journal of Experimental Psychology, 67*, 1019–1036.

Pacton, S., & Deacon, H. (2008). The timing and mechanisms of children's use of morphological information in spelling: A review of evidence from English and French. *Cognitive Development, 23*, 339–359.

Pacton, S., Fayol, M., & Perruchet, P. (2002). The acquisition of untaught orthographic regularities in French. In L. Verhoeven, C. Elbro, & P. Reitsma (Eds.), *Precursors of functional literacy* (pp. 121–136). Dordrecht, Netherlands: Kluwer.

Pacton, S., Fayol, M., & Perruchet, P. (2005). Children's implicit learning of graphotactic and morphological regularities. *Child Development, 76*, 324–339.

Pacton, S., Perruchet, P., Fayol, M., & Cleeremans, A. (2001). Implicit learning in real world context: The case of orthographic regularities. *Journal of Experimental Psychology: General, 130*, 401–426.

Pacton, S., Sobaco, A., Fayol, M., & Treiman, R. (2013). How does graphotactic knowledge influence children's learning of new spellings? *Frontiers in Psychology, 4:701.* doi: 10.3389/fpsyg.2013.00701.

Patterson, T.J., & Folk, J.R. (2014). Lexical Influences on the Sublexical System during Nonword Spelling. *SOJ Psychol 1*(3): 1–8. DOI: http://dx.doi.org/10.15226/2374-6874/1/3/00112.

Perruchet, P., & Pacton, S. (2006). Implicit learning and statistical learning: one phenomenon, two approaches. *Trends in Cognitive Sciences, 10*, 233–238.

Pollo, T.C., Kessler, B., & Treiman, R. (2005). Vowels, syllables, and letter names: Differences between young children's spelling in English and Portuguese. *Journal of Experimental Child Psychology, 92*, 161–181.

Pollo, T.C., Kessler, B., & Treiman, R. (2009). Statistical patterns in children's early writing. *Journal of Experimental Child Psychology, 104*, 410–426.

Rayner, K., White, S., Johnson, R.L., & Liversedge, S. (2006). Raeding wrods with jubmled lettres: There is a cost. *Psychological Science, 17*, 192–193.

Saffran, J.R., Aslin, R.N., & Newport, E.L. (1996). Statistical Learning by 8-Month-Old Infants. *Science, 274*, 1926–1928.

Samara, A., & Caravolas, M. (2014). Statistical learning of novel graphotactic constraints in children and adults. *Journal of Experimental Child Psychology, 121*, 137–155.

Sanchez, M., Magnan, A., & Ecalle, J. (2012). Knowledge about word structure in beginning readers: what specific links are there with word reading and spelling? *European Journal of Psychology of Education, 27*, 299–317.

Sénéchal, M., Gingras, M., & L'Heureux, L. (2016). Modeling Spelling Acquisition: The Effect of Orthographic Regularities on Silent-Letter Representations. *Scientific Studies of Reading, 2*, 155–162.

Shahar-Yames, D., & Share, D.L. (2008). Spelling as a self-teaching mechanism in orthographic learning. *Journal of Research in Reading, 31*, 22–39.

Share, D.L. (2004). Orthographic learning at a glance: On the time course and developmental onset of self-teaching. *Journal of Experimental Child Psychology, 87*, 267–298.

Share, D. (2008). Orthographic learning, phonological recoding, and self-teaching. In V. Robert (Ed.). *Advances in child development and behavior* (Vol. 36, pp. 31–82). San Diego: Elsevier.

Sobaco, A., Treiman, R., Peereman, R., Borchardt, G., & Pacton, S. (2015). The influence of graphotactic knowledge on adults' learning of spelling. *Memory & Cognition, 43*, 593–604.

Tainturier, M.J., Bosse, M.L., Roberts, D.J., Valdois, S., & Rapp, B. (2013). Lexical neighborhood effects in pseudoword spelling. *Frontiers in Psychology, 4:862. doi: 10.3389/fpsyg .2013.00862.*

Tainturier, M.J., & Caramazza, A. (1996). The status of double letters in graphemic representations. *Journal of Memory and Language, 35*, 53–73.

Treiman, R. (1993). *Beginning to spell: A study of first-grade children.* New-York: Oxford University Press.

Treiman, R. (2017). Learning to spell: Phonology and beyond. *Cognitive Neuropsychology, 22*, 83–93.

Treiman, R., Berch, D., & Weatherston, S. (1993). Children's use of phoneme–grapheme correspondences in spelling: Roles of position and stress. *Journal of Educational Psychology, 85*, 466–477.

Treiman, R., & Boland, K. (2017). Graphotactics and spelling: Evidence from consonant doubling. *Journal of Memory and Language, 92*, 254–264.

Treiman, R., & Kessler, B. (2006). Spelling as statistical learning: Using consonantal context to spell vowels. *Journal of Educational Psychology, 98*, 642–652.

Treiman, R., & Kessler, B. (2016). Choosing between alternative spellings of sounds: The role of context. *Journal of Experimental Psychology: Learning, Memory, and Cognition, 42*, 1154–1159.

Treiman, R., Kessler, B., & Bick, S. (2002). Context sensitivity in the spelling of English vowels. *Journal of Memory and Language, 47*, 448–468.

Treiman, R., Kessler, B., & Bourassa, D.C. (2001). Children's own names influence their spelling. *Applied Psycholinguistics, 22*, 555–570.

Wright, D.M., & Ehri, L.C. (2007). Beginners remember orthography when they learn to read words: The case of double letters. *Applied Psycholinguistics, 28*, 115–133.

CHAPTER 4

BAST: a Theory of Bilingual Spelling in Alphabetic Systems

Marie-Josèphe Tainturier

The main goal of this chapter is to present a theoretical framework to account for bilingual spelling abilities and to guide future research in this area. In our increasingly global world, many people will at some point in their life need to communicate in different languages. For this reason, there has been an explosion of research on language and bilingualism in the past two decades. However, most of this research concerns spoken production or, to a lesser extent, visual and spoken word recognition abilities. Surprisingly, there has so far been very little research on bilingual written production, even though there are increasingly detailed theoretical proposals regarding spelling in monolingual populations. This is surprising because written language abilities are essential in many contexts, even more so due to the widespread use of electronic means of communication. Furthermore, it is becoming increasingly common for people to have to write in more than one language. For example, one may need to send emails in English to colleagues from other countries (who may also not be English natives themselves) or use it on social platforms. In addition, most children will be taught a second language at school, and this will often rely more on written than on spoken language. Finally, studying bilingual spelling is scientifically interesting in its own right. As I hope will become clear throughout this chapter, spelling is not just like speaking, but with letters instead of sounds. It is also not just like reading 'in reverse'. Therefore, theories of bilingual spoken production are not directly transferable to written production.

In this chapter, we will propose a set of general hypotheses regarding the cognitive processes that underlie bilingual spelling abilities. Our main focus will be to provide an account of bilingual spelling in adults. In other words, this is not a learning theory, although some of our proposals have implications for learning and can also receive support from learning data. This theory of bilingual spelling in alphabetic systems (BAST) aims to account for spelling in any combination of languages using the same alphabet, although it clearly predicts an influence of the degree of similarity between languages at the lexical and orthographic levels. How the spelling system adapts to having to use different alphabets or scripts is an interesting question, but one that goes beyond

© KONINKLIJKE BRILL NV, LEIDEN, 2019 | DOI:10.1163/9789004394988_005

the scope of this chapter (for a discussion of spelling across scripts, see Weekes, Su, & To, 2013; Wilson, Kahlaoui, & Weekes, 2012).

The theory presented in this chapter is grounded in concepts derived from the monolingual spelling literature on the one hand, and from research on bilingual spoken word production on the other. The first section will summarise current knowledge on the processes involved in monolingual spelling. The second section will address key aspects of bilingual spoken word production. The third section presents our theory of bilingual alphabetic spelling (BAST). Whenever possible, experimental evidence from the literature or from ongoing studies in our own group will be used to support different aspects of our proposal. We will conclude by highlighting avenues for future research.

1   Alphabetic Spelling in Monolingual Adults

Figure 4.1 depicts a theoretical account of the processes involved in spelling single words to dictation, or from meaning (see e.g., Tainturier & Rapp, 2001; Houghton & Zorzi, 2003). This model posits two main spelling procedures. The lexical process is semantically mediated, and consists of retrieving the spelling of familiar words from long-term memory (orthographic lexicon); it is required for spelling irregular words accurately (e.g., "yacht") and is used in spelling familiar words more generally. The accuracy and speed of access to these orthographic lexemes is thought to be a function of the strength of the semantic input combined with the strength of the lexemes themselves, as determined by factors such as their frequency and possibly their age of acquisition. In addition, it is generally recognized that the semantic input will lead to the activation of a pool of orthographic lexemes related in meaning (e.g., tiger, lion, panther) which may lead to interference (Caramazza & Hillis, 1990; Breining & Rapp, in press). Note that some spelling models also include a second lexical route directly connecting phonological lexemes to orthographic lexemes bypassing semantics (e.g., Patterson, 1986). However, evidence in support of this route is scant and controversial (e.g., Hillis & Caramazza, 1995). For the sake of parsimony, we will restrict our discussion to a dual-process view of spelling, although we acknowledge that this may need adjusting should more compelling evidence for a third pathway become available.

In contrast, the sublexical process is activated by an external or internal phonological input. This process first parses phonological sequences (sound units) and then converts them into orthographic sequences (letters). In English, it is often the case that a given phoneme is associated with more than one spelling (e.g., tow, though, foe, go). In such cases, the phonology to orthog-

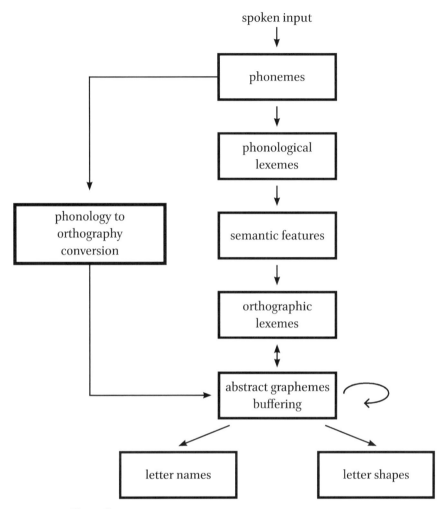

FIGURE 4.1 The spelling process

raphy conversion system (POC) will tend to apply the most frequent mappings. This is why a pseudo-word such as /fup/ is highly likely to be spelled FOOP rather than PHUPE. In addition, mapping choices are constrained by their position in the sequence; for example, POC should not produce illegal spellings such as /kus/ -> CKOOS, even though the mappings are frequent in other word positions. The POC process would be required when spelling unfamiliar words or pseudo-words (PROST), for which no prior whole word representations are available. Note that if the unfamiliar word has a low probability spelling (irregular or ambiguous spelling), POC would produce it incorrectly (i.e., phonologically plausible errors such as "cholera" -> COLLERA). On the other hand, unfamiliar words composed of common mappings (e.g., "hog") should be spelled correctly. POC is particularly important in early stages of spelling acquisition and contributes to lexical learning (e.g., Egan & Tainturier, 2011; Ehri, 1987). Although this has been less studied, it would appear that POC is influenced by the length and complexity of the sequences, by the ambiguity of the mappings (e.g., when there are options of comparable frequency) and by their similarity with familiar words in the speller's orthographic lexicon (more below).

The goal of the lexical and POC processes is to generate an ordered string of graphemes for production. At this level, the representations are still abstract in the sense that they are compatible with different forms of expression of the sequence (e.g., handwriting, typing, oral spelling). The precise nature of units at the graphemic level is still under debate (i.e., single letters, digraphs, syllabic components; Houghton & Zorzi, 2003; Tainturier & Rapp, 2004). Although it goes beyond the goals of this chapter to cover this issue in detail, let us mention that there is evidence that graphemic representations have a multi-dimensional structure that, in addition to letter identity and order, represents information about consonant/vowel status, letter doubling and some aspects of the orthosyllabic organization of the sequence (e.g., Buchwald & Rapp, 2006; Fischer-Baum & Rapp, 2014; McCloskey, Badecker, Goodman-Shulman, & Aliminosa, 1994; Tainturier & Caramazza, 1996). The strength of graphemic activation levels would be determined in part by the strength of the representations themselves (e.g., grapheme frequency), by the strengths of the inputs, and by competition amongst units.

Although the lexical and sublexical procedures involve distinct processes, they are thought to interact at the graphemic stage (see e.g., Bosse, Valdois & Tainturier 2003; Houghton & Zorzi, 2002; Rapp, Epstein & Tainturier, 2003; Tainturier, Bosse, Roberts, Valdois, & Rapp, 2013). More specifically, one proposal is that the activation of graphemic sequences is under the joint influence of lexical and sublexical sources of activation, as illustrated in Figure 4.1. The relative influence of each procedure in the selection of a graphemic sequence would be mostly determined by stimulus type. When spelling known words, the activation of letter sequences would mostly come from the lexical system, and the relative strength of this activation would increase with word frequency/familiarity. In contrast, it would mostly depend on POC when spelling new or poorly learned words. In either case, the two processes would have some degree of influence on the selection of the graphemic sequence. This joint influence can best be observed when the two processes point to different spellings. For example, it has been shown that the spelling choices for pseudo-words are influenced by word neighbors that point to alternative spelling options (e.g., Bosse et al, 2003; Tainturier et al, 2013). Similarly, in a word such as "yacht", the lexical /t/-> CHT mapping may compete with the more common /t/ -> T mapping generated by POC. This may lead to phonologically plausible errors such as YAT when the lexical representation is relatively weak, or else to an increase in spelling times (e.g., Afonso, Alvarez & Kandel, 2015; Kreiner, 1996). An additional source of lexical-sublexical interactions is feedback from the graphemic level to the lexical level (McCloskey, Macaruso, & Rapp, 1999).

Past the graphemic stage, format specific representations (e.g., upper case letter, letter name) need to be selected in preparation for motor production (we do not address these more peripheral processes in this chapter). The transition between these stages forms a bottleneck whereby graphemic sequences that were activated in parallel will need to be processed serially to support the production of individual letters in the correct order. This requires that the activation level of graphemic sequences (generated lexically and/or sublexically) be maintained during the application of sequential form selection processes (Costa, Fischer-Baum, Capasso, Miceli, & Rapp, 2011). This would be the role of a specialized short-term memory system, referred to as the "graphemic buffer".

Note that the terms "graphemic level" and "graphemic buffer" are often used interchangeably in diagrams of the spelling process. However, it is usually implied that this level involves both graphemic representations and the STM processes acting upon them. The graphemic buffer has been studied mostly through the analysis of the spelling performance of brain-damaged adults, with some recent work on developmental dysgraphia (Barisic, Kohnen & Nickels, 2017). As one would expect, graphemic buffer damage is associated with exaggerated effects of stimulus length, and is also modulated by the position of target graphemes within the sequence (e.g., Tainturier & Rapp, 2003). There is evidence that the buffering process is susceptible to both information decay and to interference (Costa et al, 2012).

2   Bilingual Spoken Word Production

Producing spoken words involves translating meanings into specific word forms. Although theories differ in the specifics of their implementation, there is general agreement that the act of producing a spoken word relies on the operation of distinct yet interconnected levels of processing: semantic, lexical and phonological (e.g., Caramazza, 1997; Dell, 1986; Dell & O'Seaghdha, 1992; Levelt, Roelofs & Meyer, 1999; Oppenheim, Dell & Schwartz, 2010). The activation of a set of semantic features corresponding to the meaning to be expressed would lead to the activation of the lexical representation of the corresponding word, and in turn to the activation of the phonological elements of that word, in preparation for articulation. Spoken word production models propose that a semantic input will activate a set of semantically related words in addition to the target itself (e.g., tiger, lion, cougar, cat) as a function of their degree of semantic overlap (e.g., Caramazza & Hillis, 1990). For example, upon presentation of a picture of a tiger, the word "lion" should be more strongly co-activated than the word "cat", which in turn would be stronger than "dog". In cascaded models (e.g., Dell, 1986), each activated lexical representation would in turn activate its constituent phonemes, even before lexical selection has been completed. Under normal circumstances, the representations corresponding to the target word would be maximally activated and thus selected for production. Nevertheless, there is some evidence that the accuracy and speed of word production may be influenced by the strength of its semantic neighbors. For example, word finding difficulties (tip of the tongue, aphasia) often lead to semantic errors such as producing 'tiger' instead of 'panther', even when there is no confusion about the meaning to be expressed. Such errors are thought to reflect this co-activation of semantically related words when the target word is temporarily unavailable (Caramazza & Hillis, 1990). Supporting evidence also comes from studies of the time taken to name pictures in various contexts designed to elicit more or less co-activation (e.g., Oppenheim et al., 2010; Vieth, McMahon & de Zubicaray, 2014). Note that although semantic neighbors are often described as competitors, the view that lexical units directly compete with each other is under debate (see e.g., Abdel Rahman & Aristei, 2010; Mahon et al, 2007; Spalek, Damian & Bölte, 2013).

Several theories and models have been proposed over the past few years to account for bilingual spoken word production (e.g., Costa, Miozzo & Caramazza, 1999; de Bot, 1992; Kroll & Tokowicz, 2005; Kroll, van Hell, Tokowicz, & Green, 2010; Strijkers, 2016) as well as for the recognition of spoken and written words in bilinguals (e.g., Dijkstra, Walter, & van Heuven, 2002; Dijkstra, Van Heuven, & Grainger, 1998; Thomas & Van Heuven, 2005; Shook & Marian, 2013). These theories have taken on board the central features of monolingual models summarized above and extended them to bilingualism. Here again, competing theories differ in their specifics but they agree on some basic principles. First, there is general agreement that bilingual word production relies on a shared or at least largely overlapping set of semantic representations across languages. This is supported by a variety of experimental evidence, such cross-language semantic priming effects (e.g., Caramazza & Brones, 1980). Second, it is generally assumed that there are distinct sets of lexical representations for each language. Third, there is ample evidence for a non-language-selective activation of lexical representations. In other words, the claim is that a semantic input would lead to the simultaneous activation of lexical representations in both languages, including the representation corresponding to the target word, its twin in the other language (translation equivalent) and, to a lesser degree, a set of semantically related words in both languages. In cascaded models, this pattern of activation would trickle down to the phonological level (e.g., Costa, Santesteban, & Caño, 2005). This co-activation has been observed even in strictly monolingual task contexts and even when the co-activation hinders performance (e.g. Colomé, 2001; Costa et al., 2000; Spalek et al., 2014; Wu, Cristino, Leek, & Thierry, 2013). For example, Colomé (2001) conducted a study in which Catalan-Spanish bilinguals decided whether a particular phoneme was part of the Catalan name of a target picture. Reaction times were slower when the phoneme was not part of the Catalan name but was part of its Spanish translation, indicating that the phonological representations of the non-target language had been activated and interfered with performance during a Catalan only task.

Additional evidence for automatic cross-linguistic lexical activation comes from multiple reports that bilingual speakers' ability to retrieve spoken words is affected by their cognate status. Cognates are translation equivalents words that are phonologically and/or orthographically similar (e.g. 'carped' in Welsh and 'carpet' in English). The key finding is that cognate words are produced faster and more accurately than non-cognate control words. This has been confirmed across a range of lexical tasks including lexical decision (Dijkstra, Miwa, Brummelhuis, Sappelli, & Baayen, 2010), picture naming (e.g. Costa, 2000; Rosselli, Ardila, Jurado, & Salvaierra, 2012; Strijkers, Costa & Thierry, 2009) and translation (e.g. De Groot, Dannenburg & Van Hell, 1994). The effect has also been documented in different language pairs, including, but not limited to, Spanish-Catalan (Costa et al, 2000), Spanish-English (Rosseli et al, 2012), Dutch-English (Dijkstra et al, 2010) and Welsh-English (Hughes, 2016).

Costa et al (2005) interpreted this 'cognate superiority effect' by appealing to the notions of cross-linguistic lexical co-activation coupled with phoneme to lexeme feedback (Dell, Burger, & Svec, 1997). The first mechanism would lead to the strong co-activation of translation equivalents irrespective of cognate status. However, cognate words would then become more activated than non-cognates because they would benefit from supporting feedback from the phonological representations they share with the target word in the other language (see Figure 4.2).

While plausible accounts have been offered to explain how word processing is influenced by representations from both the target and non-target language, a crucial question remains: If words in both languages receive comparable activation from the semantic level (by virtue of their comparable compatibility with the semantic input), how are words from the correct language ultimately

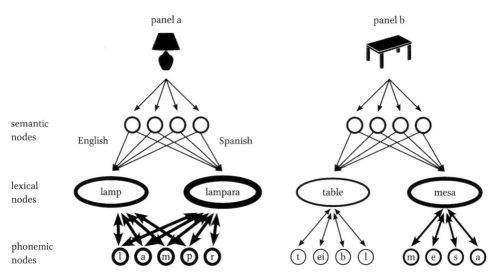

FIGURE 4.2 Schematic representation of the cognate facilitation effect (from Costa et al,
2005). In this example, the target language is Spanish. The thickness of the lines
represents relative degrees of activation.

selected for production? It is a fact that, under normal circumstances, bilingual speakers very rarely produce words in the wrong language unintentionally.
In monolingual models, the selection for production of a lexical representation is based on the system choosing the lexeme with the highest activation
level following conceptual activation (e.g., Costa et al., 2000). However, if lexical activation is entirely based on semantic activation irrespective of language,
the lexical representation in the target language may not be the most activated
(for example, if its translation is of relatively higher frequency). To solve this
problem, it has been proposed that control mechanisms, partly outside of the
lexical system itself, would either boost the activation level of units in the target
language, partly inhibit the activation level of units in the non-target language
(e.g. de Bot, 1992; Green, 1998, Kroll, Sumutka & Schwartz, 2005), or else that
the lexical selection mechanisms would only consider the activation of units
from the target language at a post-lexical stage (e.g. Costa & Caramazza, 1999;
Costa, Miozzo & Caramazza, 1999, Costa et al, 2000). Any of these processes
would minimise intrusions from the non-target language. Be this as it may, it is
clear is that early proposals of a total "shut down" of the non-target language
(e.g., McNamara & Kushnir, 1972) are not backed by current evidence.

3   Towards a Theory of Bilingual Alphabetic Spelling (BAST)

In this section, we will first present the overall architecture and general processing assumptions of BAST. We will then detail each main spelling process,
offer predictions, and present supporting evidence when available. However,
it should be noted that there is very little research on bilingual spelling that
directly addresses the focus of this chapter. That is, prior research does not
focus on bilingual spelling processes per se, but rather on related but distinct
questions such as the influence of bilingualism on metalinguistic processes
associated with spelling acquisition (e.g., Caravolas & Bruck, 1993), the possible
differences between spelling processes in deeper vs. shallower orthographies
(e.g., Caravolas, 2004), and whether preferential processing modes can transfer
from one language to another (e.g., Arab-Moghaddam & Sénéchal, 2001; Lallier & Carreiras, 2018; Lallier, Thierry, Barr, Carreiras, & Tainturier, 2018; Niolaki,
2013).

3.1   BAST: Overall Architecture and Processing Principles

BAST is essentially an adaptation to bilingual spelling of the dual process
spelling theories presented in Section 1. The bilingual elements themselves are
derived from theories of bilingual spoken word production summarized in Section 2. Indeed, it is reasonable to assume that the organization and processing
characteristics of bilingual spelling are equivalent to those that apply to spoken
word production. In keeping with models of bilingual spoken word production, we posit that access to the bilingual spelling system is non-selective, in the
sense that the representations corresponding to each language are always co-
activated to some extent. This co-activation would be modulated by the degree
of absolute and relative proficiency in each language. Nonetheless, written production is more complex than spoken production in the sense that it involves a
larger set of processes: orthography in addition to phonology, lexical and sublexical orthographic retrieval procedures and their interactions, and multiple
output modes (i.e., writing, oral spelling, typing). The general architecture of
BAST is presented in Figure 4.3.

   In short, BAST proposes the existence of distinct yet highly interconnected
orthographic lexicons for each language, feeding into a shared graphemic level.
As for spoken production, a key assumption is that lexical orthographic representations are activated by non-language-specific lexical-semantic knowledge.
Furthermore, we propose that semantic representations co-activate words
from the two languages, although units from the target language (as determined by context and speakers' intentions) may be, or may become, more
strongly activated than units from the non-target language in order to ensure

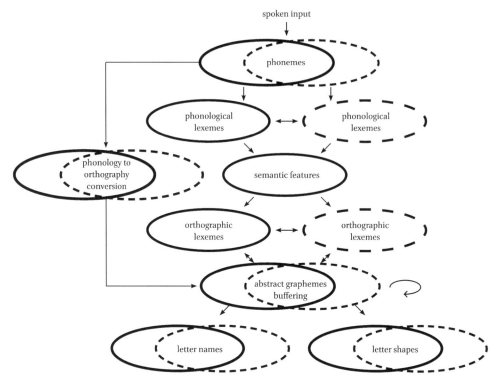

FIGURE 4.3 Bilingual alphabetic spelling. Solid vs. dashed lines represent two alphabetic languages. The overlapping ovals indicate that there is *some* overlap between the
representations in the two languages. The degree of overlap will vary across levels
of representation and across language pairs (see text).

production in the intended language. This lexical co-activation would be
stronger for highly related language pairs (e.g., English and German) than for
less related ones (e.g., English and French) due to the additional influence of
phonological and orthographic similarity (more below). With regards to the
sublexical procedures involved in spelling unfamiliar words, it is proposed that
phonological representations, activated by an external spoken input in spelling
to dictation, or by inner speech in spontaneous writing, also jointly activate
phoneme-grapheme mappings in both languages. The degree of overlap in
phonology to orthography mappings varies across language pairs. For example,
Italian and Spanish have more mappings in common than Italian and English.
The overall hypothesis is that language co-activation should lead to some predictable patterns of interactions in spelling performance. The question of how
language selection takes place goes beyond the scope of this chapter; it is a
complex and largely unresolved one in bilingual research more generally.

It should be noted that one difficulty in making specific predictions about bilingual spelling performance patterns is that it requires adopting fine-grained processing assumptions that remain controversial in monolingual research, even in word processing domains that have been extensively studied. For example, is activation cascaded or not (e.g., Buchwald & Falconer, 2014; Roux & Bonin, 2012)? Is there both activation and inhibition between levels? Is there inhibition between units at the same level? Is there feedback between levels? What is the specific format of processing units at different levels? How is letter position represented? What is the format of orthographic representations (letters, graphemes, syllables)? Most of our proposals about bilingual spelling do not critically hinge on resolving these questions. On occasion, we will adopt a position on such issues (e.g., cascaded processing), although we acknowledge the possibility of alternative accounts.

3.2   *Lexical Spelling*

As previously discussed, spelling familiar words involves the activation of orthographic lexemes from a semantic input. Semantic representations are thought to be largely overlapping in bilinguals. However, the words used to express equivalent meanings usually differ across languages, hence the distinction between an L_A and L_B orthographic lexicons. Note that we use the labels L_A and L_B in a general way to refer to the orthographic lexical knowledge of a bilingual speller of two alphabetic languages, irrespective of relative proficiency and pattern of lifelong usage. However, in this chapter we will mostly focus on spelling in proficient bilinguals.

3.2.1   Lexical Activation and Selection

In the BAST framework, the arrows from the semantic system to each orthographic lexicon represent learned associations between meaning and word forms in each language. A key postulate is that meanings will activate words in both lexicons (e.g., the meaning "pet" + "meows" would activate "cat" in English and "chat" in French). Generally speaking, the degree of activation of lexical units is a function of the strength of the input and of the units themselves. The resting level of different lexemes would be determined by a variety of factors, such as their frequency of use, as discussed in Section 1. Spelling from meaning would usually lead to the activation of several lexemes. As we have seen in Section 2, there is strong evidence that a semantic input activates a pool of semantically related lexemes. In a bilingual speller, this pool would be larger as it would include semantically related words in *both* languages (e.g., "cat" → "dog"-> "sheep" in English + "chat" → "chien" -> "mouton" in French). The arrow between the two lexicons represents direct connections between translation equivalents. This is more tentative, but is proposed by analogy to bilingual spoken word production models in which such connections are thought to play an important role in second language learning and in translation, before direct direction connections from semantics are established as proficiency in an L_A increases (see e.g., Kroll et al, 2010).

3.2.2   Graphemic Activation and Selection

Following the selection of an appropriate lexeme in the target language, its graphemic components must be retrieved for production. In Figure 4.3, we have represented this graphemic level as one of strong overlap between languages. This is because pairs of alphabetic languages share most or even all of their graphemes. As is the case for phonemes, there is compelling reason to consider that shared graphemes should be represented distinctly. Thus, the hypothesis here is that lexemes will activate graphemes from a common pool (more in Section 3.4). Given the assumptions of cascading activation and of co-activation, this means that grapheme selection will be under the joint influence of lexemes activated in the two languages: The target lexeme, its semantic neighbors, and their translations. This would lead to complex patterns of activation of graphemic units belonging to different words. The activation from semantic neighbors may create some degree of interference in grapheme selection, although this would be reduced when the target and its semantic neighbor happen to share letters in comparable position, as in "grass" and "green". Ultimately though, the graphemes associated with the target lexeme would become more strongly activated, allowing for the production of the correct sequence.

An interesting aspect of bilingual spelling is that translation equivalents are more likely to share graphemes than semantically related words within each language. This is because words in different alphabetic languages often have a common origin, which is reflected in their spelling (usually more strongly than in their phonology). For example, the explosive device that can be dropped from airplanes is written "bomb" in English, "bombe" in French, 'Bombe' in German, "bom" in Deutsch, "pomm" in Estonian, "bomba" in Spanish and Italian, etc. The relative proportion of such words, referred to as cognates, does of course vary across language pairs and is associated with language distance; for example, it is higher between different Romance languages than between Romance and Germanic languages (e.g., Schepens, Dijkstra, Grootjen and van Heuven, 2013). The relative proportion of cognates across language pairs is likely to influence learning rates and spelling performance.

3.2.3   Grapheme to Lexeme Feedback

As we have seen in Section 1, it has been proposed that the graphemic level feeds back to the orthographic lexicon. In relation to bilingualism, phoneme to lexeme feedback has been invoked to account for the cognate advantage in spoken production (see Section 2). Similarly, grapheme to lexical feedback could also lead to a cognate advantage in spelling production when translation equivalents activated lexically receive additional support from their shared graphemes. Thus, everything else being equal, cognate words should be produced faster and/or more accurately than non-cognates and could also be more resistant to damage; we are not aware of any studies having tested these predictions yet. Finally, note that cognate effects may be modulated by the joint influence of lexical and sublexical activation on grapheme selection. This point is developed in Section 3.4.

3.3   *Sublexical Spelling*

The processes that underlie lexical spelling are equivalent to those that underlie spoken word production, in the sense that they are based on learning arbitrary associations between meanings and whole word forms. However, the ability to produce unfamiliar words using learned phonology to orthography correspondences is specific to written production. As we have seen in Section 1, sublexical spelling involves converting strings of phonemes into strings of graphemes using learned associations between them (PG mappings). How would this work in bilingual spelling? In this section we will discuss the relationship between POC knowledge in different languages and propose hypotheses about the organization of the bilingual sublexical spelling system.

3.3.1   The Representation of POC Knowledge in the Bilingual Spelling
System

One central difference between POC in monolingual vs. bilingual spellers is that learned associations between phonemes and graphemes are derived from two sources of knowledge that may or may not converge. On the one hand, all alphabetic language pairs have common PG mappings. For example, /p/ -> P is highly frequent in languages that use the Latin alphabet ('pear', 'poire', 'pera', 'pedwar', etc.). PG mappings may even converge across different alphabets (e.g., /t/-> T in the Latin, Greek and Cyrillic alphabets). This point is illustrated in Figure 4.3 by the overlap between each language POC knowledge. On the other hand, most (if not all) language pairs also include language-specific mappings that can be divided into two categories. First, some mappings are 'unique' because they correspond to phonemes that do not exist in the other language; for example, the French mapping /y/-> U as in 'pur' has no relevance to English. Second,

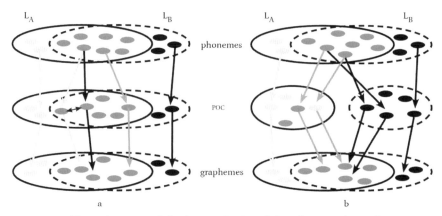

FIGURE 4.4 Alternative proposals for the organization of phonology to orthography conversion (POC) processes. Panel A: Integrated POC. Panel B: Language-specific POC.
Light grey ovals/arrows correspond to representations and mappings specific
to L$_A$, black ovals/arrows are specific to L$_B$ and dark grey ovals/arrows are not
language-specific. In both diagrams, three types of situations are illustrated: a)
unique mappings, b) divergent mappings (when a shared phoneme is associated
to different PG mappings in each language) and c) convergent mappings when a
shared phoneme is associate to the same PG mapping in each language. In Panel
A, this is expressed with a single dark grey arrow. In Panel B, there are distinct
arrows connecting shared phonemes and graphemes (see text).

phonemes that *are* used in different languages are often associated with different graphemes ('divergent' mappings). For example, the phoneme /v/ is typically spelled V in English but F in Welsh. All language pairs will rely on subsets
of shared, unique and divergent mappings in varying proportions. This raises
the question of whether POC knowledge is represented in fully distinct sets for
each language or in an integrated system (see Figure 4.4). In a fully distinct
system, each language would rely on its own set of mappings, meaning that
mappings that occur in both languages would be duplicated.

In support of an integrated view, it seems improbable that PG mappings
would be learned independently in each language (see Figueredo, 2006, for a
discussion of the transfer of spelling knowledge in ESL learners). At the very
least, one would expect that knowing that /p/ -> P in English should facilitate
the concomitant or subsequent learning of /p/ -> P in another language; such
facilitation has been reported in children learning English as a second language
(Figueredo, 2006). An advantage for shared mappings would naturally emerge
in an integrated POC system in which there would be a single language-neutral
representation of shared mappings, in addition to language specific mappings.
However, this proposal is not necessarily as straightforward as may seem. Even
when languages share mappings, their frequency of use may differ and they

may also be subject to different contextual constraints about where in a word they can be used. Clearly, an integrated system would need to include mechanisms to ensure that the sequences produced are language appropriate (as in /nuS / -> NOOSH in English but NOUCHE in French) rather than some mix of the two languages (e.g., NOOCHE or NOUSH). Indeed, mixed spellings are rare in proficient bilinguals (see below for supporting evidence), although they are common in beginning learners (e.g., James, Scholfield, Garrett, & Griffiths, 1993).

The alternative proposal is for each language to be associated with its own distinct set of mappings, including both mappings that are shared with the other language and mappings that differ. This organisation may facilitate the production of language-appropriate sequences since mappings from the target language could be maximally activated according to task constraints or context. However, the automatic co-activation of both languages would still influence activation patterns at the graphemic level. It is conceivable that there might be direct connections between mappings corresponding to the same phonemes in the two languages. These connections would be facilitatory for shared mappings and inhibitory for divergent mapping, which would reduce interference and thus the possibility of errors.

These two proposals essentially make the same predictions and, without further specification, it is unclear what type of evidence would support one over the other. Both predict a production advantage for shared mappings, although via different mechanisms: In an integrated POC system, this would be because shared mappings would have an overall higher frequency of use in relation to language-specific mappings. In the distinct POC view, the strength of each mapping would be a function of its frequency of use in each language, but an advantage may occur at the grapheme selection stage because of language co-activation resulting in a summation of activations for shared graphemes (more below). In addition, both proposals predict relatively poorer performance in the case of divergent mappings, as language co-activation would induce some competition at the grapheme selection stage. Finally, both accounts predict that mappings associated with language-specific phonemes should show little cross-linguistic influence.

One contrasting prediction that could be tested in the future is that damage to an integrated POC system should lead to more consistent error patterns across languages than damage to a distinct POC system. That is, damage to a language-neutral mapping should affect its spelling in both languages, while this would not necessarily be the case in distinct POC systems. In the following section, we will make predictions about bilingual POC processing that do not hinge on the specific representations of PG mappings across languages.

3.3.2   The Activation of POC Knowledge in Bilingual Spelling

POC knowledge is activated by an internal or external phonological input and activates graphemic sequences for output. As for lexical processing, we propose that POC knowledge is activated in both languages simultaneously. As illustrated in Figure 4.3, we posit the POC system mediates between sets of phonological and graphemic representations that overlap across languages, more or less so depending on the specific languages. In terms of the input to POC, an important difference between lexical and sublexical spelling is that POC is driven by phonology, not by meaning. Thus, the degree of cross-linguistic activation of PG mappings will depend on the sequence to be spelled including at least some common phonemes. Note that while the semantic system can be conceived as largely language-neutral, phoneme sequences rarely are. That is, even unfamiliar sequences tend to include clues to language identity, such as language-specific phonemes or phonological patterns. This will vary across language pairs and across items, and should modulate the degree of POC co-activation, and thus its potential influence on grapheme selection. As discussed in the previous subsection, PG mappings are either neutral, consistent or inconsistent across languages, leading to predictions about patterns of mutual support or interference when spelling.

Evidence from different sources provides some support for the cross-linguistic co-activation of POC knowledge. As mentioned earlier, the spelling errors of children learning a second alphabetic language are influenced by their first language. However, it is possible that such errors reflect a temporary strategy put in place to allow writing whilst sufficient knowledge of the new language's orthography is being established (Figueredo, 2006). Therefore, evidence from proficient bilingual adults is needed to establish cross-linguistic interactions in skilled spelling. In a recent study, Tainturier, Roberts & Roberts (in preparation) compared the spelling choices of monolingual English and Welsh-English proficient bilingual adults in English spelling to dictation task of pseudo-words. All pseudo-words were derived from English real words and the task instructions made it clear that the items were to be spelled as if they were invented English words. Critically, all pseudo-words included one or more phonemes that are typically spelled differently in English and Welsh. For example, the phoneme /v/ is spelled V in English but F in Welsh, and the phoneme /u/ is often spelled OO in English but is always spelled W in Welsh. Thus, the list included items such as /fup/ derived from 'food' and /nivə/ derived from 'river' (British English). Given the expertise of the bilingual participants, we expected that most of their answers would be language appropriate, as even in the presence of co-activation bilinguals should generally be able to suppress alternative spellings. This is indeed what we observed (e.g., /fup/ was generally spelled

FOOP or FUPE). However, we also expected that cross-linguistic co-activation would occasionally lead to errors consisting in applying a Welsh mapping that would be illegal in English (e.g., FWP, NIFER). This is what was observed in about 5% of the spellings produced by the bilingual group, which is largely above chance considering that monolingual controls only produced 0.5% of such errors. Thus, this study supports the hypothesis that graphemic units are activated by both languages simultaneously, and also reveals that language control processes do not fully suppress cross-language competitors. It is interesting to note that most of these productions consisted of a mix of English and Welsh mappings. For example, /fwp/ in Welsh should be spelled FFWP, not FWP (which would be read /vup/ in Welsh) and /nivə/ should be spelled NIFY in Welsh, not NIFER. This rules out that participants sometimes "forgot" to spell in English. In the future, such error corpora could be used to test additional predictions. For example, the probability of choosing a given mapping amongst alternatives in one language should be related to the degree of support it gets from the other language. Kinematic analyses of on-line spelling production (e.g., Afonso et al., 2015; Kandel, Lassus-Sangosse, Grosjacques, & Perret, 2018) may also be used to confirm the prediction that shared graphemes should be produced faster than divergent mappings.

Further support for the bilingual co-activation of POC knowledge comes from patterns of spelling deficits and of recovery in brain-damaged adults (acquired dysgraphia). First, ongoing work in our research group has revealed that some dysgraphic participants produce a very high proportion (up to 50%) of errors that mix English and Welsh mappings in a single response. Second, converging evidence comes from a recent study that attempted to restore sublexical spelling in a Welsh-English bilingual individual with acquired dysgraphia following stroke (Tainturier, Roberts & Roberts, 2011). CWS had lost the ability to select some graphemes correctly, and this in both languages (although not necessarily the same graphemes in both). In this study, training exercises were put in place in an attempt to improve the spelling of some shared (e.g., /E/-> E) and some divergent mappings (e.g., /ə/ -> U in English but Y in Welsh). The mappings were trained as part of letter sequences in one language only, and the study aimed to examine if any improvements in the treated language would generalise to the untreated language. In the treated language, both types of mappings showed large improvements following treatment; this was expected since all mappings had been directly treated. The interesting aspect of the results is that parallel improvement was observed in the untreated language, but only for shared mappings. That is, after treatment, CWS was just as likely to spell a shared mapping correctly if it was part of an English word or a Welsh word; this was still the case six weeks following the end of treatment. In contrast, divergent mappings only improved in the treated language, and this improvement itself did not last (drop from 74% correct at one week to 10% correct at six weeks). We attribute this drop to the weakening influence of the competing grapheme in the other language; indeed, the most common error type six weeks post treatment consisted in using the competing grapheme, as was the case before treatment.

3.4   Graphemic Level, Lexical/Sublexical Interactions and Buffering

The goal of the lexical and sublexical processes is to activate strings of abstract spelling units coded for position at the graphemic level prior to the selection of specific letter shapes, names or typing strokes. These abstract units (graphemes) are combined to form written words according to the orthotactic constraints of a given language. Our proposal is that the graphemic level consists of a partially overlapping set of functional spelling units that are activated in parallel by the lexical and POC systems in both languages and send feedback to orthographic lexemes.

If grapheme units are shared across languages, then their strength should be a function of their cumulative frequency of use in both languages. As a result, the relative frequency of different graphemes in a given language may differ for bilinguals vs. monolinguals would be a function of their sum frequency across languages. Overall, more frequent units should be better produced, easier to learn and more resilient to damage. In addition, frequent graphemes should provide stronger feedback to the lexeme level.

As discussed in Section 3.2, grapheme to lexeme feedback could lead to superior performance with cognate words because shared graphemes would increase the co-activation of translation equivalent words (e.g., "dance" in English and "danse" in French). Here we add that this effect could be modulated by the frequency of graphemic representations. On the other hand, feedback could also create interference from orthographically related words (e.g., "dance" and "lance"), and also contribute to "false friends" effects. By this we mean words with the same spelling but different meanings in the two languages, such as "fin" the fish appendage in English vs. "fin" meaning the end or thin in French.

3.4.1   The Size of Graphemic Units and Cross-Linguistic Overlap

Alphabetic languages share many graphemes (although they may not correspond to the same phonemes). Yet, some graphemes do not exist in all languages (e.g., Welsh has no K, French uses diacritics). In addition, alphabetic languages vary quite considerably in terms of the distributional properties of their constituent graphemes. First, graphemes vary in their relative frequency of usage (e.g., W and Y are more frequent in Welsh than in English). Second, individual graphemes are not subject to the same orthotactic constraints in different languages. For example, both English and French can use CH in syllable initial positions (though pronounced differently, e.g., /S/ in 'chaise' vs. /tS/ in 'chair'); in contrast CH final is common in English (e.g., "branch") but in French it must be followed by a vowel for the sequence to be legal (e.g., "branche"). Similarly, some letter groupings do not occur in all languages (e.g., THR* exists in English but not in French).

To complicate matters, it is not possible to fully specify the degree of overlap between languages at the graphemic level without also being more specific about the size of functional units at the graphemic level: single letters, digraphs, syllabic components? In some computational models of spelling (e.g., Houghton & Zorzi, 2003), the graphemic level stores an inventory of all the syllable onsets, vowels and codas that occur in English. Thus, some units would consist of a single letter (e.g., the onset C in CAT), a digraph (e.g., the onset CH in CHAT), a cluster (e.g., the onset CR in CROP) or a combination of the above (e.g., the onset THR in THROW). An advantage of postulating larger size units is that it is a relatively simple way to ensure that the spelling system will produce legal sequences of letters in a given language once such units are inserted in a syllabic frame. However, a corollary is that the degree of graphemic overlap between languages tends to decrease as the size of graphemic units increases, which in turn impacts on the specific predictions that can be made about cross-linguistic interactions.

In addition, the question of the size of units at the graphemic level impacts on predictions for cognateness effects. For example, the English word "cat" and the French word "chat" (/Sa/) are orthographic cognates if one defines graphemic units as single letters (three common letters) but not if they are defined as digraphs (no common units, i.e. "cat" = C+A+T but "chat" = CH+AT). Interestingly, examining the type of units that are most predictive of the strength of cognate effects may also increase our understanding of the nature of abstract graphemic representations in monolingual spellers.

3.4.2   Lexical/Sublexical Interactions

An additional source of cross-linguistic interactions relates to the joint effects of lexical and sublexical processes on graphemic activation. As we saw in Section 1, monolingual data points to interactions between lexical and sublexical procedures. More specifically, graphemic activation would be enhanced when the two processes converge on the same graphemes. In contrast, interference may occur when each procedure points to different graphemes, in a word such as "chef" for example where the sublexical process would activate SH and not

CH. In the bilingual case, the potential for interference is higher, as not only could there be a mismatch between lexical and sublexical activation within language, but also across languages. To take an extreme example involving English and French bilingual spelling, an English word such as "two" would activate competing graphemes originating from the English sublexical system (/u/-> OO) and also from the French lexical and sublexical systems (/u/-> OUT as in the word 'tout' or simply /u/-> OU, the most frequent mapping as in 'pou').

Lexical/sublexical interactions could also modulate cognate effects. Some indirect evidence is presented in Luelsdorff and Eyland (1991). In a study of 12–14 years-old German pupils learning English as a second language, Luelsdorff and Eyland report more spelling errors for cognate words that include PG mappings that are inconsistent in English and German (and which they call 'false friends', e.g., 'grass' vs. 'gras') than for control words. It remains to be seen if such factors would eliminate the cognate advantage or just reduce it.

3.4.3   Buffering

As we have seen earlier, a central aspect of the graphemic level is that once appropriate graphemic units have been selected, their level of activation needs to remain stable during the application of sequential output processes. This would be accomplished by means of a short-term memory process, often referred to as the "graphemic buffer". There is no reason to think of this process as being language-specific. Consequently, we propose a unitary buffering process operating on all sequences irrespective of language (see Roberts, Payne & Tainturier, submitted, for supporting evidence in acquired dysgraphia). However, there is evidence that the buffering process is sensitive to the strength of graphemic activation (e.g., word frequency) in addition to factors affecting buffering itself, such as stimulus length, syllabic complexity or the position of letters in the sequence. The amount of buffering needed may vary across language pairs if, say, one language has longer or more complex sequences than the other.

4   Conclusion

In summary, this chapter has introduced a theoretically motivated model of single word spelling in pairs of alphabetic languages. It also presented some supporting evidence and suggested a number of ways in which BAST could contribute to further research in the area of bilingual spelling. To quote Li (2002), "bilingualism is in dire need of formal models". Since this publication, there has been significant progress in several language domains, but cognitive theories of bilingual spelling have remained elusive. We believe that this has in turn impinged on the development of empirical studies in this area. It is our hope that BAST will provide an impetus for future work by providing a general framework to support the formulation of more specific research questions with testable predictions. It should also raise the awareness of the range of factors that should be taken into consideration when designing bilingual spelling studies. Finally, the study of bilingual spelling has the potential to shed light on some particularly thorny questions relating to monolingual spelling.

The scope of this chapter was largely limited to bilingual spelling in proficient bilingual spellers. A goal for the future would be to address additional questions: To what extent does the orthographic similarity (e.g., proportion of cognates or of shared PG mappings) between pairs of languages affects performance? Does BAST apply to bilingual spelling using different alphabets? What are the effects of expertise in the two languages (i.e., balanced vs. unbalanced bilinguals)? BAST is not a learning theory, but it does make general predictions about possible learning patterns in second language learners. In practice, BAST could contribute to the development of more principled teaching methods and also assist in the rehabilitation of spelling disorders.

Finally, it must be acknowledged that, although motivated by research in related domains, several aspects of BAST remain speculative largely due to the scarcity of directly relevant data. Future research may contradict some of its features, or indicate that alternative frameworks may have equivalent or even superior explanatory power. One limitation is that BAST is a cognitive 'verbal' theory. Given the complexity of the processes involved and the multiple sources of interactions in the system, a computational implementation would be desirable in order to generate more specific predictions about bilingual spelling performance patterns.

Acknowledgements

I gratefully acknowledge the financial support of ESRC/MRC Grant ESS/ H02526X/1, of the Bangor ESRC Impact Acceleration Account and of the University of Grenoble-Alpes Invited Researchers Scheme. Many undergraduate and graduate students have contributed to the research presented in this chapter and I thank them all collectively, with a special mention to Dr. Daniel Roberts, Dr. Jennifer Roberts, Dr. Emma Hughes, Joshua Payne and Shannon Berry.

References

Abdel Rahman, R., & Aristei, S. (2010). Now you see it … and now again: semantic interference reflects lexical competition in speech production with and without articulation. *Psychonomic Bulletin and Review, 17*, 657–661.

Afonso, O., Álvarez, C.J., & Kandel, S. (2015). Effects of grapheme-to-phoneme probability on writing durations. *Memory and Cognition, 43*, 579–592.

Arab-Moghaddam, N., & Sénéchal, M. (2001). Orthographic and phonological processing skills in reading and spelling in Persian/English bilinguals. *International Journal of Behavioral Development, 25*, 140–147.

Barisic, K., Kohnen, S., & Nickels, L. (2017). Developmental graphemic buffer dysgraphia in English: A single case study. *Cognitive Neuropsychology, 34*, 94–118.

Bosse, M.L., Valdois, S., Tainturier, M.J. (2003). Analogy without priming in early spelling development. *Reading and Writing: An International Journal, 16, 693–716*.

Breining, B. & Rapp, B. (in press). Investigating the mechanisms of written word production: insights from the written blocked cyclic naming paradigm. https://doi.org/10.1007/s11145-017-9742-4

Buchwald, A., & Rapp, B. (2006). Consonants and vowels in orthographic representation. *Cognitive Neuropsychology, 23*, 308–337.

Buchwald, A., & Falconer, C. (2014). Cascading activation from lexical processing to letter-level processing in written word production. *Cognitive Neuropsychology, 31*, 606–621.

Caramazza, A. (1997). How many levels of processing are there in lexical access? *Cognitive Neuropsychology, 14*, 177–208.

Caramazza, A., & Hillis, A.E. (1990). Where do semantic errors come from? *Cortex, 26*, 95–122.

Caramazza, A., & Brones, I. (1980). Semantic classification by bilinguals. *Canadian Journal of Psychology/Revue canadienne de psychologie, 34*, 77–81.

Caravolas, M. (2004). Spelling development in alphabetic writing systems: A cross-linguistic perspective. *European Psychologist, 9*, 3–14.

Caravolas, M., & Bruck, M. (1993). The effect of oral and written language input on children's phonological awareness: A cross-linguistic study. *Journal of Experimental Child Psychology, 55*, 1–30.

Costa, A., Colomé, A., & Caramazza, A. (2000). Lexical Access in Speech Production: The Bilingual Case. *Psicológica, 21*, 403–437.

Colomé, À. (2001). Lexical activation in bilinguals' speech production: Language-specific or language-independent? *Journal of memory and language, 45*, 721–736.

Costa, A., & Caramazza, A. (1999). Is lexical selection in bilingual speech production language-specific? Further evidence from Spanish–English and English–Spanish bilinguals. *Bilingualism: Language and Cognition, 2*, 231–244.

Costa, A., Miozzo, M., & Caramazza, A. (1999). Lexical selection in bilinguals: Do words in the bilingual's two lexicons compete for selection? *Journal of Memory and Language, 41*, 365–397.

Costa, A., Santesteban, M., & Caño, A. (2005). On the facilitatory effects of cognate words in bilingual speech production. *Brain and language, 94*, 94–103.

Costa, V., Fischer-Baum, S. Capasso, R. Miceli, G. & Rapp, B. (2011). Temporal stability and representational distinctiveness: Key functions of orthographic working memory. *Cognitive Neuropsychology, 28*, 338–362.

De Bot, K. (1992). A bilingual production model: Levelt's speaking model adapted. *Applied Linguistics 13*, 1–24.

De Groot, A.M., Dannenburg, L., & Van Hell, J.G. (1994). Forward and backward word translation by bilinguals. *Journal of memory and language, 33*, 600–629.

Dell, G.S. (1986). A spreading-activation theory of retrieval in sentence production. *Psychological review, 93*, 283–321.

Dell, G.S., & O'Seaghdha, P.G. (1992). Stages of lexical access in language production. *Cognition, 42*, 287–314.

Dell, G.S., Burger, L.K., & Svec, W.R. (1997). Language production and serial order: A fonctional analysis and a model. *Psychological Rewiew, 104*, 123–147.

Dijkstra, T., van Heuven, W.J.B., & Grainger, J. (1998). Simulating cross-language competition with the bilingual interactive activation model. *Psychologica Belgica, 38*, 177–196.

Dijkstra, T., & Walter, J.B., & van Heuven, W.J.B. (2002). The architecture of the bilingual word recognition system: From identification to decision. *Bilingualism: Language and Cognition, 5*, 175–197.

Dijkstra, T., Miwa, K., Brummelhuis, B., Sappelli, M., & Baayen, H. (2010). How cross-language similarity and task demands affect cognate recognition. *Journal of Memory and Language, 62*, 284–301.

Egan, J., & Tainturier, M.J. (2011). Inflectional spelling deficits in developmental dyslexia. *Cortex, 47*, 1179–1196.

Ehri, C.L. (1987). Learning to Read and Spell Words. *Journal of Literacy Research, 19*, 5–31.

Figueredo, L. (2006). Using the known to chart the unknown: A review of first-language influence on the development of English-as-a-second-language spelling skill. *Reading and Writing: An International Journal, 19*: 873.

Fischer-Baum, S., & Rapp, B. (2014). The analysis of perseverations in acquired dysgraphia reveals the internal structure of orthographic representations. *Cognitive Neuropsychology, 31*, 237–265.

Green, D.W. (1998). Mental control of the bilingual lexico-semantic system. *Bilingualism: Language and cognition, 1*, 67–81.

Hillis, A.E., & Caramazza, A. (1995) Converging evidence for the interaction of semantic and sublexical phonological information in accessing lexical representations for spoken output. *Cognitive Neuropsychology, 12*, 187–227.

Hughes, E.K. (2016). *Bilingual Lexical Processing: Evidence from picture naming and translation in aphasic and non-aphasic speakers.* PhD dissertation, Bangor University.

Houghton, G., & Zorzi, M. (2003). Normal and impaired spelling in a connectionist dual-route architecture. *Cognitive Neuropsychology, 20*, 115–162.

James, C., Scholfield, P., Garrett, P., & Griffiths, Y. (1993). Welsh bilinguals' English spelling: An error analysis. *Journal of Multilingual and Multicultural Development, 14*, 287–306.

Kandel, S., Lassus-Sangosse, D., Grosjacques, G., & Perret, C. (2018). The impact of developmental dyslexia and dysgraphia on movement production during word writing. *Cognitive Neuropsychology, 34*, 219–251.

Kreiner, D.S. (1996). Effects of word familiarity and phoneme-grapheme polygraphy on oral spelling time and accuracy. *The Psychological Record, 46*, 49–70.

Kroll, J.F., & Tokowicz, N. (2005). *Models of bilingual representation and processing.* In J.F. Kroll & A.M.B., de Groot (Eds.) *Handbook of bilingualism: Psycholinguistic approaches*, (pp. 531–553). Oxford University Press, New York.

Kroll, J.F., van Hell, J.G., Tokowicz, N., & Green, D.W. (2010). The Revised Hierarchical Model: A critical review and assessment. *Bilingualism: Language and Cognition, 13*, 373–381.

Kroll, J.F., Sumutka, B.M., & Schwartz, A.I. (2005). A cognitive view of the bilingual lexicon: Reading and speaking words in two languages. *International Journal of Bilingualism, 9*, 27–48.

Lallier, M., & Carreiras, M. (2018). Cross-linguistic transfer in bilinguals reading in two alphabetic orthographies: The grain size accommodation hypothesis. *Psychonomic Bulletin & Review, 25*, 386–401.

Lallier, M., Thierry, G., Barr, P., Carreiras, M., & Tainturier, M.J. (2018). Learning to read bilingually modulates the manifestations of dyslexia in adults. *Scientific Studies of Reading, 22, 335–349.*

Levelt, W.J.M., Roelofs, A., & Meyer, A.S. (1999). A theory of lexical access in speech production. *The Behavioral and Brain Sciences, 22*, 1–75.

Li, P. (2002). Bilingualism is in dire need of formal models. *Bilingualism: Language and Cognition, 5*, 213–213.

Luelsdorff, P.A., & Eyland, E.A. (1991). A psycholinguistic model of the bilingual speller. In: Joshi, R.M. (Ed.) *Written Language Disorders*. Neuropsychology and Cognition, vol. 2. Springer, Dordrecht.

McCloskey, M., Badecker, W., Goodman-Shulman, R.A., & Aliminosa, D. (1994). The structure of graphemic representations in spelling: Evidence from a case of acquired dysgraphia. *Cognitive Neuropsychology, 2*, 341–392.

McCloskey, M., Macaruso, P., & Rapp, B. (1999). Grapheme-to-lexeme feedback in the spelling system: Evidence from dysgraphia. *Brain and Language, 69*, 395–398.

McNamara, J., & Kushnir, S.L. (1972). Linguistic independence of bilinguals: The input switch. *Journal of Verbal Learning and Verbal Behaviour, 10*, 480–487.

Mahon, B.Z., Costa, A., Peterson, R., Vargas, K.A., & Caramazza, A. (2007). Lexical selection is not by competition: a reinterpretation of semantic interference and facilitation effects in the picture-word interference paradigm. *Journal of Experimental Psychology: Learning, Memory and Cognition, 33*, 503–535.

Niolaki, G. (2013) *Processes involved in spelling in bilingual and monolingual English- and Greek-speaking children with typical and atypical spelling performance.* PhD thesis. Institute of Education (University of London)

Oppenheim, G.M., Dell, G.S., & Schwartz, M.F. (2010). The dark side of incremental learning: A model of cumulative semantic interference during lexical access in speech production. *Cognition, 114*, 227–252.

Patterson, K. (1986) Lexical but nonsemantic spelling? *Cognitive Neuropsychology, 3*, 341–367

Rapp, B., Epstein, C., & Tainturier, M.J. (2002). The integration of information across lexical and sublexical processes in spelling. *Cognitive Neuropsychology, 19*, 1–29.

Roberts, J.R., Payne, J., & Tainturier, M.J. (submitted). Differential cross-linguistic generalisation patterns as a function of level of deficit in bilingual acquired dysgraphia.

Rosselli, M., Ardila, A., Jurado, M.B., & Salvatierra, J.L. (2012). Cognate facilitation effect in balanced and non-balanced Spanish–English bilinguals using the Boston Naming Test. *International Journal of Bilingualism, 18*, 649–662.

Roux, S. & Bonin, P. (2012): Cascaded processing in written naming: Evidence from the picture–picture interference paradigm. *Language and Cognitive Processes, 27*, 734–769.

Schepens, J., Dijkstra, T., Grootjen, F., & van Heuven, W.J.B. (2013). Cross-Language Distributions of High Frequency and Phonetically Similar Cognates. *PLoS ONE 8(5): e63006.* https://doi.org/10.1371/journal.pone.0063006

Shook, A., & Marian, V. (2013). The Bilingual Language Interaction Network for Comprehension of Speech. *Bilingualism: Language and Cognition, 16*, 304–324.

Spalek, K., Damian, M., & Bölte, J. (2013). Is lexical selection in spoken word production competitive? Introduction to the Special Issue on lexical competition in language production. *Language and Cognitive Processes, 28*, 597–614.

Spalek, K., Hoshino, N., Wu, Y.J., Damian, M., & Thierry, G. (2014). Speaking two languages at once: Unconscious native word form access in second language production. *Cognition, 133*, 226–231.

Strijkers, K. (2016), A Neural Assembly-Based View on Word Production: The Bilingual Test Case. *Language Learning, 66*, 92–131.

Strijkers, K., Costa, A., & Thierry, G. (2009). Tracking lexical access in speech produc-

92

TAINTURIER

tion: Electrophysiological correlates of word frequency and cognates effects. *Cerebral cortex, 20*, 912–928.

Tainturier, M.J., & Caramazza, A. (1996). The status of double letters in graphemic representations. *Journal of Memory and Language, 35*, 53–73.

Tainturier, M.J., & Rapp, B. (2001). The spelling process. In B.C. Rapp (Ed.): *What deficits reveal about the human mind/brain: A Handbook of Cognitive Neuropsychology.* (pp. 263–289) Philadelphia: Psychology Press.

Tainturier, M.J., & Rapp, B. (2003). Is a single graphemic buffer used in reading and spelling? *Aphasiology, 17*, 537–562.

Tainturier, M.J., Rapp, B. (2004). Complex graphemes as functional spelling units: Evidence from acquired dysgraphia. *Neurocase, 10*, 122–131.

Tainturier, M.J., Roberts, J., & Roberts, D. (2011). Treating sublexical spelling in bilingual acquired dysgraphia. *Procedia Social and Behavioral Sciences, 23*, 16–17.

Tainturier, M.J., Bosse, M.L., Roberts, D.J., Valdois, S., & Rapp, B. (2013). Lexical neighborhood effects in pseudo-word spelling. *Frontiers in Psychology, 4:862.* doi:10.3389/fpsyg.2013.00862.

Tainturier, M.J., Roberts, J.R., and Roberts, D.J. (in preparation). Cross-linguistic influences on the spelling choices of bilingual adults.

Thomas, M.S.C., & van Heuven, W.J.B. (2005). Computational models of bilingual comprehension. In J.F. Kroll and A.M.B. de Groot (Eds), *Handbook of bilingualism: Psycholinguistic approaches.* (pp. 202–225) Oxford University Press.

Weekes, B.S., Su, I.-F., To, C., & Ulicheva, A. (2013). Acquired dyslexia in bilingual speakers: Implications for models of oral reading. In D. Martin (Ed.) *Researching Dyslexia in Multilingual Settings.* (pp. 91–114). Bristol, UK: Multilingual Matters.

Vieth, H.E., McMahon, K.L., & de Zubicaray, G.I. (2014). Feature overlap slows lexical selection: Evidence from the picture–word interference paradigm. *The Quarterly Journal of Experimental Psychology, 67*, 2325–2339.

Wilson, M.A., Kahlaoui, K., & Weekes, B.S. (2012). Acquired dyslexia and dysgraphia in bilinguals across alphabetical and non-alphabetical scripts. In M.R. Gitterman, M. Goral, & L.K. Obler (Eds.) *Aspects of Multilingual Aphasia.* (pp. 187–204). Clevendon, UK: Multilingual Matters.

Wu, Y.J., Cristino, F., Leek, C., & Thierry, G. (2013). Non-selective lexical access in bilinguals is spontaneous and independent of input monitoring: evidence from eye tracking. *Cognition, 129*, 418–425.

CHAPTER 5

The Role of Handwriting in Reading: Behavioral and Neurophysiological Evidence of Motor Involvement in Letter Recognition

Yannick Wamain

Writing is likely one of the most remarkable motor abilities learned by humans. With speech, writing constitutes the basis of our language, which governs most the exchanges between individuals. Exactly as speech is the result of articulatory movement, the graphic trace constitutes the "end product" of the writing experience. A tight relationship links the way we write a letter with its shape. However, graphic traces have dramatically changed through history, especially because the tools required to produce them have evolved drastically. The transformations of writing tools have modified the way we learn to write. For instance, the use of a pencil instead of a feather and ink substantially modified the movement required to produce a letter. The transformation of the writing experience has impacted not only the organization of the writing production but also reading abilities.

The issues considered in the present chapter will be to understand whether the recollection of the movement required to produce the graphic trace plays a role in its visual perception. Specifically, we will investigate how the way a person writes a letter (like handwriting or typing for instance) impacts how he or she reads it. As such, we will see in a first section the key concept of the approach that considered action and perception as highly interconnected. We will present a series of behavioral and neurophysiological studies describing strong interactions between motor and perceptual processes during the perception of movements. In a second part, we will focus our attention on perception of handwritten letters. By definition, handwriting as a graphomotor behavior is a movement strongly associated with the shape of the letter produced independently to the type of script (cursive or print) and case (uppercase and lowercase) considered. Such tight relationship between movement and letter's shape resulting from an intensive motor learning is less present or absent in typing behavior. For these reasons, we will present several studies arguing that simple observation of handwritten exemplars can reactivate information about the way we produced them. The issue of the functional role of motor trace activation during visual letter recognition will then be investigated in a third part. Finally, the consequences of the strong relationship between reading and writing processing on learning will be addressed to conclude.

1   Movement Perception Is Constrained by Our Motor Knowledge

The concept of Motor-perceptual interaction was first introduced by Viviani (1990) and contains the motor behaviors that are thought to play a role in the structuration and the interpretation of our percept. Motor-perceptual interactions were especially evidenced in paradigms concerned with movement perception. The main line of research about motor-perceptual interaction postulates that the recruitment of motor knowledge during movement perception through a resonance phenomenom could be at the origin of action understanding. Thus, if perceptual and action processing are simultaneous activated during action perception, then the motor laws that govern the action behavior should also impact the way we perceive that same action (Gentsch, Weber, Synofzik, Vosgerau, & Schütz-Bosbach, 2016; Schutz-Bosbach, & Prinz, 2007).

Experiments on the *phi* movements (Shiffrar & Freyd, 1990, 1993) are particularly interesting to illustrate the impact of action laws on visual perception of biological movements. Indeed, the *phi* movement is the movement perceived by the observers when two pictures of a similar object in two different positions are successively presented. Among the different possible trajectories between the two positions of the object, the perceived movement is always the shortest trajectory between the two points (Korte, 1915). However, Shiffrar and Freyd (1990, 1993) evidenced an exception of this principle: the case of biological movement. Indeed, if we used two successive pictures presenting human body parts, the perceived movement is not the shortest but the movement respecting the anatomical constraints of the human body. This example suggests that a part of the constraints that govern our motor system also impacts visual perception of biological motion.

Studies in experimental psychology have generalized these findings and reported that at least two others of the most famous human motor laws also constrain visual perception of biological motion. It is the case for the Fitt's law (Fitts, 1954) as well as for the 2/3 power law (Lacquaniti, Terzuolo, & Viviani, 1983). The first one describes the relationship between the time needed to perform a movement and its accuracy. Thus, when individuals have to move between two targets, movement time is a function of the distance between the two targets but also of the targets' size (corresponding to the index of difficulty of the task). This law, which is likely one of the most robust laws of motor control, seems to also affect the visual perception of biological motion (Grosjean, Shiffrar, & Knoblich, 2007). In order to investigate this assumption, two pictures of a human performing a simple pointing task were alternatively presented to an observer. Based on the principle of *phi* movement, results showed that the observer perceived a movement between the two successive positions. Their task was to judge whether the movement was possible or not. The experimenters manipulated the index of difficulty of the motor task (defined by the ratio between the length of the movement and the size of the target to reach) and the interval of time between the two successive pictures (in order to obtain different speeds of movement). Results revealed that the duration of movements perceived as possible corresponded to the time required to perform the task correctly. In addition, authors found a linear relation between the index of difficulty of the task and the duration of movements perceived has possible. Such relationship was the exact translation of the Fitts' law during action perception.

The second motor law that has evidenced effects of motor behavior at the perceptual level is the 2/3 power law, which describes the relationship between movement speed and trajectory curvature (Lacquaniti et al., 1983), with the idea that the speed required to produce straight parts of a movement is greater than that required to produce trajectory parts that are curved. This effect has been shown to govern all human movements, from hand pointing tasks (Viviani, 1990; Viviani & Stucchi, 1989) to visual search tasks (deSperati & Viviani, 1997). Interestingly, when participants are instruted to adjust the speed of a dot moving on a screen around an elliptic shape with various curvatures to obtain a movement as uniform and smooth as possible. The findings showed that the speed that was preferred by the participants was not constant; rather, the preferred speed followed the 2/3 power law (Viviani & Stucchi, 1992). Together, these findings suggest that in order to perceive a movement in our environment, the perceptual system of the observers is affected by the motor laws that govern their own movements.

The involvement of motor laws in perception suggests that biological movement perception should have a special status. The experiments on point-light-diplays carried by Johansson (Johansson, 1973, 1975) have been particularly important in this respect. Indeed, while the static presentation of several dots describing a human body did not allow the recognition of the behavior, the addition of the kinematics of the movement (points in motion) provided participants with key information that allowed them the possible to perform the recognition task above chance level. It is the case that the simple passive perception of a moving dot on a screen is sufficient to give observers the ability to identify an actor's gender (Kozlowski & Cutting, 1977; Troje, Sadr, Geyer, &

Nakayama, 2006), his/her identity (Beardsworth & Buckner, 1981; Cutting & Kozlowski, 1977; Loula, Prasad, Harber, & Shiffrar, 2005) or his/her intention (Iacoboni et al., 2005). In those experiments, biological motion at the perceptual level could have a particular status because the observer used the motor knowledge stored in memory in order to recognize/understand the information perceived. In other words, our knowledge about how one performs a movement may help the recognition of the observed action. Such effects of motor knowledge on perceptual abilities could be maximized when one observes a movement for which he/she is expert. For instance, the rate of correct recognition is maximal for stimuli presenting our own walking profiles (Loula et al., 2005) in comparison to walking of other individuals.

However, we rarely have the opportunity to observe our own body in action—especially, our walking behavior. Therefore, higher recognition for our own behavior cannot be due to visual familiarity but rather must rest on the involvement of our motor knowledge. This hypothesis was corroborated by a learning experiment in which blindfolded participant had to learn new movements of danse (Casile & Giese, 2006). Results showed that performance in visual discrimination increased only for learned danse movements suggesting that development of new motor knowledge is at the basis of a better visual perception of human movements. Similar findings is now supported by numerous experiments conducted in the domain of sport sciences, suggesting that the growing motor repertories will give rise to increase perceptual abilities (Abernethy, 1990; Starkes, 1987; Williams & Davids, 1998). Basketball experts are, for instance, better to identify and anticipate about the action of others and their consequences than novices when observing basketball actions (Aglioti, Cesari, Romani, & Urgesi, 2008; Sebanz & Shiffrar, 2007). Nevertheless, closer is the observed movement to our own motor knowledge and stronger is the activation of the motor system. In this context, maximal activation of the sensorimotor network should be reached when there is a perfect match between observed and known actions (Knoblich & Flach, 2003) and helps the observer to better perceive the action. In an experiment conducted on writing behavior (Knoblich, Seigerschmidt, Flach, & Prinz, 2002), Knoblich and colleagues revealed that performances in the discrimination task were higher when observers were presented with their own writing kinematics than when presented with the kinematics of others. Hence, findings corroborate the idea that the closer the observed behavior is to our own motor repertoire, the better our ability to perceive the intention of the observed action. Yet the condition for which these motor-perceptual interactions appear may be circumscribed to body movement kinematics only. More specifically, is the impact of motor representations on the perception of biological motion limited to moving body parts? Or, alternatively, is it possible to obtain the same type of results with static pictures presenting only the outcome of the observed action?

2   Handwritten Letters as a Stimulus Implying Motion

In all the experiments presented previously, a similar type of movement (real, resume or apparent) was considered within the presented stimuli. The presence of body movement constituted indeed the key condition that was used to reveal motor-perceptual interactions. This is perfectly illustrated in the perception of Point-Light Displays for which the static presentation of points is not sufficient to afford stimulus recognition. However, some types of stimuli based on body posture appear to be sufficient to imply motion and observe motor-perceptual interactions. The most striking example is a static picture presenting a man yawning (Schurmann et al., 2005). Many other perceptual situations like scenes involving faces, objects, or letters may represent good and reliable static stimuli that induce the perception of movement. Using brain-imaging techniques, studies have revealed that several brain areas like the middle temporal cortex (MT) and medial superior temporal cortex (MST) are activated during perception of static stimuli whereas they were described as being devoted to movement analysis. More specifically, activations in these networks have been observed when movement is perceived by normal participants viewing visual scenes, both with real and apparent movement (Goebel, Khorram-Sefat, Muckli, Hacker, & Singer, 1998; Kaneoke, Bundou, Koyama, Suzuki, & Kakigi, 1997), and with imagined motor behaviors (Goebel et al., 1998; O'Craven, 1997). However, studies have also reported that similar networks are also at play during passive perception of certain types of static stimuli like for instance a picture of an athlete throwing a disc (Kourtzi & Kanwisher, 2000). The implication of motor neural network have also been reported using neurophysiological recordings (Proverbio, Riva, & Zani, 2009) with stronger activation in visual (possibly MT and MST) but also premotor and motor areas (BA 4 and 6) for static pictures implying high intensity movement (athlete in movement) in comparition to pictures suggesting less intensity movement (men doing dishes). More than activation of visual brain regions devoted to movement analysis, previous data suggested that static pictures reactive the brain networks classically involved during the planning and the execution of voluntary movements. Such phenomenom called motor resonance was not limited to scenes for which the movement was presented but appeared also when the movement was just suggested.

Taking into consideration these results as a whole, a category of stimuli may be particularly fit to reveal the motor-perceptual interactions: graphic traces. There are at least two reasons for this. First, graphic traces are likely the stimuli that are the most often observed in a static condition. Second, they are by definition the results of fine motor behaviors, especially when they are handwritten. The perfect example illustrating the relation that may exist between the abtract shape of a letter and the movement that was required to produce it comes from the kanji ideograms. Such characters are produced with a "ductus" extremely precise and codified. Thus, the order and also the direction of the different strokes are deeply learned (and cannot be mixed). And thus, the sequence of movements required to produce the character has an impact on the way we perceived it. For instance, when the sequence of strokes composing a kanji ideogram were presented stoke by stroke to the participants who had to judge the movement's direction in the last stroke, this direction was dependent on the writing experience of the participants (Li & Yeh, 2003). Indeed, opposite directions were observed for Chinese and American populations. For each population, the respective directions were in line with their classical direction of stroke writing. These data corroborate previous observations suggesting that probably the participants were able to extract informations about the writing kinematics based on the passive observation of static characters (Babcock & Freyd, 1988; Freyd, 1983). After a learning phase during which the participants were instructed on the way a character was produced (without writing it themselves), participants performed a recognition task. Performances in the test phase were impacted by the learning phase. The sequence of movements required to produce the character generated little distortions, which biased the performance in the recognition task. Performances were as if seeing the sequence of character production during the learning phase provided the participants with the means to reactivate the writing movement, which could then be available for subsequent use in the reading task.

Evidence of the reactivation of the writing movement during passive observation of characters has emerged with the development of recent neuroimaging techniques. This hypothesis was investigated by different teams with experiments on the perception of Japanese symbols (Kato et al., 1999; Matsuo et al., 2003) and roman letters (James & Gauthier, 2006; Longcamp, Anton, Roth, & Velay, 2003). In an fMRI study, Longcamp and colleagues (2003) revealed that the left premotor region (contralateral from the dominant hand) was activated during letter observation while participants did not perform any movement. Such premotor activation observed during reading was similar to the activation reported during writing experiences, suggesting that motor information related to the way a character is produced was reactivated during passive observation, even if the character was presented in a static condition. A similar conclusion was formulated on the basis of a TMS study (Papathanasiou, Filipovic, Whurr, Rothwell, & Jahanshahi, 2004). Indeed, motor evoked potentials recorded at the peripherical level significantly increased during the passive observation of letters, indicating that cortico-spinal cords classically involved during the writing movement (associated with the dominant hand) were activated by letter observation. Similar findings have been since reported by other studies conducted in fMRI (Longcamp, Hlushchuk, & Hari, 2011) and MEG (Longcamp, Tanskanen, & Hari, 2006). In these protocols, the activation of the sensorimotor region for printed and handwritten characters was compared. Based on the idea that our motor knowledge about letters is much more developed for handwritten letters in comparison to printed letters, authors expected different levels of activation of the specific sensorimotor regions used for preparing the motor system. In accordance with this hypothesis, results revealed a stronger activation of primary motor cortex (Longcamp et al., 2011) and a stronger modulation of the β rhythm (Longcamp et al., 2006), known to reflect the activity of the primary motor cortex, for handwritten letters than for printed letters. These results suggest that sensorimotor regions recruitment during passive letter observation is dependent on the amount of motor information embedded within it.

In this section, we have learned about studies that suggested that the imprint of the action associated to static handwritten letters is perceived and recognized by the observer through the recruitment of sensorimotor network(s). Such activation (comparable to the resonance phenomenom described previously) represents the perfect substrate for motor perceptual interactions and may explain the behavioral effects presented up to now. However, even if these findings are compatible with the hypothesis that the sensorimotor network plays a role in letter perception, sensorimotor activations could also result from an epiphenomenon without any functional role. In other words, simultaneous activation of the perceptual and motor systems during the learning phase could also result from the emergence of networks for which connections between perceptual and sensorimotor systems have been shaped by hebbian learning (Keysers & Perrett, 2004) without any functional role in visual recognition. This debate is the subject of the next section.

3   The Functional Role of Motor Trace Activation in Visual Letter
     Recognition

The issue of the functional role of sensorimotor activation in visual perception is still unclear. First elements to answer this issue may be found in work
assessing graphical shape perception (James & Gauthier, 2009; Wamain, Tallet, Zanone, & Longcamp, 2011, 2012). All these experiments used similar motor
interfering paradigms to make sensorimotor networks unavailable and thus,
be able to reveal the consequences on visual perception and/or recognition of
characters. For instance, in a first experiment (Wamain et al., 2011) we tested
whether the execution of a concurrent motor task (a thumb-finger opposition task) that occupies the motor networks recruited during writing deteri-
orated graphic shape discrimination. We observed a decrease in the discrimination task performance that could not be related to a general attentional
effect caused by the presence of the interfering task. Indeed, performance
decrease was only observed when the hand used to write, was mobilized by
the interfering task. Moreover, our effect appeared only for one category of
graphic traces. Furthermore, the visual discrimination of graphic traces identified as the most stable and easy to produce (stroke and ellipse with intermediate eccentricity) was affected by the execution of the concurrent motor task.
These results are in line with previous observations suggesting that sensorimotor activation is dependent on the proximity between the shapes observed
and the degree of motor knowledge of the observers (for instance Aglioti,
Cesari, Romani, & Urgesi, 2008). In addition, these results provided first evidence of the functional role of motor activations in visual graphic trace perception.
    It is the case that in past studies, the functional role of motor activations
was tested for abstract graphic traces only, using visual discrimination tasks.
In order to overpass these limits, we adapted in a second series of studies,
the motor interference paradigm in order to understand how and when the
sensorimotor activation could impact visual perception of letters (Wamain et
al., 2012). Following the rationale that the level of activation of the sensorimotor region was dependent on the amount of motor information embedded
within the letter, we chose to use three different types of letters: Printed letters (Nosuka font style), Self-handwritten letters which are the participant own
exemplars, and Non-Self-handwritten letters (exemplars produced by another
participant). Thus, the motor familiarity was manipulated along a continuum
with high, medium and low motor familiarity for Self, Non-Self handwritten
and Printed letters respectively (see Wamain et al. 2012 for a complete description of stimulus acquisition). These different exemplars of letter were then

presented to participant while he is instructed to perform a discrete motor task. This motor task was designed to provide a dynamical manipulation of the activity of the sensorimotor network. Neurophysiological recording could monitor the activity of the sensorimotor system thanks to β rhythm (around 20 Hz) recorded closed to the primary motor cortex (on the electrode c3). Indeed, a modulation of the activity of the β rhythm was observed when participant performed a motor task (Figure 5.1). Two successive states could be identified on the β rhythm modulation (around 20 Hz): First, a decrease in the amplitude of β rhythm that was associated with an activation of the sensorimotor network. This phase was followed by a second phase for which the amplitude of the β rhythm increased and was associated with an idling state of the sensorimotor network. Taking into consideration the temporal dynamics of activation of the sensorimotor network at the individual level, we presented our different types of letters (self, non-self handwritten and printed letters) in each phase of activation of the sensorimotor system: activation and idling state (see Figure 5.1). In order to measure how letters were processed, we chose other candidates than EEG rhythm: Visual Evoked Potential. Such measure corresponds to the typical electric response evoked by a stimulus and could be split into different components associated to the different steps of letter processing. Thus, while first components (like P1) refer to the processing of letter's physical properties, latter components rely to abstract identification and response planning. Our results showed that visual potentials evoked letters depended on the availability of the motor neural network (Wamain et al., 2012), but only for self handwritten letter. Findings suggest that visual perception of self-handwritten letters was the most sensitive to the motor information related to the way the letter was produced. Nevertheless, that impact of the availability of the motor neural network on the visual potentials evoked handwritten letters was visible only into two distinct time-windows: 300–350 ms and 500–600 ms after letter onset. The relative earliness of these effects strongly suggests that motor experience embedded into motor cortex could exert a top down influence on visual processing. However, even if the exact nature of such influence need to be precise, it seems unlikely that the motor experience affect abstract letter identification occurring around 170 ms after letter onset (N170 component, for instance Rey et al., 2009).

However, even if the impact of individual motor experience was visible early during letter visual processing, it remains unclear whether individual motor experiences with letters (1) contribute to the visual recognition of the character or (2) provide information about the motor trace independently from letter recognition (Barton et al., 2010). To answer this question, we used eye-tracking techniques in the Visual World Paradigm to investigate this specific

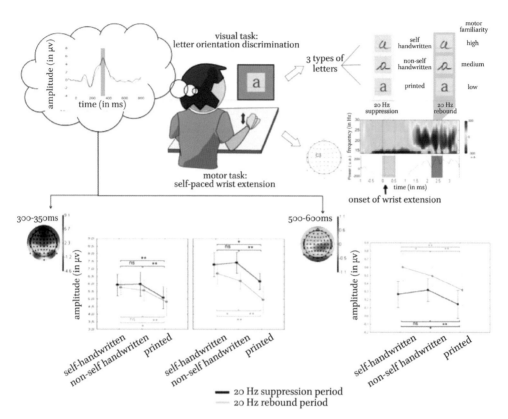

FIGURE 5.1   On the upper part, description of the dual-task procedure: Participants had to
perform simultaneously a letter orientation discrimination task (correct or mirror orientation) and a self-paced wrist extension at 5 s interval (left panel of the
figure). When a wrist extension was produced, two particular periods of the activation state of the motor cortex could be recorded under the C3 electrode: an
activation state (associated with a ~20 Hz oscillations Suppression, blue region
in the time-frequency representations in the right bottom panel of the figure)
and an "idling" state (associated with a ~20 Hz oscillations Rebound, red region).
During the dual-task procedure, three Types of Letter (Self-handwritten, Non-Self
handwritten and Printed), related to three different levels of motor familiarity,
were presented to each participant. Letters' presentation was synchronized with
these two particular periods (left top panel of the figure) while Visual Evoked
Potentials were recorded. On the lower part, main results observed on two time-
windows of VEPS: 300–350ms and 500–600ms. Error bars represent the Mean
amplitude (in μV) for each time window the 300–350 ms and 500–600 ms time-
window as a function of the Type of Letter (Self-handwritten, Non-Self handwritten and Printed) and the Period of presentation (~20 Hz oscillations Suppression
in black and ~20 Hz oscillations Rebound in grey). Each participant score was
normalized by subtracting from the original score, a participant deviation score
ADAPTED FROM WAMAIN ET AL., 2012

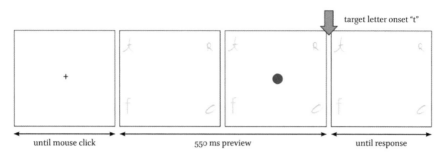

FIGURE 5.2 Example of trial used the in eye-tracking experiment. A display including the tar-
             get Letter (e.g., "t"), a script style related distractor (e.g., "r"), and two unrelated
             script style distractors (e.g., "f" and "o") was presented. Target letter name was
             delivered after 550 ms display preview (including a 50-ms red dot at the end of
             preview).

issue (Wamain & Kalenine, in preparation). Contrary to explicit discrimination
tasks, this paradigm reveals the implicit effects of the motor information—
embedded in script style—during letter recognition. More specifically, four
pictures representing different letters (a target and three distractors) were presented in the four corners of the screen. On each trial, participants heard a
letter name through speakers and were instructed to click on the image that
corresponded to the letter name (Figure 5.2).

    The time to click and the gaze position on the screen were recorded dur-
ing the entire trial sequence. As in the previous experiments, three script styles
were used allowing us to manipulate the motor familiarity of stimuli: Self, Non-
Self handwritten and Printed letters. For the critical trials, one of the distractors
was presented in the same script style as the target letter (Figure 5.3). This was
used to identify whether the script style was processed during letter recognition. The running hypothesis was that, in this case, distractors sharing the
same script style as the target letter, should attract more looks than distractors with different script styles. The main results showed that distractors with
the same script style than the target competed for attention during letter identification but only for self-handwritten letters. No competition was observed
for non-self handwritten and printed letters. In others words, the competition
effect was only observed between letters for which participants had fine motor
experience: the self-handwritten exemplars (Figure 5.3). Moreover, the competition effect with self-handwritten exemplars was exclusively observed during
the identification process, i.e., 200 ms after target letter name onset. Taking
into account that planning and execution of a saccade lasts at least 100 ms,
our results indicated that the motor information embedded within the letters
affects the early stages of visual letter identification.

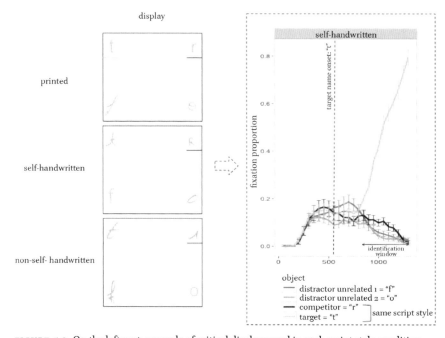

display

FIGURE 5.3 On the left part, example of critical displays used in each script style condition. The target letter is underlined in grey and the distractor letter that shared the same script style as the target in black. For instance, there were 3 displays with "t" as target letter and "r-f-o", as distractors: a Self-Handwritten display, where "t" and "r" were written by the participant while "o" was written by another scripter and "f" was printed; a Non-Self-Handwritten display, where "t" and "r" were written by another scripter while "o" was printed and "f" was written by the participant. Finally, a Printed display, where "t" and "r" were printed while "o" was written by the participant and "f" was written by other scripter. On the right part, average time course of fixations as a function of Letter Relatedness for Self-Handwritten letter script style. Each point refers to the mean fixation proportion averaged across participants and letters on a 50 ms time bin. Error bars represent individual standard errors.

Neuropsychological observations in patients have already suggested the bases of this functional role during letter identification. For instance, a case of a patient suffering from pure alexia coupled with letter visual imagery impairments was very informative (Bartolomeo, Bachoud-Lévi, Chokon, & Degos, 2002). Indeed, the patient reported difficulties in mentally evoking letter shapes while others stimuli categories (like object, face ...) were not concerned. Interestingly, his difficulties stemmed from a specific desorganisation of letter visual representations that were significantly improved every time the target letter could be written with the finger. In other words, the reactivation of the sensorimotor regions by the act of producing the writing movements improved the patient's performances in letter perception. Facilitative effects of motor trace reactivation on character recognition have already been observed both in other types of patients (Mycroft, Hanley, & Kay, 2002, Seki, Yajima, & Sugishita, 1995). Interestingly, similar conclusions have been reached in trans-cultural studies. The phenomenon named "ku-sho" represents the ability to write a character with the hand in order to recover its meaning (Sasaki, 1987). The massive impact of writing experience on the comprehension of Japanese/Chinese characters has been related to the intensive motor practice associated with the writing sequence (Naka, 1998). Overall, these data indicate that the activation of the neural network classically involved during production of a specific letter may have an impact on the visual perception and recognition of such character. More generally, investigations need now to be run to demonstrate that writing is central, not only to comprehend how fine motor knowledge is acquired but also to understand how to improve reading processes across the ages.

4   The Consequences of the Strong Relationship between Action and Perception on How We Learn to Read and Write

Debate around the disuse of handwriting in schools is systematic every time journalists publish articles on the educational issues on improving and modernizing learning programs. These questions is furthermore underlined by the transformation of our writing tools. What do you prefer? Handwriting on paper or typing on a computer pad? Pen against tablets ... a difficult battle to solve. Indeed, two distinct alternatives face each other. On the one hand, it has been argued that typing on digital devices is really simple and that this easiness may accelerate reading and writing acquisition. On the other hand, people coming from action-perception coupling fields of research postulate that sensorimotor memory traces that are constructed and consolidated during the practice of handwriting exercise facilitate written-language acquisition. Hence, the debate is a difficult one. A series of studies have now been conducted in order to evaluate the impact of several types of writing techniques on the ability to discriminate novel characters (Longcamp, Boucard, Gilhodes, & Velay, 2006; Longcamp, Zerbato-Poudou, & Velay, 2005). Especially, they compared the learning slopes in typing and handwriting tasks. Results revealed better recognition of novel characters in the handwriting condition than in the typing condition, in 3– 5 year-old children (Longcamp et al., 2005) and adults (Longcamp, Boucard, et al., 2006). Interestingly, this behavioral pattern may be due to the fact that handwriting entails an increased activation of sensorimotor networks during letter observation after training (James, 2010; James & Engelhardt, 2012; Kersey & James, 2013). The amount of time spent in performing active motor exercises may be a critical parameter enabling participation to integrate more information from the motor system within the letter recognition representations. However, most of these studies investigated the effects of the writing methods at the level of the letter. Very few studies focused on the word and results at this level of detail are more contrasted. While one study reports a superiority of handwriting over typing for spelling performances (Cunningham & Stanovich, 1990), others have not been able to replicate the effects (Ouellette & Tims, 2014; Vaughn, Schumm, & Gordon, 1992). A recent study provided an interesting contribution to the debate (Kiefer et al., 2015). Preschool children were submitted to 16 different training sessions for which eight letters of the alphabet were trained. Training was performed either by typing or by handwriting. At the word level, results revealed a superiority of handwriting training over typing training in word writing and, to a smaller extend, in word reading.

Learning to handwrite constitutes a key phase in developing the sensorimotor knowledge about a letter. This type of representation could support reading processes by facilitating letter perception and word recognition. However, the advantages that handwriting-learning should not be use as an argument to banish new technologies from schools. Further investigations are required to specify advantages and disadvantages of each learning approach. In my opinion, rather than handwriting versus typing, attention should be drawn to the question of how can one optimise the formation of specific motor representations of a letter using new technological tools. Indeed, data collected until now strongly suggest that active motor practice allows the development of letter specific motor representations that impact letter perception. The creation of a strong association between motor knowledge and the shape of the letter produced (leading to a better perception of it) may also emerge with numeric tools in specified contextual settings. This remains an important issue for future research.

5   Conclusion

To conclude, in a society where numeric tools take part of every part of our life, the question of changing writing methods from handwriting to numeric is legitimate. Like pencils several decades ago, numeric tools dramatically transform the writing experience and so, the way we learn to write a letter. These transformations of the gesture have likely consequences on the organization of the writing production and by extension on learnings and reading. Nevertheless, in the present manuscript, we developed several arguments suggesting that writing by hand (handwriting) will survive still some decades. Indeed, this type of writing allows to children to develop fine sensorimotor knowledge about letter that could participate to reading processes. Our handwritten letters are not devoted to diseappear and to be substituted by printed exemplars. Moreover, even if handwritten letters are harder to recognize than printed exemplars, they have a friendly, welcoming and familiar side. It is likely for these reasons that handwritten letters are especially present in the field of art or publicity (Mosbæk-Johannessen, 2010). Many commercials use handwritten exemplars in their logo in order to represent their product. From these giants of marketing and communication, the use of handwritten letters is unlikely to be innocuous. For many commercials, handwritten style perfectly embodies the personal touch that these brands want to represent. Nevertheless, the reasons of the familiar side of handwritten letter was not systematically investigated. Ones could argue that such feeling could result on a matching between the movement evoked by handwritten shape and movements belonging to the observers' motor repertoire. Additional research would be needed to understand whether motor resonance phenomenom could be on the basis of affective reaction evoked by logo composed by handwritten letters like for instance "Marshall".

References

Abernethy, B. (1990). Expertise, Visual Search, and Information Pick-up in Squash. *Perception, 19*, 63–77.

Aglioti, S.M., Cesari, P., Romani, M., & Urgesi, C. (2008). Action anticipation and motor resonance in elite basketball players. *Nature Neuroscience, 11*, 1109–1116.

Babcock, M.K., & Freyd, J.J. (1988). Perception of dynamic information in static handwritten forms. *The American Journal of Psychology, 101*, 111–130.

Bartolomeo, P., Bachoud-Lévi, A.C., Chokron, S., Degos, J.-D., (2002). Visually- and motor-based knowledge of letters: evidence from a pure alexic patient. *Neuropsychologia, 40*, 1363–1371.

Barton, J.J.S., Sekunova, A., Sheldon, C., Johnston, S., Iaria, G., & Scheel, M. (2010). Reading words, seeing style: The neuropsychology of word, font and handwriting perception. *Neuropsychologia, 48*, 3868–3877.

Beardsworth, T., & Buckner, T. (1981). The Ability to Recognize Oneself from a Video Recording of Ones Movements without Seeing Ones Body. *Bulletin of the Psychonomic Society, 18*, 19–22.

Casile, A., & Giese, M.A. (2006). Nonvisual motor training influences biological motion perception. *Current Biology, 16*, 69–74.

Cunningham, A.E., & Stanovich, K.E. (1990). Early spelling acquisition: Writing beats the computer. *Journal of Educational Psychology, 82*, 159–162.

Cutting, J.E., & Kozlowski, L. (1977). Recognizing friends by their walk: Gait perception without falimiarity cues. *Bulletin of the Psychonomic Society, 9*, 353–356.

deSperati, C., & Viviani, P. (1997). The relationship between curvature and velocity in two-dimensional smooth pursuit eye movements. *Journal of Neuroscience, 17*, 3932–3945.

Freyd, J.J. (1983). Representing the dynamics of a static form. *Memory & Cognition, 11*, 342–346.

Gentsch, A., Weber, A., Synofzik, M., Vosgerau, G., & Schütz-Bosbach, S. (2016). Towards a common framework of grounded action cognition: Relating motor control, perception and cognition. *Cognition, 146*, 81–89.

Goebel, R., Khorram-Sefat, D., Muckli, L., Hacker, H., & Singer, W. (1998). The constructive nature of vision: direct evidence from functional magnetic resonance imaging studies of apparent motion and motion imagery. *European Journal of Neuroscience, 10*, 1563–1573.

Grosjean, M., Shiffrar, M., & Knoblich, G. (2007). Fitts's law holds for action perception. *Psychological Science, 18*, 95–99.

Iacoboni, M., Molnar-Szakacs, I., Gallese, V., Buccino, G., Mazziotta, J.C., & Rizzolatti, G. (2005). Grasping the intentions of others with one's own mirror neuron system. *PLoS Biology, 3(3): e79.* https://doi.org/10.1371/journal.pbio.0030079.

James, K.H., & Gauthier, I. (2006). Letter processing automatically recruits a sensory-motor brain network. *Neuropsychologia, 44*, 2937–2949.

James, K.H., & Gauthier, I. (2009). When writing impairs reading: letter perception's susceptibility to motor interference. *Journal of Experimental Psychology: General, 138*, 416–431.

James, K.H., & Engelhardt, L. (2012). The effects of handwriting experience on functional brain development in pre-literate children. *Trends in Neuroscience and Education, 1*, 32–42.

Johansson, G. (1973). Visual perception of biological motion and a model for its analysis. *Perception & Psychophysics, 14*, 201–211.

Johansson, G. (1975). Visual motion perception. *Scientific American, 232*, 76–88.

Kaneoke, Y., Bundou, M., Koyama, S., Suzuki, H., & Kakigi, R. (1997). Human cortical area responding to stimuli in apparent motion. *Neuroreport, 8*, 677–682.

Kato, C., Isoda, H., Takehara, Y., Matsuo, K., Moriya, T., & Nakai, T. (1999). Involvement of motor cortices in retrieval of kanji studied by functional MRI. *Neuroreport, 10*, 1335–1339.

Kersey, A.J., & James, K.H. (2013). Brain activation patterns resulting from learning letter forms through active self-production and passive observation in young children. *Frontiers in Psychology 4*:567. doi: 10.3389/fpsyg.2013.00567.

Keysers, C., & Perrett, D.I. (2004). Demystifying social cognition: a Hebbian perspective. Trends in *Cognitive Sciences, 8*, 501–507.

Kiefer, M., Schuler, S., Mayer, C., Trumpp, N.M., Hille, K., & Sachse, S. (2015). Handwriting or Typewriting? The Influence of Pen- or Keyboard-Based Writing Training on Reading and Writing Performance in Preschool Children. *Advances Cognitive Psychololy, 11*, 136–146.

Knoblich, G., & Flach, R. (2003). Action identity: Evidence from self-recognition, prediction, and coordination. *Consciousness and Cognition, 12*, 620–632.

Knoblich, G., Seigerschmidt, E., Flach, R., & Prinz, W. (2002). Authorship effects in the prediction of handwriting strokes: evidence for action simulation during action perception. *The Quarterly Journal of Experimental Psychology, 55A*, 1027–1046.

Korte, A. (1915). Kinematoskopische Untersuchungen. *Zeitschrift für Psychologie, 72*, 194–296.

Kourtzi, Z., & Kanwisher, N. (2000). Activation in human MT/MST by static images with implied motion. *Journal of Cognitive Neuroscience, 12*, 48–55.

Kozlowski, L., & Cutting, J.E. (1977). Recognizing the sex of a walker from dynamic point-light displays. *Perception & Psychophysics, 21*, 575–580.

Lacquaniti, F., Terzuolo, C., & Viviani, P. (1983). The law relating the kinematic and figural aspects of drawing movements. Acta Psychol (Amst), 54(1–3), 115–130.

Li, J., & Yeh, S. (2003). Do "Chinese and American see opposite apparent motions in a Chinese character"? Tse and Cavanagh (2000) replicated and revised. *Visual Cognition, 10*, 537–547.

Longcamp, M., Anton, J.L., Roth, M., & Velay, J.L. (2003). Visual presentation of single letters activates a premotor area involved in writing. *NeuroImage, 19*, 1492–1500.

Longcamp, M., Boucard, C., Gilhodes, J.C., & Velay, J.L. (2006). Remembering the orientation of newly learned characters depends on the associated writing knowledge: A comparison between handwriting and typing. *Human Movement Science, 25*, 646–656.

Longcamp, M., Hlushchuk, Y., & Hari, R. (2011). What differs in visual recognition of handwritten vs. printed letters? An fMRI study. *Human Brain Mapping, 32*, 1250–1259.

Longcamp, M., Tanskanen, T., & Hari, R. (2006). The imprint of action: Motor cortex involvement in visual perception of handwritten letters. *NeuroImage, 33*, 681–688.

Longcamp, M., Zerbato-Poudou, M.T., & Velay, J. (2005). The influence of writing practice on letter recognition in preschool children: A comparison between handwriting and typing. *Acta Psychologica, 119*, 67–79.

Loula, F., Prasad, S., Harber, K., & Shiffrar, M. (2005). Recognizing people from their movement. *Journal of Experimental Psychology: Human Perception and Performance, 31*, 210–220.

Matsuo, K., Kato, C., Okada, T., Moriya, T., Glover, G.H., & Nakai, T. (2003). Finger movements lighten neural loads in the recognition of ideographic characters. *Cognitive Brain Research, 17,* 263–272.

Mosbæk-Johannessen, C. (2010). *Forensic analysis of graphic trademarks. A multimodal social semiotic approach.* University of Southern Denmark.

Mycroft, R., Hanley, J.R., & Kay, J., (2002). Preserved access to abstract letter identities despite abolished letter naming in a case of pure alexia. *Journal of Neurolinguistics, 15,* 99–108.

Naka, M. (1998). Repeated writing facilitates children's memory for pseudocharacters and foreign letters. *Memory & Cognition, 26,* 804–809.

O'Craven, K.M., Kanwisher, N.G. (1997). Visual Imagery of Moving Stimuli Activates MT/MST. Society for Neuroscience, New Orleans.

Ouellette, G., & Tims, T. (2014). The write way to spell: Printing vs. typing effects on orthographic learning. *Frontiers in Psychology, 5:117. doi: 10.3389/fpsyg.2014.00117.*

Papathanasiou, I., Filipovic, S.R., Whurr, R., Rothwell, J.C., Jahanshahi, M., (2004). Changes in corticospinal motor excitability induced by non-motor linguistic tasks. *Experimental Brain Research, 154,* 218–225.

Proverbio, A.M., Riva, F., & Zani, A. (2009). Observation of static pictures of dynamic actions enhances the activity of movement-related brain areas. PLoS One, 4(5), e5389.

Repp, B.H. (1987). The Sound of 2 Hands Clapping—an Exploratory-Study. Journal of the Acoustical *Society of America, 81,* 1100–1109.

Sasaki, M. (1987). Why do Japanese Write Characters in Space? *International Journal of Behavioral Development, 10,* 135–149.

Schurmann, M., Hesse, M.D., Stephan, K.E., Saarela, M., Zilles, K., Hari, R., et al. (2005). Yearning to yawn: the neural basis of contagious yawning. *Neuroimage, 24,* 1260–1264.

Schutz-Bosbach, S., & Prinz, W. (2007). Perceptual resonance: action-induced modulation of perception. *Trends Cognitive Sciences, 11,* 349–355.

Sebanz, N., & Shiffrar, M. (2007). Bluffing bodies: Inferring intentions from actions. *Perception, 36,* 176–176.

Seki, K., Yajima, M., & Sugishita, M., 1995. The efficacy of kinesthetic reading treatment for pure alexia. *Neuropsychologia, 33,* 595–609.

Shiffrar, M., & Freyd, J.J. (1990). Apparent Motion of the Human-Body. *Psychological Science, 1,* 257–264.

Shiffrar, M., & Freyd, J.J. (1993). Timing and apparent motion path choice with human body photographs. *Psychological Science, 4,* 379–384.

Starkes, J.L. (1987). Skill in Field Hockey: The nature of the cognitive advantage. *Human Kinetics Journals, 9,* 146–160.

Troje, N.F., Sadr, J., Geyer, H., & Nakayama, K. (2006). Adaptation aftereffects in the perception of gender from biological motion. *Journal of Vision, 6,* 850–857.

Tse, P.U., & Cavanagh, P. (2000). Chinese and Americans see opposite apparent motions in a Chinese character. *Cognition, 74*, B27–32.

Vaughn, S., Schumm, J.S., & Gordon, J. (1992). Early spelling acquisition: Does writing really beat the computer? *Learning Disability Quarterly, 15*, 223–228.

Viviani, P. (1990). Motor-perceptual interactions: the evolution of an idea. In M. Piatelli Palarini (Ed.), *Cognitive science in Europe: issues and trends* (pp. 11–39): Golem.

Viviani, P., & Stucchi, N. (1989). The effect of movement velocity on form perception: geometric illusions in dynamic displays. *Perception & Psychophysics, 46*, 266–274.

Viviani, P., & Stucchi, N. (1992). Biological movements look uniform: evidence of motor-perceptual interactions. *Journal of Experimental Psychology: Human Perception and Performance, 18*, 603–623.

Wamain, Y., Tallet, J., Zanone, P.-G., & Longcamp, M. (2011). Biological Geometry Perception: Visual Discrimination of Eccentricity Is Related to Individual Motor Preferences. *PLoS ONE 6(1): e15995*. https://doi.org/10.1371/journal.pone.0015995.

Wamain, Y., Tallet, J., Zanone, P.-G., & Longcamp, M. (2012). Brain responses to handwritten and printed letters differentially depend on the activation state of the primary motor cortex. *NeuroImage, 63*, 1766–1773.

Wamain, Y., & Kalénine, S. (in preparation). The power of handwriting: Eye Tracking evidence that individual motor experience impacts letter identification.

Williams, A.M., & Davids, K. (1998). Visual search strategy, selective attention, and expertise in soccer. *Research Quarterly for Exercise and Sport, 69*, 111–128.

CHAPTER 6

Struggling with Writing: an Examination of Writing Difficulties in Specific Language Impairment, Developmental Dyslexia and Developmental Coordination Disorder

Olivia Afonso, Vincent Connelly and Anna L. Barnett

Writing is a complex process involving perceptual, motor and linguistics skills. During writing acquisition children have to develop these skills while their working memory capacities are still limited (Berninger & Amtmann, 2003). Given the complexity of writing production in general and writing acquisition in particular, it is not surprising that many children struggle to learn to write. Children with developmental dysgraphia, for example, manifest a primary impairment in writing ability and different subtypes have been described depending on the specific aspects of writing affected (e.g., lexical access, phonology-to-orthography conversion, motor processes). However, handwriting difficulties are also common in a wide range of other developmental disabilities, even if the core deficit affects a different cognitive or motor process. The fact that these developmental disabilities are not primarily defined by the presence of writing impairments may lead to these difficulties being under-identified and/or undertreated. The potential negative consequences for academic and professional development may be extensive for these individuals, given the increasing importance of written communication in modern societies. In this chapter we review the evidence obtained about the writing difficulties often observed in three different developmental disabilities: Specific Language Impairment (SLI), Developmental Dyslexia (DD), and Developmental Coordination Disorder (DCD). There is not only a clinical need for a better understanding of the writing difficulties in individuals with one or more of these disabilities. From a theoretical point of view, the study of writing performance in these groups offers a unique window to the connections between writing and other closely-related domains such as speech production (SLI), reading (DD) and movement control (DCD).

1   Defining Specific Language Impairment, Developmental Dyslexia,
       and Developmetal Coordination Disorder

Although there is considerable co-occurrence of SLI, DD, and DCD, these are
rather different disabilities in which one specific domain of human performance is primarily affected. SLI (also referred to as language learning disability, LLD) is a heterogeneous category including children who have difficulties
producing and understanding language, although they generally have more
problems with oral language production than with receptive language (Dockrell, Lindsay, Roulston, & Law, 2014). In the fifth edition of the Diagnostic and
Statistical Manual of Mental Disorders (DSM-V, 2013), the American Psychological Association (APA) uses the term Communication Disorder to refer to those
cases in which language is underdeveloped as in the clinical description of SLI
(Hulme & Snowling, 2009). DD is described as reduced reading achievement
and DCD as poor motor coordination. In the three cases, these difficulties cannot be explained by intellectual ability, little opportunity to develop the skill
or the existence of a neurological condition. Moreover, difficulties must affect
daily living activities and academic or professional activities. Interestingly, in
each of the three categories writing is specifically mentioned as a skill potentially affected.

   Although the study of writing difficulties in these groups is relatively limited, there is growing evidence indicating that writing difficulties are in fact
frequently present in individuals with SLI, DD or DCD. One common charac-
teristic seems to be the production of shorter texts than their peers (Bishop
& Clarkson, 2003; Connelly, Campbell, McLean, & Barnes, 2006; Rosenblum &
Livneh-Zirinski, 2008). However, this is just a superficial similarity, since thorough assessment and a number of experimental studies analysing measures of
the writing product and the writing process have revealed clear differences in
the nature of the writing difficulties experienced by these three groups.

2   Specific Language Impairment: the Impact of Morphological
       Deficits in Word Writing

SLI is a category in which children with impaired language comprehension
and/or production and typical nonverbal ability are included. One of the core
impairments in SLI seems to affect the processing of morpho-syntactic information (Gopnik & Cargo, 1991; Hulme & Snowling, 2009; Rice, 2000). For this
reason, more studies have been conducted at the text and sentence level than at
the word level both in oral and written production research. Although previous

literature has mainly focused on difficulties with oral language, it is acknowledged that written production is frequently impaired in children with SLI
(Bishop & Clarkson, 2003; Critten, Connelly, Dockrell, & Walter, 2014; Mackie
& Dockrell, 2004; Mawhood, Howlin, & Rutter, 2000). These difficulties affect
writing dynamics. Connelly, Dockrell, Walter, and Critten (2012) reported that
English speaking children around 11 years of age produced fewer words, shorter
writing bursts and more pauses associated with misspellings than typically-
developing peers of the same age. Both oral language measures of vocabulary
and written spelling accuracy continue to predict written production for pupils
with SLI throughout primary to the end of secondary school (Dockrell, Lindsay, & Connelly, 2009; Dockrell, Lindsay, Connelly, & Mackie, 2007). Stothard,
Snowling, Bishop, Chipchase and Kaplan (1998) tested adolescents who had
been identified to have SLI when they were 4 years of age (Bishop & Edmundson, 1987) to evaluate the evolution of their language difficulties. They observed
that even a sub-group considered to have resolved their speech-expression
difficulties at $5^{1/2}$ years continued to show reading and spelling difficulties.
Mawhood et al. (2000) found that adults that had been diagnosed as having
a developmental language disorder during childhood still had difficulties with
written language, with spelling difficulties more prevalent than reading difficulties. Windsor, Scott, and Street (2000) observed that similar difficulties were
observed in spoken and written samples of language production in individuals
with LLD, but that the impairments were exacerbated in the written domain.
These findings suggest that writing difficulties in SLI might outlast and in some
cases exceed the severity of the problems observed in oral production.

The writing impairment observed in SLI seems to mirror the difficulties
experienced with spoken language. One of the hallmarks of the speech production of individuals with SLI is the presence of more grammatical errors
than those made by their chronological-age matched peers (Rice, 2000; Rice,
Wexler, & Cleave, 1995). Errors exhibited by individuals with SLI in spoken language typically include the omission of copulas and auxiliary verbs (Grela &
Leonard, 2000; Rice et al., 1995; Watkins, Rice, & Moltz, 1993), the past tense
marker -ed (Joanisse & Seidenberg, 1998; Marshall & van der Lely, 2012; Rice et
al., 1995) and the third person marker -s (Hayiou-Thomas, Bishop, & Plunkett,
2004; Hulme & Snowling, 2009). Thus, it is widely accepted that children with
SLI have particular difficulties with verb morphology. Grela and Leonard tested
the usage of verbs by 4–6 year-old children with SLI in a story-completion task.
The children were told a story while the experimenter recreated it with animate
and inanimate figures. The children were asked to orally narrate the end of the
action performed by a given character. This task required the use of sentences
including auxiliary forms of the verb *be* (e.g., *The dog is running*). Children with

SLI were significantly more likely to omit the auxiliary verb than their peers matched by mean-length of utterance (a measure assumed to reflect linguistic productivity). A similar tendency to omit auxiliary verbs was observed in written production by Mackie and Dockrell (2004). These authors found that English children with SLI produced more whole-word syntax errors in their narratives than their chronological-age (CA) and language-age (LA) matched peers. Differently, Windsor et al. (2000) did not find significant differences in the percentage of errors made in the use of the verb *be* in either the spoken or written productions of 10–12 year-old children with LLD in comparison to the CA or LA matched groups. Given the limited number of studies addressing this issue, it remains to be seen whether the differences in age of the children tested in these studies could explain the different pattern of results obtained. By the age of 10 years, initial difficulties with the learning of the rules of use of auxiliary verbs may have been resolved as a result of experience at school.

More research has been conducted on the difficulties shown by English speakers with SLI with inflectional and derivational morphology (Gopnik & Crago, 1991). In their study, Gopnik and Crago observed that in a family with members with and without SLI, affected members showed impaired performance in tests requiring generation of plural forms (*-s*), past tense marked forms (*-ed*) and derivational morphemes (*sunny*, given *sun*). Although other studies have also detected problems in plural generation in SLI (Windsor et al., 2000), it is widely assumed that verb morphology is more problematic than noun morphology for individuals with SLI (Hayiou-Thomas et al., 2004; Hulme & Snowling, 2009). Several studies assessing the spoken production of children with SLI have shown that they use the past tense marker *-ed* less frequently than their peers (King, Schelletter, Sinka, Fletcher, & Ingham, 1995; Rice et al., 1995; Windsor et al., 2000). Although considerably less research has been conducted on irregular past tense production, it seems that children with SLI produce similar error rates as younger children matched by LA (Oetting & Horohov, 1997; Rice, Wexler, Marquis, & Hershberger, 2000). In written production, difficulties in the use of the *-ed* past tense marker have also been observed (Larkin, Williams, & Blaggan, 2013; Mackie & Dockrell, 2004), in some cases being even greater than difficulties exhibited in spoken language (Windsor et al., 2000). Windsor and colleagues observed that, in the written task, all errors made by 10–12 year-old children with SLI in regular past tense were incorrect zero-marked forms (*help* instead of *helped*). These authors reported that this tendency to use bare-stem forms was also present in the SLI children's spelling of irregular verbs (using, for example, *grow* instead of *grew*), with the number of overgeneralisations of the regular *-ed* past tense marker being considerably less frequent. Although more research is needed on the written production of irregular past tense forms in SLI, these findings are in line with the reduced number of overgeneralised past tense forms observed in spoken production in children with SLI compared to the CA and LA matched groups (Oetting & Horohov, 1997). However, other studies have reported different patterns in the written and spoken products of individuals with SLI. While many studies have observed particular difficulties with inflectional morphology in spoken production (e.g., Marshall & Van Der Lely, 2007), Critten and colleagues did not find differences in spelling accuracy for inflectional morphemes between a group of 9–10 year-old children with SLI and a group of peers matched by spelling ability (SA), but only in spelling accuracy for derivational morphemes. Interestingly, children with SLI produced a higher proportion of phonologically implausible errors and a fewer proportion of phonologically plausible errors than children in the CA and LA groups only in derived morphemes. Mackie and Dockrell (2004) observed in the writing of individuals with SLI inflectional morphology errors that they did not make in spoken production, suggesting that the problems exhibited by this group in writing could not be solely explained by the deficit in oral production. In sum, it seems that difficulties with expressive oral language in SLI may affect also written word production. Specifically, the production of verbs seem to be impaired in children with this disorder, with inflectional morphology representing a particular challenge. However, more evidence is necessary to determine whether or not all the impairments observed in writing can be accounted for by the level of oral language development as there are some problems interpreting results in this area due to interactions with spelling knowledge (e.g., Dockrell & Connelly, 2009; 2013).

3   Spelling Difficulties in Developmental Dyslexia

The presence of word-level difficulties in dyslexia are well-documented both in reading and writing (Connelly & Dockrell, 2015; Sumner, Connelly, & Barnett, 2014b; Wimmer & Mayringer, 2002). Children and adults with DD exhibit poor spelling (Afonso, Suárez-Coalla, & Cuetos, 2015; Berninger, Nielsen, Abbott, Wijsman, & Raskind, 2008; Connelly et al., 2006) and pause more during writing (Sumner, Connelly & Barnett, 2013; 2014a). More specifically Sumner et al., (2014a) observed that differences in the number of words produced by children with dyslexia and their SA-matched peers were mainly due to the number of pauses produced within misspelled words. Furthermore, these pauses are longer than those produced by typically-developing CA matched peers even in words correctly spelled (Afonso et al., 2015). Regarding handwriting speed, it seems that children with DD are not slower than typically-developing peers.

In their study, Sumner and colleagues (2014a) observed that both groups were equally fast when pauses were excluded from the analyses. The impact of poor spelling on the temporal aspects of writing is not limited to composing tasks. Over 50% of the variability in performance of children with dyslexia on a sentence copying task was predicted by spelling ability, and the children were slower than their same age peers but no slower than a group of children matched for spelling ability (Sumner et al., 2014a). Word level production rates remain slow into adolescence even when keyboarding (Torrance, Ronneberg, Johansson, & Uppstad, 2016). Thus, previous evidence seems to indicate that writing difficulties in DD are related to spelling processes and not to handwriting.

   Although the precise underlying cause of reading difficulties in DD remains controversial, there is extensive agreement about the fact that these problems are related to impaired phonological skills (Hulme & Snowling, 2009). Thus, it seems reasonable to think that spelling difficulties often observed in children and adults with DD may stem from impaired phonological representations. Some findings support this claim (Angelelli, 2004; Caravolas, Hulme, & Snowling, 2001; Caravolas & Volín, 2001; Friend & Olson, 2010; Goswami & Bryant, 1990; Shaywitz & Shaywitz, 2005). Children with DD who are speakers of languages with transparent orthographies, such as Czech or Italian, have been reported to produce more phonologically non-plausible errors (Caravolas & Volín, 2001) and more minimal distance errors (Angelelli, 2004). Minimal distance errors consist of the substitution of one letter by another that differs only in one phonetic feature. These types of errors are thought to reflect difficulties to correctly apply the phonology-to-orthography conversion rules. However, other authors have suggested that the main writing impairment in dyslexia affects orthographic lexical representations (Angelelli, Judica, Spinelli, Zoccolotti, & Luzzatti, 2004; Angelelli, Notarnicola, Judica, Zoccoloti, & Luzzatti, 2010; Di Betta & Romani, 2006). Angelelli et al. (2004) observed in a sample of Italian children with dyslexia that although some of these children made minimal distance errors, the main problem concerned the spelling of words with unpredictable transcription. As these words necessarily require the retrieval of the appropriate orthographic representation, these authors concluded that the main deficit responsible for the spelling problems in DD was better explained by a selective impairment to the orthographic lexicon. In a study in which online measures of the written responses of Spanish adults with and without dyslexia were analysed, Afonso and colleagues (2015) observed that the group with DD showed enhanced word frequency effects in written latencies compared to the control group. However, phonology-to-orthography consistency effects were similar in both groups, suggesting that the main differences between adults with and without DD were at the lexical level of processing. In this study, individuals with DD also exhibited stronger word length effects. This may indicate some difficulty in maintaining long words in orthographic working memory in the group with dyslexia. It has been recently proposed that reading difficulties in dyslexia may be due to impaired ability to consolidate in long-term memory serial-order representations maintained in short-term memory (Bogaerts, Szmalec, Hachmann, Page, & Duyck, 2015; Szmalec, Page, & Duyck, 2012). Although this hypothesis has not been directly tested as an explanation for word writing difficulties in DD, the remarkably serial nature of writing production provides an especially interesting context to address this issue.

Although less studied than phonological deficits, difficulties with the use of morphological information during spelling have also been reported in children with DD in comparison to typically developing chronological age-matched children. However, results have been less consistent in those studies including a reading or spelling ability-matched control group. A number of studies have failed to find differences between children with DD and a group of younger children with the same spelling ability in their use of morphological information to correctly spell inflected or derived words (Bourassa & Treiman, 2008; Bourassa, Treiman, & Kessler, 2006). These results point to a delay in the development of morphological ability rather than to the existence of a specific deficit affecting morphological processing in DD. Nevertheless, in some studies individuals with DD have been observed to perform more poorly than their younger peers in morphological spelling tasks (Carlisle, 1987; Egan & Pring, 2004; Hauerwas & Walker, 2003). For example, in Egan and Pring's study 11–12 year-old children with DD showed specific difficulties to spell regular past tense verb forms. It is worth noting that differently from other studies and from the evidence accumulated for SLI children, in this study the -ed past tense marker was more often substituted by -t or -d (generating phonologically plausible errors) than completely omitted (zero-marking). As the authors suggested, it is necessary to further address the relation that may exist between this particular pattern of spelling errors and the poor level of development of the orthographic lexicon of children with DD. The fact that these children may know the spelling of only a reduced set of words may lead to overreliance on phonological spelling strategies in DD.

Some evidence suggests that different spelling deficits in DD might be detected depending on the age of the groups tested. Initial difficulties with the learning of phonological-to-orthography conversion patterns may be overcome with formal instruction. In line with this idea, Angelelli and colleagues (2010) observed that Italian children with DD in Grade 3 (8–9 years old) produced all type of errors, while in Grade 5 (10–11 years old) they committed mainly phonologically-plausible errors. Other authors have also claimed that spelling and reading impairments in DD may vary as a function of age (Afonso et al., 2015; Landerl & Wimmer, 2000; Snowling & Nation, 1997). In a study conducted with adult English speakers, Di Betta and Romani (2006) asked participants to learn new words in association to pictures. These authors did not obtain a strong correlation between the score obtained in this written word learning task and phonological awareness. These findings led the authors to conclude that the writing impairments shown by adults with DD could not be explained by the phonological deficits usually reported in children. More studies comparing different age groups with the same tasks and variables are necessary in order to obtain a complete picture of the development of the spelling deficits related to DD over time.

Whether or not these spelling difficulties are exclusively linked to the reading deficits is a question requiring further research. To the best of our knowledge, studies systematically investigating this issue have not been conducted to date. Although some authors have claimed that spelling impairments largely mirror reading impairments in dyslexia (Angelelli et al., 2004), it is revealing that spelling difficulties persist into adulthood even to the point of representing the major reason for complaint in adults with DD (Di Betta & Romani, 2006; Holmes & Castles, 2001). This might be due to the fact that spelling is more difficult than reading also for typically-developing individuals (see Bosman & Van Order, 1997). This is in part due to the higher level of consistency in orthography-to-phonology correspondences than in phonology-to-orthography correspondences (Ziegler, Jacobs, & Stone, 1996). It is possible that some of the spelling difficulties experienced by individuals with DD can be ameliorated by improving reading ability, while other problems may need to be directly addressed. In any case, evidence strongly supports the idea that writing difficulties present in DD primarily concern the word level. Regardless of the characteristics of the specific language of the individuals assessed, spelling seems to be the main process impaired. Whether this impairment is connected to orthographic or phonological deficits or both is an issue that warrants further investigation.

4   Difficulties with Motor Aspects of Writing: the Case of Developmental Coordination Disorder

The fine motor coordination difficulties experienced by children with DCD impact their development of handwriting skill. Learning to handwrite involves learning to maintain an adequate posture and pencil grasp, something that can be difficult for individuals with DCD. Unsurprisingly, difficulties with handwriting are one of the most common reasons for referral to occupational therapists for individuals with DCD (Asher, 2006; Prunty, Barnett, Wilmut, & Plumb, 2013). As for children with SLI and DD, children with DCD have been found to produce fewer words than typically-developing children in their written productions (Barnett, Henderson, Scheib, & Schulz, 2011; Prunty et al., 2013; Rosenblum & Livneh-Zirinski, 2008). Detailed analyses of the handwriting process have shown that this reduced productivity of the writing of children with DCD may be due not to slower movement execution but to longer pausing during production. In a study conducted with 8–14 year-old children with DCD, participants completed the four handwriting tasks of the Detailed Assessment of Speed of Handwriting (DASH; Barnett, Henderson, Scheib, & Schulz, 2007) on a digitising writing tablet (Prunty et al., 2013). The findings revealed that the group with DCD and the control group did not significantly differ in their execution speed, but in the percentage of time they spent pausing. Other studies have confirmed this tendency of children with DCD to pause longer (Prunty et al., 2013; Rosenblum & Livneh-Zirinski, 2008) and more often (Prunty et al., 2014) during writing. Specifically, Prunty and colleagues observed that children with DCD produced more and longer pauses of above 10 seconds. Based on previous studies (Alamargot, Plane, Lambert, & Chesnet, 2010), the authors associated this type of pausing to higher-order processes related to planning and formulation of forthcoming ideas. However, children with DCD produced these longer pauses within an idea. This result was interpreted as a lack of automation of the handwriting skill in the group with DCD which would hinder the ability to concurrently engage in higher-order writing processes. The idea that motor aspects of writing are the main difficulty in DCD is both intuitive and supported by evidence. In the same study, Prunty and collaborators conducted an analysis of the position of pauses. Results revealed that individuals with DCD paused longer than controls within illegible words. Rosenblum and Livneh-Zirinski (2008) also reported less legible writing in Hebrew and more letter corrections in a group of 7–10 year-old children with DCD than in a CA matched group. In sum, it seems that children with DCD may experience problems in correctly and fluently forming letters.

Although it seems clear that the main difficulties with written production in DCD are related to handwriting, poor spelling has also been reported in these children. English-speaking children with DCD aged between 8–14 years have been observed to produce more spelling errors in free-writing tasks (Prunty, Barnett, Wilmut, & Plumb, 2016) and in assessment tests (Dewey, Kaplan, Crawford, & Wilson, 2002). In spite of these findings, spelling deficits have not been consistently reported. However, recent evidence suggests that spelling and handwriting abilities are closely related during writing acquisition (Afonso, Suárez-Coalla, González-Martín, & Cuetos, 2018; Berninger & Amtmann, 2003; Bosga-Stork, Ellis, & Meulenbroek, 2016), so impairments to motor aspects of writing seems to be likely to have a negative impact on spelling ability. The fact that both skills compete for limited resources (e.g., working memory resources) and have to be learned simultaneously may lead to considerable mutual influence between these processes. If children with DCD experience difficulties in fully automatizing handwriting movements, they may have little resources available to focus on spelling. Thus, word production in DCD can be affected both at the spelling and at the motor execution level. More evidence is needed to determine whether spelling difficulties in DCD are circumscribed to a particular point of development or are a persistent deficit in DCD. Additionally, an analysis of the type of spelling errors made by children and adults with DCD may provide more information about the cause of these spelling problems. To the best of our knowledge, results of such an analysis have not been yet reported.

5   Conclusions

Learning to write is a complex task that requires mastering linguistic and motor processes. Even writing words in isolation exerts considerable demands in terms of morphological processing, lexical access, phonology-to-orthography conversion, working memory resources and motor execution. If any of the involved processes are affected, writing difficulties may appear, with the consequent impact for academic progress. Several developmental disabilities are associated with writing difficulties, but they are likely to be caused by different underlying impairments. Although written word production is slower and/or less accurate in SLI, DD and DCD compared to typically-developing children of the same age, the specific processes affected seem to be different in each group. Children and adolescents with SLI have particular problems with inflectional morphology, which mostly affects verb production. Conversely, individuals with DD seem to use morphological information as expected given their reading and spelling ability, but, they produce errors and a pattern of within-word pauses consistent with poor phonological awareness and reduced orthographic lexical information. Little is yet known about the linguistic variables that affect spelling in DCD, but it is clear from the evidence that motor aspects of writing are the primary level of impairment. However, some results suggest that the interaction between central and peripheral aspects of word writing especially during early writing acquisition may also produce spelling difficulties in children with DCD. In sum, problems affecting word writing in these disorders might be linked to primary deficits in spoken language, reading and movement coordination respectively, so different methods of assessment and intervention have to be considered.

Finally, it must be highlighted that the study of writing abilities in these populations is still relatively limited. More information is needed about the specific processes affected and the prevalence of the writing difficulties in each case. Moreover, clarity in understanding developmental difficulties in word writing is limited by the lack of commonality in methods of participant sampling and task design. This line of research would also contribute to our understanding of the relationships between writing and other cognitive domains (such as oral language production, reading and movement) that have been understudied in typical development.

References

Afonso, O., Suárez-Coalla, P., & Cuetos, F. (2015). Spelling impairments in Spanish dyslexic adults. *Frontiers in Psychology, 6. doi: 0.3389/fpsyg.2015.00466*

Afonso, O., Suárez-Coalla, P., González-Martín, N., & Cuetos, F. (2018). The impact of word frequency on peripheral processes during handwriting: A matter of age. *The Quarterly Journal of Experimental Psychology, 71,* 695–703.

Alamargot, D., Plane, S., Lambert, E., & Chesnet, D. (2010). Using eye and pen movements to trace the development of writing expertise: case studies of a 7th, 9th and 12th grader, graduate student, and professional writer. *Reading and Writing, 23,* 853–888.

American Psychiatric Association. (2013). *Diagnostic and Statistical Manual of Mental Disorders* (5th Ed.). Arlington, VA: American Psychiatric Publishing.

Angelelli, P. (2004). I disturbi de lettro-scritura in et età evolutiva. *Quaderni di didattica della scrittura, 2,* 59–81.

Angelelli, P., Judica, A., Spinelli, D., Zoccolotti, P., & Luzzatti, C. (2004). Characteristics of Writing Disorders in Italian Dyslexic Children. *Cognitive and Behavioral Neurology, 17,* 18–31.

Angelelli, P., Notarnicola, A., Judica, A., Zoccolotti, P., & Luzzatti, C. (2010). Spelling impairments in Italian dyslexic children: Phenomenological changes in primary school. *Cortex, 46,* 1299–1311.

Asher, A.V. (2006). Handwriting instruction in elementary schools. *American Journal of Occupational Therapy, 60,* 461–471.

Barnett, A., Henderson, S., Scheib, B., & Schulz, J. (2007). *The detailed assessment of speed of handwriting.* London: Harcourt Assessment.

Barnett, A., Henderson, S., Scheib, B., Schulz, J. (2011). Handwriting difficulties and their assessment in young adults with DCD: Extension of the DASH for 17–25 year olds. *Journal of Adult Development, 18*, 114–121.

Berninger, V.W. & Amtmann, D. (2003). Preventing written expression disabilities through early and continuing assessment and intervention for handwriting and/or spelling problems: Research into practice. In Swanson, H.L., Harris, K. & Graham, S. (Eds.). *Handbook of learning difficulties.* (pp. 345–363). New York & London. Guildford Press.

Berninger, V.W., Nielsen, K.H., Abbott, R.D., Wijsman, E., & Raskind, W. (2008). Writing problems in developmental dyslexia: Under-recognized and under-treated. *Journal of School Psychology, 46*, 1–21.

Bishop, D.V.M., & Clarkson, B. (2003). Written language as a window into residual language deficits: A study of children with persistent and residual speech and language impairments. *Cortex, 39*, 215–237.

Bishop, D.V.M., & Edmundson, A. (1987). Language impaired 4-year-olds: Distinguishing transient from persistent impairment. *Journal of Speech and Hearing Disorders, 52*, 156–173.

Bogaerts, L., Szmalec, A., Hachmann, W.M., Page, M.P.A., & Duyck, W. (2015). Linking memory and language: Evidence for a serial-order learning impairment in dyslexia. *Research in Developmental Disabilities, 43–44*, 106–122.

Bosga-Stork, I., Bosga, J., Ellis, J.L., & Meulenbroek, R.G.J. (2016). Developing interactions between language and motor skills in the first three years of formal handwriting education. *British Journal of Education, Society & Behavioural Science, 12*, 1–13.

Bosman, A.M.T., & Van Orden, G.C. (1997). Why spelling is more difficult than reading. In C.A. Perfetti, L. Rieben, & M. Fayol, (Eds.), *Learning to spell: Research, theory, and practice across languages* (pp. 173–194). Hillsdale, NJ: Lawrence Erlbaum Associates.

Bourassa, D.C., & Treiman, R. (2008). Morphological constancy in spelling: a comparison of children with dyslexia and typically developing children. *Dyslexia, 14*, 155–169.

Bourassa, D.C., Treiman, R. & Kessler, B. (2006). Use of morphology in spelling by children with dyslexia and typically developing children. *Memory & Cognition, 34*, 703–714.

Caravolas, M., Hulme, C., & Snowling, M.J. (2001). The foundations of spelling ability: Evidence from a 3-year longitudinal study. *Journal of Memory and Language, 45*, 751–774.

Caravolas, M., & Volín, J. (2001). Phonological spelling errors among dyslexic children learning a transparent orthography: the case of Czech. *Dyslexia, 7*, 229–245.

Carlisle, J.F. (1987). The use of morphological knowledge in spelling derived forms by learning-disabled and normal students. *Annals of Dyslexia, 27*, 90–108.

Connelly, V. & Dockrell, J.E. (2015). Writing development and instruction for students with learning disabilities: Using diagnostic categories to study writing difficulties. In C. MacArthur, S. Graham, J. Fitzgerald (Eds) *Handbook of Writing Research, 2nd Edition.* (pp. 349–363). New York: Guildford Publications.

Connelly, V., Campbell, S., MacLean, M., & Barnes, J. (2006). Contribution of lower order skills to the written composition of college students with and without dyslexia. *Developmental Neuropsychology, 29,* 175–196.

Connelly, V., Dockrell, J.E., Walter, K., Critten, S. (2012). Predicting the Quality of Composition and Written Language Bursts From Oral Language, Spelling, and Handwriting Skills in Children With and Without Specific Language Impairment. *Written Communication, 29,* 278–302.

Critten, S., Connelly, V., Dockrell, J.E., & Walter, K. (2014). Inflectional and derivational morphological spelling abilities of children with Specific Learning impairment. *Frontiers in Psychology, 5:948. doi: 10.3389/fpsyg.2014.00948.*

Dewey, D., Kaplan, B., Crawford, S., & Wilson, B.N. (2002). Developmental coordination disorder: Associated problems in attention learning and psychological adjustment. *Human Movement Science, 21,* 905–918.

Di Betta, A.M., & Romani, C. (2006). Lexical learning and dysgraphia in a group of adults with developmental dyslexia. *Cognitive Neuropsychology, 23,* 376–400.

Dockrell, J.E., & Connelly, V. (2009). The impact of oral language skills on the production of written text. *British Journal of Educational Psychology Monograph Series II, Teaching and Learning Writing, 6,* 45–62.

Dockrell, J.E., Lindsay, G., & Connelly, V. (2009). The impact of specific language impairment on adolescents' written text. *Exceptional Children, 75,* 427–446.

Dockrell, J.E., Lindsay, G., Connelly, V., & Mackie, C. (2007). Constraints in the production of written text in children with SLI. *Exceptional Children, 73,* 147–164.

Dockrell, J.E., Lindsay, G., Roulstone, S., & Law, J. (2014). Supporting children with speech, language and communication needs. *International Journal of Language & Communication Disorders, 49,* 543–557.

Egan, J., & Pring, L. (2004). The Processing of Inflectional Morphology: A Comparison of Children with and without Dyslexia. *Reading and Writing: An International Journal, 17,* 567–591.

Friend, A., & Olson, R.K. (2010). Phonological spelling and reading deficits in children with spelling disabilities. *Scientific Studies of Reading, 12,* 90–105.

Goswami, U., & Bryant, P. (1990). *Phonological Skills and Learning to Read.* Hove: Lawrence Erlbaum Associates Ltd.

Gopnik, M., & Crago, M.B. (1991). Familial aggregation of a developmental language disorder. *Cognition, 39,* 1–50.

Grela, B.G., & Leonard, L.B. (2000). The influence of argument structure complexity on the use of auxiliary verbs by children with SLI. *Journal of Speech, Language, and Hearing Research, 43,* 1115–1125.

Hauerwas, L.B., & Walker, J. (2003). Spelling of inflected verb morphology in children with spelling deficits. *Learning Disabilities Research & Practice, 15,* 25–35.

Hayiou-Thomas, M.E., Bishop, D.V.M., & Plunkett, K. (2004). Simulating SLI: General cognitive processing stressors can produce a specific linguistic profile. *Journal of Speech, Language and Hearing Research, 47,* 1347–1362.

Holmes, V.M., & Castles, A.E. (2001). Unexpectedly poor spelling in university students. *Scientific Studies of Reading, 5,* 319–359.

Hulme, C., & Snowling, M.J. (2009). *Developmental Disorders of Language, Learning and Cognition.* Oxford: Wiley-Blackwell.

Joanisse, M.F., & Seidenberg, M.S. (1998). Specific language impairment: A deficit in grammar or processing? *Trends in Cognitive Sciences, 2,* 240–247.

King, G., Schelletter, C., Sinka, I., Fletcher, P., & Ingham, R. (1995). Are English-speaking SLI children with morpho-syntactic deficits impaired in their use of locative-contact and causative alternating verbs? *University of Reading Working Paper in Linguistics, 2,* 45–65.

Landerl, K., & Wimmer, H. (2000). Deficit of phonemic segmentation are not the core problem of dyslexia: Evidence from German and English children. *Applied Psycholinguistics, 21,* 243–262.

Larkin, R.F., Williams, G.J., Blaggan, S. (2013). Delay or deficit? Spelling processes in children with specific language impairment. *Journal of Communication Disorders, 46,* 5–6

Mackie, C., & Dockrell, J.E. (2004). The Nature of written language deficits in children with SLI. *Journal of Speech, Language, and Hearing Research, 47,* 1469–1483.

Marshall, C., & van der Lely, H.K.J. (2012). Irregular past tense forms in English: how data from children with specific language impairment contribute to models of morphology. *Morphology, 22,* 121–141.

Mawhood, L., Howlin, P., & Rutter, M. (2000). Autism and developmental receptive language disorder: A comparative follow-up in early adult life. *Journal of Child Psychology and Psychiatry, 41,* 561–578.

Oetting, J.B., & Horohov, J.E. (1997). Past-Tense Marking by Children With and Without Specific Language Impairment. *Journal of Speech, Language, and Hearing Research, 40,* 62–74.

Prunty, M., Barnett, A.L., Wilmut, K., & Plumb, M. (2013). Handwriting speed in children with Developmental Coordination Disorder: Are they really slower? *Research in Developmental Disabilities, 34,* 2927–2936.

Prunty, M.M., Barnett, A.L., Wilmut, K., & Plumb, M.S. (2014). An examination of writing pauses in the handwriting of children with Developmental Coordination Disorder. *Research in Developmental Disabilities, 35,* 2894–2905.

Prunty, M.M., Barnett, A.L., Wilmut, K., & Plumb, M.S. (2016). Visual perceptual and handwriting skills in children with Developmental Coordination Disorder. *Human Movement Science, 49*, 54–65.

Rice, M.L. (2000). Grammatical symptoms of specific language impairment. In D.V.M. Bishop & L.B. Leonard (Eds.), *Speech and language impairments in children: Causes, characteristics, intervention and outcome* (pp. 17–34). East Sussex, England: Psychology Press Ltd.

Rice, M.L., Wexler, K., & Cleave, P.L. (1995). Specific language impairment as a period of extended optional infinitive. *Journal of Speech and Hearing Research, 38*, 850–863.

Rice, M.L., Wexler, K., Marquis, J., & Hershberger, S. (2000). Acquisition of irregular past tense by children with specific language impairment. *Journal of Speech, Language, and Hearing Research, 43*, 1126–1145

Rosenblum, S., & Livneh-Zirinski, M. (2008). Handwriting process and product characteristics of children diagnosed with developmental coordination disorder. *Human Movement Science, 27*, 200–214.

Shaywitz, S.E., & Shaywitz, B.A. (2005). Dyslexia (specific reading disability). *Biological Psychiatry, 57*, 1301–1309.

Snowling, M., & Nation, K. (1997). Language, phonology and learning to read. In C. Hulme and M. Snowling (Eds.). *Dyslexia: Biology, Cognition and Intervention* (pp. 153–166). London: WhurrPublishers.

Stothard, S.E., Snowling, M.J., Bishop, D.V.M., Chipchase, B.B., & Kaplan, C.A. (1998). Language impaired preschoolers: A follow-up into adolescence. *Journal of Speech, Language, and Hearing Research, 41*, 407–418.

Sumner, E., Connelly, V., & Barnett, A.L. (2013). Children with dyslexia are slow writers because they pause more often and not because they are slow at handwriting execution. *Reading & Writing, 26*, 991–1008.

Sumner, E., Connelly, V. & Barnett, A. (2014a). The influence of spelling ability on handwriting production: Children with and without dyslexia. *Journal of Experimental Psychology: Learning Memory and Cognition. 40*, 1441–1447.

Sumner, E., Connelly, V., & Barnett, A. (2014b). Dyslexia and expressive writing in English. In B. Arfe, J.E. Dockrell, & V.W. Berninger (Eds.), *Writing development and instruction in children with hearing, speech, and oral language difficulties.* (pp. 188–200). Oxford: Oxford University Press.

Szmalec, A., Page, M.P.A., & Duyck, W. (2012). The development of long-term lexical representations through Hebb repetition learning. *Journal of Memory and Language, 67*, 342–354.

Torrance, M., Ronneberg, V., Johansson, C. and Uppstad, P.H., (2016). Adolescent weak decoders writing in a shallow orthography: process and product. *Scientific Studies of Reading, 20*(5), 375–388.

Watkins, R., Rice, M.L., & Moltz, C. (1993). Verb use by language-impaired and normally developing children. *First Language, 13*, 133–143.

Wimmer, H., & Mayringer, H. (2002). Dysfluent reading in the absence of spelling difficulties: A specific disability in regular orthographies. *Journal of Educational Psychology, 94*, 272–277.

Windsor, J., Scott, C.M., & Street, C.K. (2000). Verb and noun morphology in the spoken and written language of children with language learning disabilities. *Journal of Speech, Language, and Hearing Research, 43*, 1322–1336.

Ziegler, J.C., Jacobs, A.M., & Stone, G.O. (1996). Statistical analysis of the bidirectional inconsistency of spelling and sound in French. *Behavior Research Methods, Instruments, & Computers, 28*, 504–515.

PART 2

Methodological Section

∴

CHAPTER 7

Task Differences and Individual Differences in Skilled Spelling

Patrick Bonin and Alain Méot

> Man has an instinctive tendency to speak, as we see in the babble of our young children, whereas no child has an instinctive tendency to bake, brew, or write.
>
> CHARLES DARWIN (1871)

∴

1   Introduction

Writing is a less frequent activity than speaking, even though as claimed by Rapp and Dufor (2011): "(...) *as electronic communication increases, the time some people spend in written communication, through activities such as e-mailing, texting, chatting, instant messaging, tweeting, etc., may come close to or even surpass the time spent speaking.*" (p. 4067) and as the quotation of Charles Darwin (1871), taken from his book *The descent of man*, indicates, writing, unlike speaking, is not instinctive (see also Pinker, 1994, for the view that speaking is an instinct).

The different studies described below relate to the production of isolated words. Some readers might ask themselves why certain researchers have decided to focus on isolated words given that people rarely engage in the production of single words, such as, for instance, writing down a word from a picture (an experimental task that has often been used to study spelling in adults, see below). The reason is that focusing on isolated words makes it possible to isolate different parameters (e.g., frequency, length) and to study their influence more systematically. This is not to say that it is not possible to investigate specific parameters in text production, but it has turned out to be somewhat more difficult. A general assumption has been that studying the written production of isolated words is fundamental because producing texts or sentences necessarily involves the production of individual words. Moreover, patients who suffer from language production damage are often impaired at the level of individual words. Therefore, for many years in our own work, we have designed different kinds of studies in which participants have had to write down single words from different inputs: from pictures or spoken words. In this chapter, we hope to convince readers that this research strategy has been fruitful.

Different tasks have been used to investigate the issue of the different units and the mechanisms that are involved in skilled word spelling: Written naming, spelling to dictation and immediate copying (in the reminder of this chapter we will focus on written naming and spelling to dictation; readers who are interested in the copying task are referred to Lambert, Alamargot, & Fayol, 2012). The use of these three tasks has made it possible to investigate several important issues in writing, such as the role of phonological codes in skilled written naming (e.g., Bonin, Fayol, & Gombert, 1997; Bonin, Fayol, & Peereman, 1998; Bonin, Peereman, & Fayol, 2001), the role of syllables in written naming and copying (Sausset, Lambert, Olive, & Larocque, 2012), the locus[1] of word frequency in written naming (e.g., Bonin, Fayol, & Chalard, 2001; Qu, Zhang, & Damian, 2016), in spelling to dictation (Bonin, Laroche, & Perret, 2016; Shi Min & Richard Liow, 2016), or in copying (e.g., Lambert, Alamargot, Larocque, & Caporossi, 2011) as well as the dynamics of the information flow in written naming (e.g., Roux, & Bonin, 2012; Bonin, Roux, Barry, & Canell, 2012) to name a few. Up to now, however, these tasks have been used separately. As a result, we still do not know exactly whether the effects that are observed in a given spelling task can be generalized to another spelling task. Moreover, the issue of individual differences within a given spelling task, as well as across spelling tasks, has not as yet been investigated thoroughly. In this chapter, we will review some recent studies that have addressed these issues. To begin with and to permit readers to gain a better understanding of the rationale underpinning these studies, we recap the line of reasoning followed in some earlier studies that made use of either written naming or spelling to dictation in adults.

---

1   The locus of a variable corresponds to a processing level within a cognitive architecture where it may have an effect.

2   Using Single Tasks to Investigate Spelling Processes: What Have We Learned from the Use of Either Written Naming or Spelling to Dictation?

Picture naming is a task that has been frequently used to study spoken language production. It is a simple experimental task during which adults have to say aloud the name of a picture as quickly as possible after its presentation on a computer screen. It has often been assumed that picture naming operationalizes an ecological production situation in which adults start with a communicative intention (Bock & Levelt, 1994). Thanks to this task, it is possible to measure the time taken to name pictures, i.e., onset naming latencies, which corresponds to the time that elapses from the onset of picture presentation through to the start of articulation of the picture name. The picture naming task has also been used to investigate written langage production. In order to record onset latencies, a digitizer pad is used, e.g., WACOM pad (UltraPad A5), equipped with a stylus linked to a computer.

The picture naming task can be combined with the interference paradigm. This experimental technique has been, and still is, widely used to investigate the nature of the representations that are involved in spoken or in written naming and the time when these are activated (e.g., Schriefers, Meyer, & Levelt, 1990). In this technique, a target is defined, and most often corresponds to pictures. The targets are accompanied by distractors, e.g., the written word *frog* in the middle of a picture of a DOG. Participants are required to name (or to write down) targets as quick as possible while ignoring the distractors. There can be different types of relations between the targets and the distractors (note that the distractors can be presented in their written or spoken form). For instance, targets and distractors can be semantically related as in "rabbit-DOG", or they can be phonologically related as in "blog-DOG". The distractors used as controls are often unrelated words, e.g., "house-DOG", but other types of control distractors are sometimes used such as strings of "xxx", or non-linguistic symbols, e.g., "&&&". The time taken to process the targets with different types of distractors is analyzed (as is the accuracy of the processing). Compared to unrelated word distractors, semantic or phonological distractors can slow down or, in contrast, accelerate the processing of the targets. Another key aspect of this technique is that the interval between the onset of targets and distractors can be manipulated, i.e., SOA = Stimulus Onset Asynchrony. The distractors can be presented simultaneously with the targets (SOA = 0 ms), slightly before (negative SOAs) or after (positive SOAs) the targets. Likewise, it is possible to obtain information about the representations that are relevant at a given moment in processing and not, or less, relevant at another moment.

In one study, Bonin and Fayol (2000) attempted to determine the extent to which written and spoken naming share similar or, on the contrary, mobilize different representations and processes. The authors' line of reasoning was that the observation of similar effects during the same temporal windows in both output modalities would suggest the involvement of similar representations and processes. In this study, the picture-word interference paradigm was used to investigate the time-course of activation of semantic and lexical representations. As described above, in this paradigm, participants have to name pictures that are accompanied by linguistic or nonlinguistic distractors that have to be ignored.[2] The time taken to name targets, i.e., preparation latencies, is measured. In Bonin and Fayol's (2000) Experiment 1, pictures were presented with spoken word distractors that were semantically related (e.g., *toe* for FINGER) or unrelated to the targets (e.g., *lemon*). Two different SOAs were used: –150 ms and 0. In another experiment (Experiment 3), target pictures had to be named and were accompanied by word distractors that resulted from the crossing of the semantic relatedness and orthographic relatedness factors. Similarly, there were semantically and orthographically related distractors (e.g., *caravane* [caravan] for CAMION [TRUCK]), distractors that were only semantically related (*hélicopter* [helicopter]), distractors that were only orthographically related (*carotte* [carrot]) and unrelated word distractors (*noix* [walnut]). In Experiment 1, both speaking and writing were investigated whereas in Experiment 3, only writing was investigated.

Several important findings emerged from Bonin and Fayol's (2000) study. Firstly, the time course of semantic code activation—as indexed by the semantic interference effects, e.g., longer naming latencies for the drawing of a FOX when *dog* is presented as a word distractor compared to the unrelated distractor *house*—were obtained at the same SOA in speaking and writing, thus suggesting that similar semantic representations are involved in both output modalities. Secondly, orthographic/phonological effects were also observed at the same SOAs in both modalities. Last, but not least, as found in spoken naming, there was a reliable reduction of semantic interference (in fact, the semantic interference effect was eliminated) on written naming latencies when distractors were both semantically and orthographically related. The latter finding, which has led to some controversial discussions in the past (Roelofs, Meyer, & Levelt, 1996; Starreveld & La Heij, 1995, 1996), was interpreted by Bonin and Fayol (2000) as suggesting that the lexico-semantic (or lemma) and

---

2 Several variants of the interference paradigm exist, for example both the targets and the distractors can be pictures: the picture-picture interference paradigm. The latter paradigm has been successfully used to study written naming (Roux & Bonin, 2012).

the word-form (or lexeme) levels in writing are not serial and discretely connected. In effect, according to the additive factors logic (Sternberg, 1969),[3] if semantic interference has an effect at the lexico-semantic (or lemma) level and phonological/orthographic facilitation takes place at a different processing level, namely the word-form (or lexeme) level then, if the discrete-serial account is correct, we should have observed that the effects of the two variables were additive.

In a related vein, Bonin, Chalard, Méot and Fayol (2002) used the multiple regression approach to investigate the determinants of both spoken and written naming latencies. They used line-drawings taken from the Snodgrass and Vanderwart (1980) database and took account of picture and word characteristics that were normed in French by Alario and Ferrand (1999). Again, the general hypothesis was that whenever similar processes and representations are used in both production modalities, one should observe that naming latencies are predicted by the very same determinants. This prediction was borne out. Bonin et al. (2002) observed that the main determinants of naming speed were the same in both writing and speaking, namely name agreement, image agreement and age-of-aquisition. To illustrate, the observation that image agreement was a reliable determinant of naming speed in both production modes was taken to suggest that in both speaking and writing, there is a common level of structural representation (the level of object recognition in Figure 7.1). This level of representations has been assumed to correspond to canonical visual descriptions of objects. Moreover, the observation that age-of-acquisition (AoA) had a reliable influence was taken to indicate that either the same representations, i.e., phonological word-forms, are accessed, and if this is the case, mediate access to orthographic codes in written naming, i.e., obligatory phonological mediation (see below), or that orthographic representations themselves are impacted by the age at which they are learned due to the implication of the same learning principles that apply to both phonological and orthographic lexical representations. At the time the Bonin et al. (2002) study was conducted the idea that AoA effects are rooted in the lexical phonology of the words was generally thought to account for these effects (see Johnston & Barry, 2006, and Juhasz, 2005, for reviews). It is important to stress that the locus/i and the mechanisms underpinning AoA effects in word production are still a matter of debate (e.g., Perret, Bonin, Laganaro, 2014).

---

3 The additive factors logic is based on the idea that when two factors affect theoretically independent stages within a cognitive architecture, this should result in additivity in mean RTs, that is to say there should be two main effects corresponding to the two factors, but no interaction.

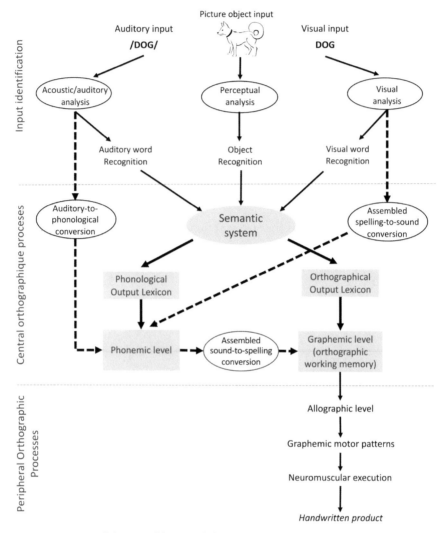

FIGURE 7.1 General theoretical framework for understanding the component processes
              involved in written object naming, spelling to dictation and immediate copying
              (the components belonging to the lexical pathway are presented against a gray
              background and the components relating to the nonlexical pathway are shown in
              bold dotted lines)
              FIGURE ADAPTED FROM BONIN, P., MÉOT, A., LAGARRIGUE, A., AND ROUX,
              S. (2015). WRITTEN OBJECT NAMING, SPELLING TO DICTATION, AND IMME-
              DIATE COPYING: DIFFERENT TASKS, DIFFERENT PATHWAYS? QUARTERLY
              JOURNAL OF EXPERIMENTAL PSYCHOLOGY, 68, 1268–1294

The logic suggested by Bonin and colleagues (Bonin & Fayol, 2000; Bonin et al., 2002) was recently adopted by Perret and Laganaro (2012). In this study, the researchers investigated written and spoken naming using EEGs. A high-density EEG was recorded for healthy adults during a handwritten and a spoken picture naming task involving the same line-drawings of objects. The authors performed waveform analyses and topographical pattern analyses on stimulus- and response-aligned ERPs in order to cover the entire word encoding phase. They found that speaking and writing from pictures started to diverge and to display different and modality specific topographical configurations from around 260 ms, a time-window corresponding to the start of word-form encoding in speaking (Indefrey, 2011). Importantly, Perret and Laganaro (2012) reached similar conclusions to Bonin and colleagues regarding the question of shared and different levels of processing in speaking and writing, namely that written and spoken word production share the conceptual and the lexical-semantic levels (often referred to as lemmas) and differ at the level of word-form encoding.

But is writing fully dependent upon speaking? Is it the case that what we learn from speaking generalizes directly to writing? As we have seen, speaking and writing do share some processing levels but there are also some differences that have been explored in a number of studies.

The hypothesis that writing and speaking differ at the level of word-form encoding has been explored in the theoretical framework of the obligatory phonological mediation view as compared to the orthographic autonomy view. There are two views of the role of phonological codes in conceptually-driven writing. According to the obligatory phonological mediation (OPM) view (Geschwind, 1969; Luria, 1979), phonological codes have to be retrieved in order to derive the orthography of the words, whereas the orthographic autonomy (OA) view (Rapp, Benzing., & Caramazza, 1997) holds that orthographic codes can be accessed independently of the retrieval of phonological codes (via the link from the semantic level to the orthographic output lexicon in Figure 7.1). The OPM has been challenged on the basis of analyses of the spelling and naming performances of patients. Certain patients are able to produce the correct written forms of words that they cannot produce orally (Rapp, Benzing, & Caramazza, 1997), or produce them orally as nonwords (Rapp & Caramazza, 1997). There are also descriptions of patients who make different semantic errors in the two production modalities (Miceli, & Capasso, 1997; Miceli, Capasso, & Caramazza, 1999), a pattern that cannot be easily accounted for if the same phonological codes underpin both production modes. The patterns of spelling performances of these brain-damaged patients are more in line with the OA view. In healthy adults, the role of phonological codes in the access to orthographic codes has been investigated in a series of factorial studies that used written picture naming tasks (Bonin et al., 1998; Bonin et al., 2001). The findings were consistent with the following conclusions: (1) Phonological codes are not obligatory to write down words from conceptual input; (2) In line with the OA view, orthographic codes can be accessed directly from semantic codes; (3) Although not obligatory, phonological codes can play a role in orthographic encoding. Some more recent studies (especially those conducted by Markus Damian's team) suggest that phonological codes could play a greater role in written naming than initially thought (e.g., Damian & Qu, 2013; Damian, Dorjee, & Stadthagen-Gonzalez, 2011; Qu, Damian, Zhang, & Zhu, 2011; Zhang & Damian, 2010). By contrast, other findings suggest that orthographic codes can be derived without the (prior) involvement of phonology, and thus independently of phonology, in alphabetic languages (e.g., Bonin et al., 1998; Roux & Bonin, 2012), as well as in Chinese (e.g., Zhang & Wang, 2016), a non-alphabetic language in which orthographic and phonological characteristics can are easier to distinguish between. Thus, it is clear that there are major discrepancies in the findings concerning the role of phonology in written naming that are, at the moment, difficult to resolve and that will require future studies.

Turning to (written) spelling to dictation, the theoretical framework that has guided research on healthy adults and patients is the dual-route view of spelling which is supported by various lines of evidence (see Tainturier & Rapp, 2001 for a review). We will consider one recent proposal of this view, namely the dual-route view of spelling put forward by Tainturier and Rapp (2001). According to this view, two routes, or processing pathways, are available to produce the spelling of both familiar and unfamiliar words in educated adults: a lexical and a nonlexical route (Figure 7.1). The spoken input is first analyzed at the perceptual level. This level is shared by both routes. From the perceptual level, phonological word-forms are used to access semantic codes, the latter making it possible to activate of several orthographic word-forms within the orthographic (output) lexicon, one of which will be selected for further encoding. The nonlexical route makes use of the sublexical phonological units—most probably phonemes—activated at the perceptual level and the latter are converted into orthographic sublexical units (graphemes). This route assembles spelling by relying on the most frequent correspondences between phonemes and graphemes (e.g., Sanders & Caramazza, 1990). Both routes provide outputs at the level of graphemes (graphemic level in), a level which is also conceptualized as an orthographic working memory (Purcell, Turkeltaub, Eden, & Rapp, 2011). Finally, several peripheral processes are involved in deriving a written trace from the grapheme level in the case of handwriting. Given that the nonlexical route produces a phonologically plausible spelling output for irregular words whereas the lexical route makes available the correct spelling response, a conflict is assumed to arise at the grapheme level and is thought to take some time to resolve. This view therefore predicts that words with multiple phonology-to-orthography renderings will be produced more slowly than words with one-to-one renderings. To illustrate, compare *tank* and *tube* in French. The word *tank* has multiple renderings at the level of the rime (/âk/ can be produced as *anque* or *ank*) whereas this is not the case for the word *tube*. In real-time studies (e.g., Bonin et al., 2001), it has been found that "tank-like words" take longer to produce (in writing) than "tube-like words". Such phenomena are referred to as consistency/irregularity effects.

In the Bonin and Méot (2002) study, the goal was to investigate the determinants of spelling to dictation latencies (and errors). Adults had to write down on a graphic tablet nouns that were orally presented. A multiple regression was performed on the onset latencies. The reliable predictors of spelling latencies were acoustic duration, objective word frequency, PO consistency and word length. Interestingly, consistency effects were found to interact with word frequency, with the result that consistency effects were stronger with low-frequency words than with high-frequency words. This finding is consistent with the prediction of the dual-route view because the dual-route view assumes that consistency effects are the result of a competition between the outcomes of the lexical and nonlexical routes (Tainturier & Rapp, 2001).

The research that has been conducted on written word production from either conceptual inputs (e.g., pictures in written picture naming) or auditory inputs (e.g., spoken words in spelling to dictation) has made it possible to delineate the most important lexical or semantic characteristics that influence word writing speed. At a theoretical level, these studies have helped to constrain certain views of spelling production in adults. It is now clear that when participants write down words from a perceptual input, such as a pictorial representation, there are many processing levels that are shared with the speaking of the same words. However, unlike speaking, writing does not obligatorily require the involvement of phonological codes. Finally, in spelling to dictation, two routes rather than one are involved when writing down familiar words. A nonlexical route is required for spelling unknown words or pseudowords. However, when spelling, it is possible that some individuals rely more on one route than on the other. This is precisely the question that we now address below.

3   Individual Differences in (Written) Spelling to Dictation

The issue of individual differences has begun to be addressed quite extensively in the field of visual word recognition (Yap, Balota, Sibley, & Ratcliff,
2012). In a recent study, Bonin, Méot, Millotte and Barry (2013) investigated the
issue of individual differences in handwritten spelling to dictation. The participants were all students (80 from the University of Bourgogne) and a large
number of monosyllabic words were used (164 monosyllabic nouns). The theoretical framework used to guide the different hypotheses that were tested
was the dual-route view of spelling (Tainturier & Rapp, 2001). As described
in greater detail earlier, most researchers assume that two routes are available to spell words to dictation. To recap briefly, one route is a lexical route in
which the spellings of known words are retrieved from an orthographic long-
term memory, whereas the other route is a nonlexical route in which individual phonemes derived from the spoken input are converted into graphemes
by applying sets of phoneme-to-grapheme correspondences. Given that the
French orthographic system is highly inconsistent (Peereman & Content, 1999),
it is not unreasonable to hypothesize that certain spellers rely more on lexical knowledge whereas, perhaps, the opposite is true for other spellers. The
idea that there are trade-offs among spellers in the use of the two routes
was inspired by word reading studies aimed at identifying reading profiles on
the basis of the participants' tendency to rely on one of the two routes: 'lexical readers' versus 'non-lexical readers'. However, evidence supporting such
profiles has been rather scarce (Burt & Heffernan, 2012). We reasoned that
if individuals are able to exert some degree of 'control' over the use of the
two routes, namely the lexical route, which is sensitive to word frequency,
and the non-lexical route, which is sensitive to PO consistency, one prediction would be that a trade-off between word-frequency and PO consistency
variables should be found. However, this type of trade-off between the different types of knowledge could be modulated by the level of exposure to print
among participants. It is a popular belief that individuals who read a lot and
possess a rich vocabulary tend to be good spellers. However, to our knowledge,
there is little evidence to support such a claim. Consequently, all the participants performed a vocabulary test taken from Deltour (1993) at the end of the
experimental session (they had to select the synonym corresponding to different words). The experiment took place during two sessions separated by at
least one week. During a testing session, the participants listened (via head-
phones) to individual words that had been recorded by a female speaker and
had to write down each word they heard using a graphic tablet. The preparation
latencies were recorded. Linear mixed models with by-participants random

slopes[4] were run on the latencies (and spelling errors), with several independent variables included in the equation model, that is to say: acoustic duration (in ms), orthographic length, word frequency, frequency trajectory, bigram frequency, phonological neighbors, PO consistency and imageability.

The most important findings were as follows.

1. As far as fixed effects are concerned, we found that several variables reliably predicted the preparation latencies: acoustic duration, word length, word frequency and PO consistency. The pattern of results was consistent with previous findings (Bonin & Méot, 2002; Bonin, Barry, Méot, & Chalard, 2004). Second, we found that the participants' mean latencies (and standard deviations) were very reliable both within and between sessions. We think that this finding is good news for researchers who want to study spelling performance based on the use of groups of individuals who are generally tested in a single session.

2. It should be remembered that we expected that spellers who were more sensitive to word frequency should be less sensitive to PO consistency (and vice versa). However, the by-participants random slopes did not enable us to identify different types of spellers on the basis of their reliance on one of the two routes (a reliance that could be dispositional and stable). This finding accords with a previous study by Bonin, Collay, Fayol and Méot (2005) who also found no evidence of strategic control over the non-lexical route in spelling to dictation. This does not mean that individual writing profiles cannot be identified since, in text production, Levy and Ransdell (1995) were able to identify writing profiles extending through the processes of planning, text generation, reviewing and revising during different writing sessions. Finally, in visual word recognition, Yap et al. (2012) also did not find evidence of a trade-off between sensitivity to different types of information (e.g., lexical versus nonlexical information).

3. Examining the distributions obtained from within-participants regression analyses, we found that there was substantial variability in the magnitude of the effects that were produced by the participants. Take, for instance, the case of word frequency which has been reported in various spelling to dictation studies (Bonin & Méot, 2002; Bonin et al., 2004). We observed that, even though the regression coefficients for the effect

---

4   The inclusion of random slopes makes it possible to obtain estimations of the effects of independent variables (IV) at the participants level, which can be used to differentiate participants on their relative sensitivity to the dimensions under investigation. These effects can also be related with certain other characteristics of the participants (e.g., a vocabulary test).

of word frequency were negative for the majority of the participants, these coefficients were nevertheless subject to a certain level of variability. These individual analyses contribute to our understanding of how the effects of the different variables do or do not correspond to those obtained at the level of groups of participants or at the level of items. Also, the direction and relative magnitudes of the effects observed at the level of individual participants were generally consistent with those observed in the by-items analyses.

4.   Finally, turning to the impact of vocabulary scores, we found that individuals who achieved high vocabulary scores wrote down the words more quickly and made fewer spelling errors (including both phonological plausible errors and orthographic errors). They were therefore more accurate than those who had poorer vocabulary scores.

4   How Far Can What We Learn from Written Naming Be Generalized to Other Spelling Tasks?

In a recent study, Bonin, Méot, Lagarrigue and Roux (2015) addressed the general question of the extent to which what we learn from written naming generalized to other spelling tasks. More precisely, Bonin et al. (2015) addressed the issue of how the spellings of the words that people know are derived from three different types of input: pictures, spoken words and visually presented words. Indeed, a key issue is the extent to which these three spelling tasks rely on similar or different processing pathways.

As can seen from Figure 7.1, there are components that are exclusively dedicated to a given task only such as object recognition in object naming, auditory word recognition in spelling to dictation, and visual word recognition in immediate copying. There are components that are shared by the three tasks, that is to say the orthographic output lexicon and sublexical conversion processes. Finally, there are processes dedicated to the planning and execution of the handwriting trace. Most views of word spelling assume that two processing pathways, and not only one, are available to derive the spelling of words.

The primary goal of Bonin et al.'s (2015) study was to shed light on the contribution of these two pathways in written naming, spelling to dictation and copying. In this study, participants took part in three different sessions that were separated by at least one week. They had to perform either written naming, spelling to dictation or immediate copying from the same set of word stimuli in a given writing session. Thus, the participants performed *the three tasks with the same items*. Multiple regression analyses were performed on the preparation latencies. Several characteristics of the words were taken into account, including imageability, a variable that is assumed to index semantic code activation, i.e., a semantic variable (Evans, Lambon Ralph, & Woollams, 2012); word frequency was used to index the involvement of the lexical pathway (Bonin et al., 2012) and PO consistency was used to index the involvement of the nonlexical pathway (Bonin et al., 2001). Important characteristics of the pictures and of the auditory/visual words were also taken into account in the multiple regression analyses. Among the findings, three are worthy of note.

First of all, word frequency was reliable in all tasks, but it was stronger in written naming than in the other two spelling tasks. This suggests that, perhaps, there is no one single locus in picture naming, spelling to dictation and copying. Indeed, we recently addressed the issue of the locus of word frequency in spelling to dictation (Bonin et al., 2016) in the light of a study by Chua and Rickard Liow (2014) that claimed to have provided evidence that word frequency effects in spelling to dictation are located at the level of spoken word recognition, and not at at the level of the orthographic word-forms as traditionally assumed (Delattre, Bonin, & Barry, 2006). In this study, we used the additive factors logic (Sternberg, 1969) (see also Footnote 3): If word frequency in spelling to dictation influences a processing level—the orthographic output level—which is different from that influenced by phonological neighborhood density—spoken word recognition—then the impact of the two factors should be additive; otherwise their impact should be overadditive if their effects occur at the same processing level, namely spoken word recognition. In line with the hypothesis that word frequency has its locus at the orthographic word-form level, we found that both factors had a reliable influence on the spelling latencies but did not interact. It is important to note that our hypothesis of a word-form locus of word frequency effects in handwritten spelling to dictation is reinforced by the findings of Bonin et al. (2015). Across the three tasks, as we noted, word frequency effects were stronger in written naming latencies than in the other two tasks, namely spelling to dictation and immediate copying, where they were nearly the same, thus suggesting that the latter two spelling tasks very likely share a common level at which frequency effects occur, namely the orthographic output level.

Second, PO consistency was reliable only in spelling to dication. This is a very important finding. The pattern of findings suggests that the lexical pathway is involved in all spelling tasks, although it makes a stronger contribution in written naming than in the other two tasks, and that the nonlexical pathway is reliably dominant only in spelling to dictation. In Bonin et al. (2001), consistency effects were found in written naming but only when the inconsistent units were located at the beginning of the words, not at the middle or at the end. It is important to stress, however, that Bonin et al.'s (2001) study is the sole study to have found initial consistency effects in written naming latencies. Phonology may play a role in written naming (e.g., Damian & Qu, 2013; Damian et al., 2011; Qu et al., 2011; Zhang & Damian, 2010) under certain conditions, but certainly not a strong role.

Third, imageability was found to have an effect on written naming performance only. This effect was clearly anticipated because written naming is a conceptually-driven naming task (Bonin & Fayol, 2000) and imageability is thought to index semantic code activation (Evans et al., 2012). The finding that imageability was not reliably observed in spelling to dictation and in immediate copying is not surprising because it is assumed that semantics is less involved in these tasks than in written naming (Bonin et al., 2004).

In sum, even though some factors have an effect in all spelling tasks, as in the case of word frequency, there are also effects that are more specific to certain spelling tasks, e.g., PO consistency in spelling to dictation. The theoretical implication is therefore that different processing pathways underpin different (written) spelling tasks. Given these findings, researchers now know that the experimental task chosen to investigate spelling may be not neutral regarding the variables that are investigated.

5   Conclusion

Readers may be surprised by the paucity of the studies that have been devoted to the investigation of individual differences in written naming as well as those focusing on the issue of functional similarities vs. differences in the different tasks in which participants are asked to spell words. As long as 1988, Ellis has claimed that it is important to distinguish between the processing components that are or are not shared between writing and speaking. Despite this until recently, only a few studies have addressed this problem. However, as we have reported in this chapter, the situation is now changing since there have been some recent studies on this issue. For instance, some recent work has investigated the question of the similarities in the processing levels involved in typing compared to handwriting (Pinet, Ziegler, & Alario, 2016; see also Scaltritti, Arfé, Torrance, Peressotti, 2016). However, there is still a great need for research comparing different spelling tasks because several important issues remain. Just to take one example, the involvement of semantic codes is stronger in written naming than in spelling to dictation, but what precise role does semantics play in spelling to dictation? Several pathways have been postulated in spelling to dictation. In the literature, certain researchers have suggested the existence of "direct" lexical routes (e.g., Hillis, 2001) in spelling to dictation as well as in copying. In spelling to dictation, it has been postulated that there is a direct link from the auditory word recognition level to the phonological output lexicon. The spelling performance of certain brain-damaged patients is consistent with the existence of such a nonsemantic pathway, for instance patients who suffer from damage at the semantic level as well as damage in the use of the PO conversion procedure but who are still able to produce the correct spellings of a number of words in spelling to dictation, including irregular ones (Patterson, 1986; Rapcsak & Rubens, 1990; Roeltgen, Rothi, & Heilman, 1986). However, the studies of healthy adults tell us little about the issue of the existence and the use of a nonsemantically-mediated lexical route. It thus remains an important issue to determine whether a direct (nonsemantic) lexical pathway is available when writing familiar words to dictation.

One way to pinpoint more precisely which processing levels are shared in different spelling tasks would be to investigate, for instance, the levels at which different psycholinguistic variables exert their influence by means of Event-Related Potentials and spatiotemporal segmentation analysis, because EEG recordings permit the continuous tracking of periods of stable electrophysiological activity (see Laganaro, 2014 for a thorough description). One straighforward methodological implication of Bonin et al.'s (2015) findings is that researchers should be very careful when choosing the task they use to investigate spelling since certain psycholinguistic effects are reliably found in certain spelling tasks and not in others.

From an educational perspective, research comparing different spelling tasks is important because the way the spellings of words are produced (e.g., handwriting, using a keyboard) certainly matters. Even though it has been claimed that, since we are now living in a digital age, there is no need to learn how to write with pens, recent research casts doubt on such a claim (Longcamp, Zerbato-Poudou, & Velay, 2005). Likewise, it has been shown that handwriting contributes to the visual recognition of letters (Longcamp, Lagarrigue, & Velay, 2010) and that learning how to write letters is beneficial to children's recognition of them (Longcamp et al., 2005), which is a core component of reading. What is more, adult students who take course notes by hand understand more deeply and remember information much better than students who take notes on a laptop (Mueller, & Oppenheimer, 2014). Finally, a recent study (Mangen, Anda, Oxborough, & Brønnick, 2015) compared memory for words (assessed by free recall and recognition) that had been spelled by hand, by using a conventional keyboard or on a virtual iPad keyboard. Participants were instructed to write down words (one list per writing modality) read out loud to them in the three writing modalities. In free recall (and not in recognition), the participants remembered the words better when these had been written in the handwriting condition compared to when they had been produced via the two types of keyboards. Thus, these findings strongly suggest that learning handwriting is still important in children and that adults should continue to use a pen to take notes or to produce longer texts. Handwriting constituted a cultural revolution in human beings and we hope it will continue to be used in the future in addition to typing using modern technologies such as iPads or smarphones.

References

Alario, F.-X., & Ferrand, L. (1999). A set of 400 pictures standardized for French: Norms for name agreement, image agreement, familiarity visual complexity, image variability, and age of acquisition. *Behavior Research Methods Instruments & Computers, 31,* 531–552.

Bock, K., & Levelt, W.J.M. (1994). Language production: Grammatical encoding. In M.A. Gernsbacher (Ed.), *Handbook of Psycholinguistics* (pp. 945–984). London: Academic Press.

Bonin, P., & Fayol, M. (2000). Writing words from pictures: What representations are activated and when? *Memory & Cognition, 28,* 677–689.

Bonin, P., & Méot, A. (2002). Writing to dictation in real time in adults: What are the determinants of written latencies? In S.P. Shohov (Ed.), *Advances in psychology research* (pp. 139–165). New York: Nova Science Publishers.

Bonin, P., Fayol, M., & Chalard, M. (2001). Age of acquisition and word frequency in written picture naming. *Quarterly Journal of Experimental Psychology, 54A,* 469–489.

Bonin, P., Fayol, M., & Gombert, J.E. (1997). Role of phonological and orthographic codes in picture naming and writing: An interference paradigm study. *Current Psychology of Cognition, 16,* 299–320.

Bonin, P., Fayol, M., & Peereman, R. (1998). Masked form priming in writing words from pictures: Evidence for direct retrieval of orthographic codes. *Acta Psychologica, 99,* 311–328.

Bonin, P., Laroche, B., & Perret, C. (2016). Locus of word frequency effects in spelling to dictation: Still at the orthographic level! *Journal of Experimental Psychology: Learning, Memory, and Cognition, 42,* 1814–1820.

Bonin, P., Peereman, R., & Fayol, M. (2001). Do phonological codes constrain the selection of orthographic codes in written picture naming? *Journal of Memory and Language, 45,* 688–720.

Bonin, P., Barry, C., Méot, A., & Chalard, M. (2004). The influence of age of acquisition in word reading and other tasks: A never ending story. *Journal of Memory Language, 50,* 456–476.

Bonin, P., Chalard, M., Méot, A. & Fayol, M. (2002). The determinants of spoken and written picture naming latencies. *British Journal of Psychology, 93*, 89–114.

Bonin, P., Collay, S., Fayol, M., & Méot, A. (2005). Attentional strategic control over sublexical and lexical processing in written spelling to dictation in adults. *Memory & Cognition, 33*, 59–75.

Bonin, P., Méot, A., Lagarrigue, A., & Roux, S. (2015). Written object naming, spelling to dictation, and immediate copying: different tasks, different pathways? *Quarterly Journal of Experimental Psychology, 68*, 1268–1294.

Bonin, P., Méot, A., Millotte, S., & Barry, C. (2013). Individual differences in adult handwritten spelling-to-dictation. *Frontiers in Psychology, 4:402. doi: 10.3389/fpsyg.2013 .00402.*

Bonin, P., Roux, S., Barry, C., & Canell, L. (2012). Evidence for a limited-cascading account of written word naming. *Journal of Experimental Psychology: Learning, Memory and Cognition, 38*, 1741–1758.

Burt, J.E., & Heffernan, M.E. (2012). Reading and spelling in adults: Are there lexical and sublexical subtypes. *Journal of Research in Reading, 35*, 183–203.

Chua, S.M., & Rickard Liow, S.J. (2014). The locus of word frequency effects in skilled spelling-to-dictation. *The Quarterly Journal of Experimental Psychology, 67*, 1720–1741.

Damian, M.F., & Qu, Q. (2013). Is handwriting constrained by phonology? Evidence from Stroop tasks with written responses and Chinese characters. *Frontiers in Psychology, 4:765. doi: 10.3389/fpsyg.2013.00765.*

Damian, M.F., Dorjee, D., & Stadthagen-Gonzalez, H. (2011). Long-term repetition priming in spoken and written word production: Evidence for a contribution of phonology to handwriting. *Journal of Experimental Psychology: Learning, Memory & Cognition, 37*, 813–826.

Darwin, C. (1871/2014). *The Descent of Man.* CreateSpace Independent Publishing Platform.

Delattre, M., Bonin, P., & Barry, C. (2006). Written spelling to dictation: Sound-to-spelling regularity affects both writing latencies and durations. *Journal of Experimental Psychology: Learning, Memory, and Cognition, 32*, 1330–1340.

Ellis, A.W. (1988). Modelling the writing process. In G. Denes, C. Semenza, P. Bisiacchi, & E. Andreewsky (Eds), *Perspectives in cognitive neuropsychology* (pp. 189–211). London: Lawrence Erlbaum Associates.

Evans, G., Lambon Ralph, M., & Woollams, A. (2012). What's in a word. A parametric study of semantic influences on visual word recognition. *Psychonomic Bulletin & Review, 19*, 325–331.

Geschwind, N. (1969). Problems in the anatomical understanding of the aphasias. In A.L. Benton (Ed.), *Contributions to clinical neuropsychology* (pp. 107–128). Chicago, IL: Aldine.

Hillis, A.E. (2001). The organization of the lexical system. In B.C. Rapp (Ed.): *What deficits reveal about the human mind/brain: A Handbook of Cognitive Neuropsychology*. (pp. 185–210) Philadelphia: Psychology Press.

Indefrey, P. (2011). The spatial and temporal signatures of word production components: A critical update. *Frontiers in Psychology, 2:255. doi: 10.3389/fpsyg.2011.00255.*

Johnston, R.A., & Barry, C. (2006). Age of acquisition and lexical processing. *Visual Cognition, 13,* 789–845.

Juhasz, B.J. (2005). Age-of-acquisition effects in word and picture identification. *Psychological Bulletin, 131,* 684–712.

Laganaro, M. (2014). ERP topographic analyses from concept to articulation in word production studies. *Frontiers in Psychology, 5:493. doi: 10.3389/fpsyg.2014.00493.*

Lambert, E., Alamargot, D. & Fayol, M. (2012). Why use a copy task to study spelling in handwriting? In Fayol, M., Alamargot, D., & Berninger, V. (Eds.) *Written Translation of Thought to Written Text While Composing: Advancing Theory, Knowledge, Research Methods and Tools, and Applications* (pp. 339–357). Psychology Press. (USA).

Lambert, E., Alamargot, D., Larocque, D., & Caporossi, G. (2011). Dynamics of the spelling process during a copy task: Effects of regularity and frequency. *Canadian Journal of Experimental Psychology, 65,* 141–150.

Levy, M.C., & Ransdell, S. (1995). Is writing as difficult as it seems. *Memory & Cognition, 23,* 767–779.

Longcamp, M., Lagarrigue, A., & Velay, J.-L. (2010). Contribution de la motricité graphique à la reconnaissance visuelle des lettres. *Psychologie Française, 55,* 181–194.

Longcamp, M., Zerbato-Poudou, M.-T., & Velay, J.-L. (2005). The influence of writing practice on letter recognition in preschool children: A comparison between handwriting and typing. *Acta Psychologica, 119,* 67–79.

Luria, A.R. (1970). *Traumatic aphasia.* The Hague: Mouton.

Mangen, A., Anda, L.G., Oxborough, G.H., & Brønnick, K. (2015). Handwriting versus keyboard writing: Effect on word recall. *Journal of Writing Research, 7,* 227–247.

Miceli, G., & Capasso, R. (1997). Semantic errors as neuropsychological evidence for the independence and the interaction of orthographic and phonological word forms. *Language and Cognitive Processes, 12,* 733–764.

Miceli, G., Capasso, R., & Caramazza, A. (1999). Sublexical conversion procedures and the interaction of phonological and orthographic lexical forms. *Cognitive Neuropsychology, 16,* 557–572.

Mueller, P.A., & Oppenheimer, D.M. (2014). The pen is mightier than the keyboard. Advantages of longhand over laptop note taking. *Psychological Science, 25,* 1159–1168.

Patterson, K.E. (1986). Lexical but nonsemantic spelling? *Cognitive Neuropsychology, 3,* 341–367.

Peereman, R., & Content, A. (1999). LEXOP: A lexical database providing orthography-phonology statistics for French monosyllabic words. *Behavior Research Methods, Instruments, & Computers, 31,* 376–379.

Perret, C., & Laganaro, M. (2012). Comparison of electrophysiological correlates of writing and speaking: A Topographic ERP analysis. *Brain Topography, 25,* 64–72.

Perret, C., Bonin, P., Laganaro, M. (2014). Exploring the multiple-loci hypothesis of AoA effects in spoken and written object naming using a topographic ERP analysis. *Brain and Language, 135,* 20–31.

Pinet, S., Ziegler, J.C., & Alario, F.-X. (2016). Typing is writing: Linguistic properties modulate typing execution. *Psychonomic Bulletin & Review, 23,* 1898–1906.

Pinker, S. (1994). *The Language Instinct.* New York, NY: Harper Perennial Modern Classics.

Purcell, J., Turkeltaub, P., Eden, G., & Rapp, B. (2011). Examining the central and peripheral processes of written word production through meta-analysis. *Frontiers in Psychology, 2:239. doi: 10.3389/fpsyg.2011.00239.*

Qu, Q., Damian, M., Zhang, Q., & Zhu, X. (2011). Phonology contributes to writing: Evidence from written word production in a nonalphabetic script. *Psychological Science, 22,* 1107–1112.

Qu, Q., Zhang, Q., & Damian, M.F. (2016). Tracking the time course of lexical access in orthographic production: An event-related potential study of word frequency effects in written picture naming. *Brain and Language, 159,* 118–126.

Rapp, B., & Dufor, O. (2011) The neurotopography of written word production: an fMRI investigation of the distribution of sensitivity to length and frequency. *Journal of Cognitive Neuroscience, 23,* 4067–4081.

Rapp, B., & Caramazza, A. (1997). The modality specific organization of grammatical categories: Evidence from impaired spoken and written sentence production. *Brain and Language, 56,* 248–286.

Rapp, B., Benzing, L., & Caramazza, A. (1997). The autonomy of lexical orthography. *Cognitive Neuropsychology, 14,* 71–104.

Rapcsak, S.Z., & Rubens, A.B. (1990). Disruption of semantic influence on writing following a left prefrontal lesion. *Brain and Language, 38,* 334–344.

Roelofs, A., Meyer, A.S., & Levelt, W.J.M. (1996). Interaction between semantic and orthographic factors in conceptually driven naming: Comment on Starreveld and La Heij (1995). *Journal of Experimental Psychology: Learning, Memory, & Cognition, 22,* 246–251.

Roeltgen, D.P., Rothi, L.G., & Heilman, K.M. (1986). Linguistic semantic agraphia: A dissociation of the lexical spelling system from semantics. *Brain and Language, 27,* 257–280.

Roux, S., & Bonin, P. (2012). Cascaded processing in written naming: Evidence from the picture-picture interference paradigm. *Language and Cognitive Processes, 27,* 734–769.

Sanders, R.J., & Caramazza, A. (1990). Operation of the phoneme-to-grapheme conversion mechanism in a brain injured patient. *Reading and Writing, 2*, 61–82.

Sausset, S., Lambert, E., Olive, T., & Larocque, D. (2012). Processing of syllables during handwriting: Effects of graphomotor constraints. *Quarterly Journal of Experimental Psychology. 65*, 1872–1879.

Scaltritti, M., Arfé, B., Torrance, M., & Peressotti, F. (2016). Typing pictures: Linguistic processing cascades into finger movements. *Cognition, 156*, 16–29.

Schriefers, H., Meyer, A.S., & Levelt, W.J.M. (1990). Exploring the time-course of lexical access in language production: Picture-word interference studies. *Journal of Memory and Language, 29*, 86–102.

Shi Min, C., & Richard Liow, S.J.R. (2014). The locus of word frequency effects in skilled spelling-to-dictation. *Quarterly Journal of Experimental Psychology, 67*, 1720–1741.

Snodgrass, J.G., & Vanderwart, M. (1980). A Standardized set of 260 pictures: Norms for Name agreement, Image Agreement, Familiarity, and Visual Complexity. *Journal of Experimental Psychology: Human Perception and Performance, 6*, 174–215.

Starreveld, P.A., & La Heij, W. (1995). Semantic interference, orthographic facilitation and their interaction in naming tasks. *Journal of Experimental Psychology: Learning, Memory, & Cognition, 21*, 686–698.

Starreveld, P.A., & La Heij, W. (1996). The locus of orthographic-phonological facilitation: Reply to Roelofs, Meyer, and Levelt (1996). *Journal of Experimental Psychology: Learning, Memory, & Cognition, 22*, 1–4.

Sternberg, S. (1969). The discovery of processing stages: Extensions of Donders' method. In W.G. Koster (Ed.), Attention and performance II: Proceedings from a symposium on attention and performance. *Acta Psychologica, 30*, 276–315.

Tainturier, M., & Rapp, B. (2001). The spelling process. In B. Rapp (Ed.), *The handbook of cognitive neuropsychology: What deficits reveal about the human mind.* (pp. 263–289) Psychology Press.

Yap, M.J., Balota, D.A., Sibley, D.E., & Ratcliff, R. (2012). Individual differences in visual word recognition: Insights from the english lexicon project. *Journal of Experimental Psychology: Human Perception Performance, 38*, 53–79.

Zhang, Q., & Damian, M.F. (2010). Impact of phonology on the generation of handwritten responses: Evidence from picture-word interference tasks. *Memory & Cognition, 38*, 519–528.

Zhang, Q., & Wang, C. (2016). The temporal courses of phonological and orthographic encoding in handwritten production in Chinese: An ERP study. *Frontiers in Human Neuroscience, 10:417. doi: 10.3389/fnhum.2016.00417.*

CHAPTER 8

Measuring Writing Durations in Handwriting Research: What Do They Tell Us about the Spelling Process?

Olivia Afonso and Carlos J. Álvarez

Writing is a complex activity recruiting many different modules of processing. These processes range from higher-order levels of planning and revision to lower-order levels of motor performance. In the last decades several models of writing have tried to identify the main processing steps involved in writing production (Bonin, Méot, Lagarrigue, & Roux, 2015; Bonin, Pereeman, & Fayol, 2001; Kandel, Peereman, Grosjacques, & Fayol, 2011; Van Galen, 1991). It has become clear that any model of writing needs to differentiate between *central* and *peripheral processes*. In the context of isolated words production, central processes refer to those involved in the retrieval and processing of abstract representations required to access and maintain the orthographic form to be produced (also referred to as *spelling*). Peripheral processes refer to the processes required to execute the movements intended to produce the physical written response. Similar spelling processes are necessary to produce a word regardless of the writing modality (e.g., handwriting, typewriting, oral spelling), while peripheral processes considerably vary across writing modalities. This distinction between central and peripheral processes is well supported by early and recent evidence from studies conducted with participants with and without neurological damage (Ellis, 1979; Purcell, Turkeltaub, Eden, & Rapp, 2011; Weingarten, 2005). However, growing evidence suggests that central and peripheral processes influence each other (Kandel & Perret, 2015; Lambert, Alamargot, Laroque, & Caporossi, 2011: Roux, McKeeff, Grosjacques, Afonso, & Kandel, 2013). Although this influence is currently almost undisputed in the literature, authors have been relatively unspecific about the explanatory underlying mechanisms. In this chapter we describe some theoretical and methodological issues related to the study of the impact of central processes on peripheral processes during handwriting. We also summarise the evidence obtained supporting the incidence of this impact and discuss some of the hypotheses that have been sketched to account for these findings. For reasons of simplicity, we will focus on the literature of research conducted with adult participants. Some evidence suggests that central processes have not the same impact on writing durations in adulthood than during writing acquisition (Afonso, Suárez-Coalla, González-Martín, & Cuetos, 2018; Kandel & Perret, 2015). It is necessary to extend the research about these potential differences to clarify which claims are valid for each group of age.

1   Do Central Processes Influence Peripheral Processes? A Methodological Question

Whether or not central processes have an impact on peripheral processes is not only an interesting theoretical question, but it has also a critical impact on methodological decisions. The field of handwriting research is now characterized by a growing proportion of studies that investigate spelling processes by measuring writing durations. Although it seems clear that writing durations reflect to some extent increased loads of processing at the central modules of the writing system, a detailed explanation about how abstract representations may affect motor processes is not yet available. This is probably one of the reasons underlying the huge variability in the methods used to measure writing durations. Without agreement in the field about the best way of measuring peripheral processes to gain insight into central processes, studies have reported rather different dependent variables that might be measuring different things. In this chapter we will focus on four different measures of peripheral processing: whole-word durations, inter-letter intervals (ILIs), mean stroke durations and letter durations. ILIs refer to the time between the end of a letter and the initiation of the next one. Word and letter durations are usually reported as the total time between the first contact of the pen in a digitizing tablet and the last pen lift (thus, they include within word pauses).

Mean strokes durations refer to the results of dividing a letter's duration by the number of strokes that form that letter, being strokes usually defined on the basis of the presence of tangential velocity minima in the velocity profile (see Kandel & Spinelli, 2010). Do all these measures give us the same information about spelling? This is a question of paramount importance for the cognitive study of writing research, since in this field writing durations have been most frequently reported in studies addressing the spelling process.

2   The Spelling Process: Evidence of Its Influence on Writing
       Durations

In his influential model of handwriting, van Galen (1991) proposed a series of
hierarchically-ordered modules that could be activated in parallel. Modules
higher in this hierarchy provided the input for lower levels, and then they could
deal with forthcoming units. In this model, van Galen claimed that the spelling
module deals with word-size units. This means that orthographic representations are retrieved or generated for whole words.

    Although van Galen described a spelling module in which diverse routes
were not differentiated, it is now widely assumed that spelling can be achieved
by resorting to (at least) two different types of information: lexical and sublexical information (Caramazza, 1988; Rapp, Epstein, & Tainturier, 2002; Tainturier & Rapp, 2000). Lexical information can be gathered for known words by
accessing orthographic word-level representations stored in the orthographic
lexicon. Sublexical information consists of a set of language-specific rules linking phonemes-to-graphemes. This information would be especially useful to
generate a plausible spelling for unknown words, but it would be rather inef-
fective for spelling irregular words. Regardless of the route followed to access
it, the retrieved orthographic representation must be maintained in a short-
term memory system (Caramazza, Miceli, Villa, & Romani, 1987; Fischer-Baum,
McCloskey, Rapp, 2010; Hillis & Caramazza, 1989) so-called orthographic working memory (OWM) system. This allows for graphemes to be serially selected in
the correct order and submitted to the peripheral levels of processing (allographic selection, size control and muscular adjustment) while the rest of
graphemes in the OWM system are kept active for subsequent production. How
exactly graphemes are represented and selected in the OWM is a largely unex-
plored question, but this is bound to be a crucial matter in our understanding
of the connections between spelling and peripheral levels of processing. Not
in vain in the widely accepted van Galen's view of the writing production process OWM would be the last component within of central modules that is active
before peripheral modules begin if a dual-route model is assumed. It is important to notice that while van Galen's model posits that higher-level modules
may be active at the same time that lower-level modules operate, the OWM
system *needs* to be active during peripheral processing to maintain the rest
of letters to-be-produced. This makes it a particularly good candidate to play
a role in the interplay between linguistic and motor processes. Surprisingly,
little has been said about this possibility in previous literature and no efforts
have been made to determine the influence of OWM in writing durations. Thus,
with virtually no experimental evidence regarding this issue, it is impossible to

estimate the influence of working memory processes during the actual writing production process. However, in a study conducted with adults with and without dyslexia (Afonso, Suárez-Coalla, & Cuetos, 2015) word length effects (which are assumed to arise at the OWM level of processing) were observed to affect the ILIs duration. This evidence suggests that increased load of processing at the OWM level affects how quickly the production of a given grapheme is initiated, but systematic studies are required to elucidate the extent of these effects. More research has been conducted about the impact on peripheral processes of both the lexical and sublexical routes for spelling.

It has been repeatedly observed that phonological and orthographic sublexical units mediate the kinematics of word production. One of the most studied effects has been the syllable boundary effect (Álvarez, Cottrell, & Afonso, 2009; Kandel, Álvarez, & Vallée, 2006; Lambert, Sausset, & Rigalleau, 2015; Sausset, Lambert, Olive, & Laroque, 2012). The typical result is that participants produce longer ILIs durations in inter-syllabic than in intra-syllabic intervals. ILIs durations have also been observed to be sensitive to other linguistic units that seem to reflect the involvement of the sublexical route, phoneme-to-grapheme (P-G) consistency and P-O regularity. P-O inconsistency refers to the fact that a phoneme may be spelled in more than one way, while P-O irregular correspondences are those instances of inconsistency in which the phoneme is represented by means of a grapheme that is not the most frequent for that phoneme. P-O regularity has been found to affect whole-word writing durations (Delattre, Bonin, & Barry, 2006; Lambert et al., 2011) and mean stroke durations (Kandel & Perret, 2015; Roux et al., 2013). In a language with a very regular orthography like Spanish, longer ILIs have been obtained before P-G inconsistent segments (those with more than one possible graphemic representation) than P-O consistent words (Afonso, Suárez-Coalla, et al., 2015). Longer ILIs have also been reported before complex than simple graphemes, both in Spanish and French (Afonso, Álvarez, & Kandel, 2015). The presence of a morphemic boundary seems to increases ILI durations as well (Kandel, Álvarez, & Vallée, 2008). These results have been interpreted as evidence of linguistic (central) factors affecting motor (peripheral) processes during handwriting. Evidence supporting the claim that lexical variables affect handwriting durations have been more limited. Word frequency has not been found to affect writing durations produced by adult writers, even though an effect of this variable is consistently observed to have an impact on writing latencies (Delattre et al., 2006; Lambert et al., 2011). However, word frequency has been observed in several studies to affect writing durations in children (Afonso et al., 2018; Søvik, Arntzen, Samuelstuen, & Heggberget, 1994). Thus, it has been proposed that lexical variables affect writing durations only at early stages of handwriting acquisition, when handwriting has not been fully automatized (Afonso et al, 2018). Roux and colleagues (2013) did report a significant difference between words and pseudowords in mean stroke durations, which would reflect effects of lexical access on the duration of the motor processes. However, this lexicality effect appeared only in the third position of the stimuli tested. It seems that the effect of lexical variables during handwriting production is at best inconsistent in adults.

As mentioned above, a key factor to take into account is that different studies have reported different measures of the online written production. ILIS durations, whole-word durations, letter durations and mean stroke durations have been indistinctively used, frequently to assess the effect of linguistic variables on peripheral processes. Thus, all these measures have been interpreted to reflect the interaction between central and peripheral processes to the same extent. But, is this justified? We propose that it is more and more necessary to address what each of these measures can tell us about the writing process and that, at this point of development of the field, they must be interpreted with caution for different reasons.

Whole-word durations were initially measured to address the impact of central processes on peripheral processes (Bonin et al., 2001). This measure can be very useful in experiments using, for example, priming paradigms (either explicit or implicit). In this type of experiments the same set of words can be compared across different conditions. However, word durations have obvious limitations in order to test for the effect of variables requiring the use of different items per condition. Different letters have different durations, so it is impossible to separate effects due to peripheral factors (different letter-shapes) from the effect of the central variables manipulated in the study. For this reason, this measure is currently rarely used in writing research. More common is reporting mean stroke durations (Kandel, Perreman, & Ghimenton, 2014; Kandel & Perret, 2015; Roux et al., 2013). This measure refers to the result of dividing a letter's duration by the number of strokes needed to produce it. For example, given a duration of 420 ms for a letter A (which is typically formed by 3 strokes), its mean stroke duration would be 140 milliseconds (420/3). This measure was developed in an attempt to make those durations obtained for different letters comparable and represented a great opportunity for handwriting researchers to extend the phenomena that they were able to study. But this measure has important limitations too. No all strokes have the same duration. Besides differences in length and curvature, it has also been shown that strokes with different directionality have different velocity profiles (Teulings & Schomaker, 1993; van Galen, 1991; Wing, 1978). This means that letters with the same number of strokes may have different durations. In order to confirm this claim, we conducted an analysis on the letter durations of a small set of stimuli used in one of our previous experiments. The experiment used a paired-associate learning task, in which participants are required to learn pairs of words. In the test phase the first words act as prompt and the second word is the response that participants have to produce. One of the responses was the Spanish word BANANA, which was produced 24 times in upper-case letters by 6 Psychology students from the University of La Laguna. We conducted a t-test on the durations of letter *N* (in both positions) with the duration of letter *A* (in fourth and sixth position). Although both letters have three strokes, durations for letter *A* were significantly longer than for letter *N*, $t(11) = 4.93$, $p < .001$, with mean letter durations of 315 and 266 ms respectively. This difference can be at least partially due to the fact that letter *A* usually is produced including a within in-air pause and letter *N* does not. In any case, this example illustrates that ignoring letter identity and only considering the number of strokes to compare letter durations may not be the best way to extract conclusions from handwriting movements. We propose that experimental designs allowing for measuring the same letter (or letters) in the same position in different words can be the most recommendable procedure to analyse writing durations in those cases in which the same word cannot be compared across conditions. Several studies have used this methodology and they have observed effects of variables linked to linguistic variables in writing durations (Afonso, Álvarez, et al., 2015; Kandel et al., 2014). Another issue is whether these linguistic variables affect the actual writing movements or only the in-air pen time. In writing research durations are not usually submitted to different analyses including or not in-air pen times. Predictions to this regard will depend on the assumptions one makes about the specific mechanisms responsible for the appearance of effects of central variables on writing durations. Although these assumptions are seldom described in detail in the literature, it is worthwhile to briefly refer to the differences between potential alternative positions that authors may take of the relationship between central and peripheral processes.

3 Different Accounts for the Effects of Central Processes on Peripheral Processes

3.1 *Central Processes Do Not Really Affect Peripheral Processes*
Some studies have failed to find evidence of central processing on writing durations (Damian & Stadthagen-González, 2009). However, a sceptic position about the existence of a real interaction between central and peripheral processes can be maintained even taking into account some of the effects of central variables that have been found after the written response had been

initiated. Some effects of linguistic variables on writing durations most consistently observed in the literature have been obtained in analyses conducted on ILIs durations (Álvarez et al., 2009; Kandel et al., 2006). Since in these intervals writing movements are not actually being executed, it is possible to argue that these findings could not reflect a true interaction between central and peripheral processes, but some kind of "switching" between them. Linguistic variables might be used to segment the written response in the OWM system rather than to have a direct effect on motor modules. It is also possible that orthographic representations may need to be refreshed during handwriting, yielding to effects on response duration. This re-activation of central representations may occur during pauses between writing periods, instead of during the performance of the actual writing movements. It has been frequently claimed that effects of central variables on ILIs durations reflect interaction between central and peripheral processes because they occur after the response has been initiated. This claim seems to assume that the whole word is the unit of motor programming in handwriting. However, according to van Galen's model (1991) the module of allographic selection (the first motor module included in his model) deals with grapheme-size units. Thus, ILIs durations may reflect OWM processes, influence of the P-G correspondences (which could in turn affect selection/maintenance in the OWM system through links of this system with the phonological loop), or re-activation of the lexical representation before motor modules are activated for the production of the corresponding grapheme. This means that graphemes would be selected in the OWM system in serial order to be processed at the following stages (e. g., peripheral processes), and that this selection could be affected by lexical or sublexical central variables. These effects would occur at a central and not a peripheral level of processing. From to this point view, only effects on letter duration would undoubtedly support the hypothesis that central processes have an impact on peripheral processes. As mentioned above, effects of linguistic factors on letter durations have actually been reported (Afonso, Álvarez, et al., 2015; Kandel et al., 2014; Kandel & Spinelli, 2010). Thus, specific mechanisms accounting for those effects should be considered.

3.2 Information Cascades from Central to Peripheral Levels of Processing

The debate about the staged or cascaded nature of the writing system has been inherited from the field of speech production research (Goldrick & Blumstein, 2006). Cascading activation refers to the fact that information flows from higher to lower levels of processing before target units have been selected. In opposition to cascaded models, stage models claim that higher levels of processing must be finished before lower levels can be active. Bonin and Fayol (2010) obtained evidence supporting the idea that information cascades from the semantic to the phonological/orthographic levels of processing in the writing system. These authors observed that the semantic interference produced by distractor words when naming a target picture was modulated by the phonological and orthographic relationship of the distractors with the target's name. More recently, Roux and Bonin (2012) found using a picture-picture interference paradigm that the name of the non-target picture was activated at the grapheme level, suggesting cascading of activation from the lexical to the grapheme level of processing. It has been repeatedly argued that effects of lexical or sublexical variables on writing durations reveal cascading of information from the spelling module to the motor modules. Increased writing durations are interpreted as an effect of unfinished spelling processes that are resolved during writing. This explanation could account for effects observed in both letter and ILI durations. Nonetheless, this point of view requires accepting that the spelling process might be unfinished until approximately 2 seconds after stimuli presentation. This seems a particularly long time in those studies using a copying task, in which effects on the duration of letters located at medial positions of the word have been observed in several studies (Afonso, Álvarez et al., 2015; Afonso, Suárez-Coalla, et al., 2015) although the spelling of the word has been given to the participants.

Moreover, effects should be observed at all the positions within the word previous to the conflict resolution. Some variables observed to impact letter durations have shown inconsistent effects across different letter positions rather than a stable and continued effect (Roux et al., 2013). Some evidence suggests that some sublexical variables affect writing duration locally to the position of the target unit (grapheme or syllable) and not all the letters of a word (Afonso, Álvarez, et al., 2015). Conversely, Roux et al. (2013) reported evidence in line with the idea of a sustained effect until the position of conflict. These authors conducted a study testing the effect of regularity and measured mean stroke durations for all letter positions. In this study, longer mean stroke durations for irregular words were observed in almost every position located before the irregularity. However, the fact that these letters were not matched across conditions makes difficult to determine to what extent they are due to differences in letter shape. In a different study, Kandel and colleagues (2014) tested the effect of gemination (letter doubling) in writing durations. In this case the first three letters of the word were identical in the geminated and non-geminated conditions (for example, LISSER vs LISTER). The results showed significantly longer mean strokes durations in the first three letters for words with doubled letters. This finding provides striking evidence for the idea of a conflict persisting during the execution of the written response until the position of conflict is reached. More studies in which the duration of letters matched across conditions are measured are necessary to confirm whether effects of lexical and sublexical variables appear locally or affect the production of the whole written response. In any case, that central processes cascade to affect peripheral processes is probably the most widespread interpretation given to the effects of central variables observed on writing durations.

3.3   *Central and Peripheral Processes Compete for Shared Resources*

As mentioned above, according to van Galen's model of handwriting production (1991) central and peripheral modules are engaged in parallel, with higher-order modules dealing with units that are further ahead in the response. This is different from the cascading activation hypothesis in several aspects. For example, in this hypothesis central effects observed on the writing durations of a specific unit (e.g., a given letter) would be due to central processing of a different unit. In other words, central effects would be detectable by measuring writing durations because of the sharing of resources between the processes involved in real-time stroke production and the concurrent preparatory processing of forthcoming segments. This is in line with the idea that spelling and handwriting share, among other resources, working memory capacity (Berninger & Amtmann, 2003). Although it is difficult to experimentally test some of the predictions that would derive from this hypothesis, if competition for shared resources is assumed more local effects should be expected than from the point of view of cascaded activation. Previous evidence does suggest that effects of variables tapping at the central levels of processing observed in writing durations manifest themselves in segments of the response located just before the manipulated segment (Afonso, Suárez-Coalla, et al., 2015: Kandel et al., 2008; Kandel et al., 2011; Kandel et al., 2014; Lambert, et al., 2011; Sausset, et al., 2012). In their study, Lambert and colleagues (2011) asked participants to write down a sequence of four words in which the third word was the target. By measuring both eye and pen movements, these authors demonstrated that participants were engaged in spelling processes of the target word while writing the previous word. Moreover, several authors have observed that sublexical variables are processed in the ILI previous to the execution of the target segment. This evidence includes (but it is not restricted to) effects of P-G consistency (Afonso, Álvarez et al., 2015; Afonso, Suárez-Coalla, et al., 2015), letter doubling (Kandel et al., 2015), grapheme complexity (Kandel & Spinelli, 2010), and syllable structure (Kandel et al., 2006; Álvarez et al., 2009). In order to clarify this issue, specific studies must be designed to establish how the position of observed effects changes depending on the variable manipulated. For example, semantic effects should be observed at earlier moments of the written response than word frequency effects and word frequency effects should appear earlier than sublexical effects. The higher in the hierarchy of processing, the earlier the effect should be observed in the response. Unfortunately, such a prediction has been more assumed than experimentally tested.

4   Conclusions

Although a growing number of studies have reported writing durations as a measure of central processing during handwriting, little is known about the mechanisms that would explain the effect of linguistic and cognitive variables in motor processes. How this influence becomes effective is not a minor detail for writing research. Instead, the mechanisms thought to underlie the observed effects of syllabic and morphemic structure, probability of the P-G correspondences, word frequency, graphemes complexity or gemination, determine their interpretation. At this point of the development of writing production research we face the difficult challenge of unifying methodology and theory to allow for the discipline to gain maturity. It is imperative that a consensus is reached about the implications of using one measure or another in the analyses of the written response. Although writing latencies seem to be used and reported in a fairly consistent manner, much work is yet necessary to unify the way of analysing and interpreting data concerning pen movements. Furthermore, theoretical proposals are yet underspecified and require more detail to establish precise predictions that can be experimentally tested.

References

Afonso, O., Álvarez, C.J., & Kandel, S. (2015). Effects of grapheme-to-phoneme probability on writing durations. *Memory & Cognition, 43*, 579–592. doi: 10.3758/s13421-014-0489-8

Afonso, O., Suárez-Coalla, P., & Cuetos, F. (2015). Spelling impairments in Spanish dyslexic adults. *Frontiers in Psychology, 6.* doi: 0.3389/fpsyg.2015.00466

Afonso, O., Suárez-Coalla, P., González-Martín, N., & Cuetos, F. (2018). The impact of word frequency on peripheral processes during handwriting: A matter of age. *Quarterly Journal of Experimental Psychology, 71*(3), 695–703. doi.org/10.1080/17470218.2016.1275713

Álvarez, C.J., Cottrell, D., & Afonso, O. (2009). Syllabic effects in inter-letter intervals when handwriting single words in Spanish. *Applied Psycholinguistics, 30*, 205–223.

Berninger, V., Amtmann, D. (2003). Preventing written expression disabilities through early and continuing assessment and intervention for handwriting and/or spelling problems: Research into practice. In: H.L. Swanson, K. Harris, & S. Graham (Eds.), *Handbook of Research on Learning Disabilities* (pp. 345–363). New York: Guilford.

Bonin, P., & Fayol, M. (2000). Written picture naming: What representations are activated and when? *Memory & Cognition, 28*, 677–689.

Bonin, P., Méot, A., Lagarrigue, A., & Roux, S. (2015). Written object naming, spelling-to-dictation, and immediate copying: Different tasks, different pathways? *Quarterly Journal of Experimental Psychology, 68*, 1268–1294.

Bonin, P., Peereman, R., & Fayol, M. (2001). Do phonological codes constrain the selection of orthographic codes in written picture naming? *Journal of Memory and Language, 45*, 688–720.

Caramazza, A. (1988). Some aspects of language processing revealed through the analysis of acquired dysgraphia: The lexical system. *Annual Review of Neuroscience, 11*, 395–421.

Caramazza, A., Miceli, G., Villa, G., & Romani, C. (1987). The role of the graphemic buffer in spelling: Evidence from a case of acquired dysgraphia. *Cognition, 26*, 59–85.

Damian, M.F., & Stadthagen-Gonzalez, H. (2009). Advance planning of form properties in the written production of single and multiple words. *Language and Cognitive Processes, 24*, 555–579.

Delattre, M., Bonin, P., & Barry, C. (2006). Written spelling to dictation: Do irregularity effects persist on writing durations? *Journal of Experimental Psychology: Learning, Memory, and Cognition, 32*, 1330–1340.

Fischer-Baum, S., McCloskey, M., & Rapp, B. (2010). Representation of letter position in spelling: Evidence from acquired dysgraphia. *Cognition, 115*, 466–490.

Goldrick, M., & Blumstein, S.E. (2006). Cascading activation from phonological planning to articulatory processes: Evidence from tongue twisters. *Language & Cognitive Processes, 21*, 649–683.

Hillis, A.E. & Caramazza, A. (1989). The graphemic buffer and attentional mechanisms. *Brain and Language, 36*, 208–235.

Kandel, S., Álvarez, C.J., & Vallée, N. (2006). Syllables as processing units in a handwriting production. *Journal of Experimental Psychology: Human Perception and Performance, 32*, 18–31.

Kandel, S., Álvarez, C.J., & Vallée, N. (2008). Morphemes also serve as processing units in handwriting production. In M. Baciu (Ed.), *Neuropsychology and Cognition of language Behavioral, Neuropsychological and Neuroimaging Studies of Spoken and Written Language* (pp. 87–100). Kerala, India: Research Signpost.

Kandel, S., Peereman, R., & Ghimenton, A. (2014). How do we code the letters of a word when we have to write it? Investigating double letter representation in French. *Acta Psychologica, 148*, 56–62.

Kandel, S., Peereman, R., Grosjacques, G., & Fayol, M. (2011). For a psycholinguistic model of handwriting production: Testing the syllable-bigram controversy. *Journal of Experimental Psychology: Human Perception and Performance, 37*, 1310–1322.

Kandel, S., & Perret, C. (2015). How does the interaction between spelling and motor processes build up during writing acquisition? *Cognition, 136*, 325–336.

Kandel, S., & Spinelli, E. (2010). Processing complex graphemes in handwriting production. *Memory & Cognition, 38*, 762–770.

Lambert, E., Sausset, S. & Rigalleau, F. (2015). The ortho-syllable as a processing unit in handwriting: the mute e effect. *Reading and Writing: An Interdisciplinary Journal, 28*, 683–698.

Lambert, E., Alamargot, D., Larocque, D., & Caporossi, G. (2011). Dynamics of the spelling process during a copy task: Effects of regularity and frequency. *Canadian Journal of Experimental Psychology, 65*, 141–150.

Purcell, J.J., Turkeltaub, P.E., Eden, G.F., & Rapp, B. (2011). Examining the central and peripheral processes of written word production through meta-analysis. *Frontiers in psychology, 2:1, doi:10.3389/fpsyg.2011.00239.*

Rapp, B., Epstein. C., & M.-J. Tainturier (2002). The integration of information across lexical and sublexical processes in spelling. *Cognitive Neuropsychology, 19*, 1–29, 2002.

Roux, S., McKeeff, T.J., Grosjacques, G., Afonso, O., & Kandel, S. (2013). The interaction between central and peripheral processes in handwriting production. *Cognition, 127*, 235–241.

Sausset, S., Lambert, E., Olive, T., & Laroque, D. (2012). Processing of syllables during handwriting: Effects of graphomotor constraints. *The Quarterly Journal of Experimental Psychology, 65*, 1872–1879.

Søvik, N., Arntzen, O., Samuelstuen, M., & Heggberget, M. (1994). Relations between linguistic word groups and writing. In C. Faure, G. Lorette & A. Vinter (Eds.), *Advances in handwriting and drawing: A multidisciplinary approach* (pp. 231–246). Paris: Europia.

Tainturier, M.J., & Rapp, B. (2000). The spelling process. In B. Rapp (Ed.), *What deficits reveal about the human mind: A handbook of cognitive neuropsychology.* (pp. 263–289) Philadelphia, PA: Psychology Press.

Teulings, H.L., & Schomaker, L.R.B. (1993). Invariant properties between stroke features in handwriting. *Acta Psychologica, 82*, 69–88.

Van Galen, G.P. (1991). Handwriting: Issues for a psychomotor theory. *Human Movement Science, 10*, 165–191.

Weingarten, R. (2005). Subsyllabic units in written word production. *Written Language & Literacy, 8*, 43–61.

Wing, A.M. (1978). Response timing in handwriting. In G.E. Stelmach (Ed.), *Information processing in motor control and learning* (pp. 153–172). New York: Academic Press.

CHAPTER 9

Analyzing Variability in Upper-Case Letter Production in Adults

Laurence Séraphin-Thibon, Silvain Gerber and Sonia Kandel

1 Introduction

Unlike speech acquisition, learning how to write results from formal explicit instruction. Its proficiency requires a long learning period (Chartrel & Vinter, 2004) that is cognitively very demanding (Bourdin, & Fayol, 1994; Olive & Kellogg, 2002). The reason why it is so long is that there are many processing levels that must interact to turn an idea into a written text (Hayes, 2012). The children have to learn that to write a text they have to organize ideas into a succession of logical events. There will be one or several paragraphs devoted to each event. To produce these paragraphs, the children must understand that they have to generate sentences that convey meaningful statements. The semantic aspects of the sentences will be related to the meaning of each word. The children know how to produce them orally. Learning how to write requires that they acquire knowledge on which letters make up which words. However, knowing the letters is not enough. The children must learn how to produce them. This implies that they need to acquire proficiency in movement execution and manual dexterity. The present study focuses on letter production. When the children learn how to write, they are taught rules that will constrain a certain number of parameters for letter production. For example, all vertical lines should be produced from top to bottom. It is like a "grammar of action" (Goodnow & Levine, 1973) that specifies letter shape and determines stroke order and direction (Van Sommers, 1984). Learning the rules renders letter production "efficient". On one hand, they render writing legible because the children have to learn to reproduce a specific geometric pattern. On the other, letters can be produced in many ways. Following rules decreases movement variability and increases efficiency because it limits the number of strokes for letter production (Thomassen, Tibosch & Maarse, 1989).

At the beginning of the learning processes, the application of these rules during letter production involves a strong cognitive load. Letter writing is time and energy consuming. With practice, the children memorize these rules and the need for important attentional and mneumonic resources decreases progressively. This increases movement fluency and speed. When the cognitive load does not constitute an obstacle for movement production, letter writing will become automatic. Cognitive resources will mainly be devoted to other functions of writing like text composition and syntax processing (Berninger & Winn, 2006). It becomes an instrument for communication. Automation also implies, however, that the child introduces other movement patterns that are easier for him/her to produce. So, at this time, writing becomes a personal "blend" of geometric and kinematic adjustments to the grammar of action rules. Adult writing is the result of the stabilization through repetition of this personal writing. This implies that adult writing presents similarities but also variability. Variability is one of the major issues in handwriting research. Most writing studies based their movement time analyses and normalization procedures on a "theoretical" counting of stroke production during letter writing (e.g., Meulenbroek & van Galen, 1990 for cursive lower-case letters) or a limited quantity of data (e.g., Spinelli et al., 2012 for print upper-case letters). The goal of the present study was to provide an empirical stroke execution reference that specifies the most frequent movement patterns in upper-case letter production.

We write to communicate contents and meanings. If we write fast we will be able to transmit more information. We also need to write fast so we do not forget the sentences we planned. These sentences are stored temporarily in working memory. Writers who produce irregular or unreadable letters have difficulties in writing long texts because the mechanical aspects of writing consume the cognitive resources that are needed to focus on the orthographic and informational aspects of the paragraph (Graham, Harris & Fink, 2000). Another essential aspect of writing is legibility. We have to write fast, but not too fast, because we have to produce letter shapes that need to be clear enough so they can be read by other people. So, when a child learns to write, he/she needs to consider both aspects. Learning to write efficiently consists of a trade-off between writing speed and legibility. The writing rules or "grammar of action" that are taught at school are the basis to achieve this trade-off. With practice, the child will assimilate all the rules until he/she writes clear and fast enough as to communicate effectively. Once writing automation is achieved writing patterns will become more and more personal (Mojet, 1991).

The aim of this study was to gain understanding on how variable writing becomes when motor production becomes personal. The other goal of this study was to provide an empirical methodological basis for writing experiments that require movement time normalization on the basis of stroke number. Several studies investigating the impact of the linguistic components of writing applied this kind of normalization. For example, Kandel, Peereman,

Grosjaques, and Fayol (2011) examined the impact of syllable structure and bigram frequency in adult handwriting. They had to compare movement time for writing French words that differed on these aspects (e.g., VILAIN (naughty) vs. VOLEUR (thief)). The V is the same for both words, so there is no need to normalize, but most of the remaining letters in the words are not the same. The authors had to find a way to compare them. To compare letters that are made up of a different number of strokes (e.g. I in VILAIN has three strokes and O in VOLEUR has 2 strokes), they normalized the letter duration values with respect to the number of strokes per letter. For example, if the durations for I and O were both 300 ms, the mean stroke durations were 300/3 = 100 ms and 300/2 = 150, respectively. With this method, they presented adult data indicating that word production is mostly programmed syllable-by-syllable. This writing strategy can by modified if there is a low frequency bigram within the initial syllable.

The normalisation procedure used in Kandel et al. (2011) was described more formally by Spinelli et al. (2012). They presented a table in which they determine the stroke number for each upper-case letter of the alphabet. However, we are not sure that this procedure can be generalized because the data it relied on is rather limited. Indeed, there was only one participant. She was instructed to write ten times each letter in upper-case, one after the other, as she usually writes them. It is also noteworthy that the stroke count Spinelli et al presented concerned writing time. That is, the time when the tip of the pen touched the surface of the digitizer (pressure > 0). They did not consider in air movements (pressure = 0), like the ones we do to change location and write the horizontal line of an A (see Figure 9.1). Noting "in air movements" could be useful, since they add supplementary movement time that is not always considered in handwriting studies. These points may produce biases in movement duration data that could question the theoretical implications of these experiments.

To examine this issue, we conducted an experiment in which the participants wrote the alphabet in upper-case letters on a digitizer. We counted the number of strokes per letter, and distinguished "on surface strokes" from "in air movements". On this basis, we examined the variability of each letter of the alphabet across participants. We also considered the impact of instructing the participants to follow a particular model or letter shape and compared it to a situation of "spontaneous writing".

2   Method

2.1   *Participants*

Forty-two adults participated in the experiment (21 participants in the "without model" writing condition and 21 participants in the "with model" writing condition). All the participants were right-handed, had normal or corrected-to-normal vision, and no motor or hearing disorders. They were unaware of the purpose of the experiment. They gave written consent for their participation in the experiment. The study received approval from the CERNI, which is the ethical committee for Cognitive Science experiments in Grenoble.

2.2   *Material and Procedure*

The participants had to write the letters of the alphabet in upper-case. Letter presentation and movement analysis were controlled by *Ductus* (Guinet & Kandel, 2010). We presented the letters in upper-case on the center of a laptop screen. The letters were presented in Calibri font size 72 (e.g., E, T, A, F). We chose this font because we found that it was the font that respected the best handwritten upper-case letter patterns. Some fonts, like "Times New Roman", present wheelbases on the top and bottom of the letters that are not done in handwriting. The letters were presented in alphabetic order, by groups of six. They were preceded by a fixation point (500 ms duration). The participants had to write the letters on a paper stuck to a digitizer (Wacom Intuos 3—A5, sampling frequency 200 Hz, accuracy 0.02 mm). The digitizer was connected to the laptop that monitored the handwriting movements. The participants had to write with a special pen (Intuos Inking Pen) on a 20.5×19.5 cm lined paper, landscape format (spacing between lines = 0.7 cm). The participants were instructed to start writing as soon as possible and write the letters four times in upper-case. In one condition, we asked them to write the letters following the shape of the letter presented in the screen ("with model" condition; WM hereafter). In the other condition, we gave no particular instruction and they had to write the upper-case letters "as they usually did" ("without model" condition; WOM hereafter). We tested the participants individually in a quiet room. The experiment lasted approximately 10 minutes.

2.3   *Data Processing and Analysis*

We segmented each letter into strokes. As can be observed in Figure 9.1, the first stroke for letter A concerned the initial movement (from points 1 to 2), the second stroke referred to the segment between points 2–3, there was an in-air movement at points 3–4 and a final stroke from point 4 to 5. We used

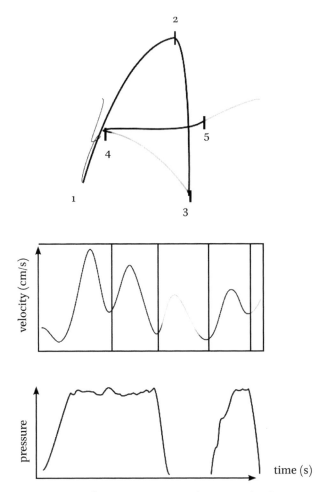

FIGURE 9.1   Stroke segmentation procedure. Example of a participant who wrote letter A. The black lines correspond
to writing time with ink on the paper (pressure >
0 on the pressure profile). The grey lines are movements that do not touch the surface of the digitizer
(pressure = 0 on the pressure profile). The numbers
and the corresponding dashes indicate the beginning
and end of each stroke. Between 3 and 4 there is an
in-air movement. Velocity profile: tangential velocity
as a function of time. Pressure profile: Pen tip pressure as a function of time

the definition of "stroke" presented by Teulings (1996): "... when recording the movement of the pen tip during fluent writing the tangential (or absolute) velocity time function will show a sequence of unimodal peaks: the ballistic strokes".

We counted the number of strokes for each letter in each condition. The number of "in air" movements were counted separately. An "in air" movement refers to a movement within the production of a letter that does not touch the surface of the digitizer (pressure = o; points 3–4 in Figure 9.1). The "in air" movements can be monitored because the digitizer detects the pen 6 mm above its surface. The first step of the data analysis consisted in segmenting the letters into strokes. Letter onset corresponded to pressure > o after letter presentation. Each stroke corresponded to the movement on the surface of the digitizer between two consecutive velocity minima (Figure 9.1). Letter end corresponded to pressure = o after its last stroke.

We recorded 4368 data points. There were 12 productions that were not exploitable (0.3 % of the data) so we excluded them from the analyses. First, we conducted a descriptive analysis to gain understanding on production variability. Then, we conducted statistical analyses to examine whether the instruction to follow a model during writing had an impact on the number of strokes produced. To do so, we compared the distributions of the two conditions (WM vs WOM) for each letter. We considered stroke number as an ordered variable with 7 levels. We conducted an ordered logit regression (Tutz & Hennevogl, 1996) using the ordinal package (Christensen, 2015) and the lsmeans package (Russell, 2016), provided by R-software (R Core Team, 2014, version 3.0.1). The model included three fixed-effect factors: Condition (with model vs. without model), Letter (the 26 letters of the alphabet) and their interaction. Participants were considered as a random effect. We report the significant differences.

3   Results and Discussion

3.1   *Number of Strokes*

Table 9.1 presents the number of strokes produced for each letter with and without model. It is difficult to establish a "variability threshold" to determine when there is variability and when there is not. Therefore, we quantified the amount of letters that were produced with the same number of strokes by at least 75 % (range 75–100 %) and 50 % (range 50–74 %) of the observations. The analysis in this section is descriptive.

There were 7 letters produced with the same number of strokes in at least 75 % (range 75–100 %) of the observations in both conditions: L, T, U, V, X were

TABLE 9.1A Number of strokes produced for each letter with model. The numbers indicate the percentage of observations (the highest percentage is in bold).

Nb of strokes (wm)	1	2	3	4	5	6	7
A			**50**	44	5	1	
B			6	13	**54**	26	1
C	11	**85**	4	1			
D		12	43	43	2		
E		1	23	**70**	1		5
F			**54**	46			
G		7	**60**	31	2		
H			**93**	7			
I	**99**	1	0				
J	25	**73**	2				
K			**88**	12			
L	2	**98**	0				
M			8	**52**	39		
N			36	**64**			
O	1	**62**	29	2	6		
P	2	6	**51**	33	7		
Q		2	**57**	36	5		
R			10	**58**	30	2	
S		15	**81**	4			
T		**93**	7				
U	5	**88**	5	2			
V		**100**	0				
W			1	**99**			
X		**100**	0				
Y		**82**	15	2			
Z			**98**	2			

produced with 2 strokes, W with 4 strokes, and Z with 3 strokes. In the "with model" condition, there were 6 other letters for which we observed the same number of strokes in at least 75% of the observations: I = 1 stroke, C and Y = 2 strokes, K, H and S = 3 strokes. In the "without model" condition, these 6 letters presented more variability but represented at least 50% (range 50–74%) of the observations: C = 1 stroke (39%) or 2 strokes (53%), H = 3 strokes (71%)

TABLE 9.1B Number of strokes produced for each letter without model. The numbers indicate the percentage of observations (the highest percentage is in bold).

Nb of strokes (WOM)	1	2	3	4	5	6	7
A			29	**67**	4		
B			8	37	**40**	13	1
C	39	**53**	8				
D		18	**54**	28			
E		7	25	**54**	12	1	
F		5	**52**	42	1		
G	4	23	**48**	21	5		
H		1	**71**	23	5		
I	29	2	**67**	1			
J		32	**65**	2			
K		7	**57**	36	0		
L	11	**89**	0				
M		1	10	**58**	31		
N			39	**61**	0		
O	8	**67**	23	2			
P		18	**61**	20	1		
Q		12	**65**	22	1		
R			14	**70**	1		
S	6	25	**58**	11	0		
T		**100**					
U	6	**83**	8	2			
V		**100**					
W			4	4	**87**	6	
X		**100**					
Y		45	**55**				
Z		4	**76**	20			

or 4 strokes (23 %), I = 1 stroke (29 %) or 3 strokes (67 %), K = 3 strokes (57 %) or 4 strokes (36 %), S = 2 strokes (25 %) or 3 strokes (58 %), Y = 2 strokes (45 %) or 3 strokes (55 %).

There were 10 letters that were produced with the same number of strokes in at least 50 % of the productions in both conditions: A = 3 strokes WM condition (50 %) or 4 strokes WOM condition (67 %), E = 4 strokes in WM condition

(70 %) or 5 strokes WOM condition (54 %), F = 3 strokes, J = 2 strokes WM condition (73 %) or 3 strokes WOM condition (65 %), M = 4 strokes, N = 4 strokes, O = 2 strokes, P = 3 strokes, Q = 3 strokes, R = 4 strokes. In the WM condition, B was produced with 5 strokes in 54 % of the observations, whereas in the WOM condition it was produced with 4 strokes in 37 % of the productions and 5 strokes in 40 % of the productions. Likewise, in the WM condition, G was produced with 3 strokes in 60 % of the observations, whereas in the WOM condition it was produced with 2 strokes in 23 % of the productions, 3 strokes in 48 % of the productions and 4 strokes in 21 % of the productions. The inverse was observed for D: in the WM condition it was produced with 3 strokes 43 % of the productions and 4 strokes in other 43 % of them; in the WOM condition it was produced with 3 strokes in 54 % of the observations.

To summarize, 7 letters (L, T, U, V, W, X, Z) were written with the same number of strokes in the range 75–100 % of the observations. When considering the range 50–74 % of the observations, there were 12 more letters (C, E, F, H, K, M, N, O, P, Q, R, S) written with the same number of strokes, irrespective of the instructions. This makes a total of 19 letters out of 26. In addition, when presenting the model, 13 out of 26 letters were written with the same number of strokes in at least 75 % of the observations. Without the model, only 7 letters were written with the same number of strokes in at least 75 % of the observations. If we consider the range 50–74 % of the observations, then 25 letters in the WM condition and 24 letters in the WOM condition were produced with the same number of strokes. There was only one letter (D) in the WM condition and two letters (B and G) in the WOM condition that were produced differently in less than 50 % of the observations

When comparing statistically the *distribution* of the number of strokes of each letter as a function of condition, we observed a significant impact of the instructions in 13 out of 26 letters: A, H, R ($p < .05$), D, G, O, Q ($p < .01$), B, C, J, P ($p < .001$), and I, Y ($p < .0001$). When the distributions differed, we observed that writing the letters with the model produced less variability than without a model (except for D). It is noteworthy that 9 of these letters presented curved lines that require rotation movements for production. The distributions were more extended when having to write the letters with the model. For example, letter C in the WM condition varied from 1 to 4 strokes and in the WOM condition varied from 1 to 3. For the remaining letters, which are made up of straight lines, the effect of the instruction was to produce them with less strokes.

Table 9.2 presents the most frequent number of strokes produced for each letter with and without model. It revealed that there are 5 letters for which the number of strokes is not the same in the WM and WOM conditions: A, D, I, J, and Y. The statistical analyses of their distribution indicated that the

TABLE 9.2   Most frequent number of strokes for each letter when produced with and without model

Nb of strokes	With model	Without model
A	3	4
B	5	5
C	2	2
D	3 or 4	3
E	4	4
F	3	3
G	3	3
H	3	3
I	1	3
J	2	3
K	3	3
L	2	2
M	4	4
N	4	4
O	2	2
P	3	3
Q	3	3
R	4	4
S	3	3
T	2	2
U	2	2
V	2	2
W	4	4
X	2	2
Y	2	3
Z	3	3

instruction to follow the model constrains even more the number of strokes produced (except for D).

We also compared our stroke count with the one presented by Spinelli et al. (2012). In their experiment, one individual wrote the letters with no particular instruction, like in our "without model" condition. Their stroke count excluded in air movements. The comparison indicated that there are 8 letters (A, C, G,

I, N, P, R, Y) that differ in stroke numbers with our WOM condition. The differences are of only one stroke, except for I. All these letters had an agreement of at least 50%, except for G, which is one of the most variable letters of the alphabet with respect to the number of strokes.

In sum, and from a descriptive point of view, we globally observed that there are letters that are more variable than others. This suggests that the rules that were learnt during writing acquisition are still applied in many cases when we write the letters.

3.2   *In Air Movements*

Table 9.3 presents the number of "in air" movements produced for each letter with and without model. There were 17 letters in the WM and 16 letters in the WOM conditions that presented very little variability in the number of in air movements (range 75–100% of the observations). There were 9 letters in the WM and 10 letters in the WOM conditions that presented more variability (50–74%). There were no letters that presented less than 50% variability. These results therefore revealed that there is little variability in the number of in air movements.

It is interesting to point out that 17 letters in the WM condition and 16 letters in the WOM condition were mostly produced without any in air movement. Only 7 letters in the WM condition and 7 letters in the WOM condition were produced with one in air movement. The in air movement always corresponded to a straight line that was either horizontal (e.g., A, T) or slanted (e.g., K, X, Y). There were only 2 letters in the WM condition and 3 letters in the WOM condition that were produced with two in air movements. In other words, we observed that a majority of the upper-case letters were produced without any in air movements (23–26% of the alphabet was produced with one in air movement).

TABLE 9.3A Number of in air movements produced for each letter with model. The numbers indicate the percentage
of observations (the highest percentage is in bold).

Nb of in air movements (WM)	0	1	2	3
A	5	**73**	23	0
B	**67**	32	1	0
C	**100**	0	0	0
D	**56**	44	0	0
E	5	23	**58**	14
F	0	**58**	42	0
G	**82**	18	0	0
H	5	13	**82**	0
I	**100**	0	0	0
J	**100**	0	0	0
K	13	**62**	25	0
L	**100**	0	0	0
M	**77**	23	0	0
N	**74**	23	4	0
O	**100**	0	0	0
P	**70**	30	0	0
Q	8	**92**	0	0
R	**71**	29	0	0
S	**100**	0	0	0
T	8	**92**	0	0
U	**100**	0	0	0
V	**100**	0	0	0
W	**88**	12	0	0
X	0	**99**	1	0
Y	19	**81**	0	0
Z	**99**	1	0	0

TABLE 9.3B Number of in air movements produced for each letter
without model. The numbers indicate the percentage
of observations (the highest percentage is in bold).

Nb of in air movements (WOM)	0	1	2
A	0	**91**	9
B	70	25	5
C	100	0	0
D	66	34	0
E	1	34	**65**
F	1	**63**	36
G	100	0	0
H	15	23	**62**
I	29	18	**53**
J	11	**88**	1
K	27	**57**	15
L	100	0	0
M	**82**	11	7
N	**93**	2	5
O	100	0	0
P	**79**	21	0
Q	1	**99**	0
R	**90**	10	0
S	100	0	0
T	1	**99**	0
U	100	0	0
V	**95**	5	0
W	**63**	32	5
X	4	**96**	0
Y	**60**	40	0
Z	**69**	31	0

4 Conclusion

This experiment is a first attempt to quantify production variability in handwriting. It also aimed at providing a methodological contribution to handwriting studies in which movement time data is normalized on the basis of stroke

number. To do so, the participants had to write the letters of the alphabet in upper-case format on a digitizer. They were instructed either to follow the model of the letter presented on the screen or to write it spontaneously.

The data revealed that there were 19 letters that were produced, in at least 50% observations, with the same number of strokes, irrespective of the experimental instructions. This means that 7 letters are the ones that vary the most. Furthermore, among these letters, only 3 of them presented less than 50% agreement in the observations. In addition, the majority of the letters (17 letters) were produced without in air movements and 7 letters with one in air movement. In air movements were always done at the end of the production and concerned straight lines. The results also indicated that the instructions to follow a specific model could have an impact on the number of strokes for certain letters. This study revealed that the participants produced many letters with the same number of strokes. The instruction to follow the model seemed to affect more letters A, D, I and J. It is therefore likely that the "grammar of action" we learned during the writing acquisition period could prevail on our production strategies in adulthood.

We also compared the data of the present study to the table defining stroke numbers presented by Spinelli et al. (2012). We observed discrepancies of one stroke in seven letters. This comparison shows the importance of the present methodological contribution and sheds some light into possible biases of previous experiments with upper-case writing (e.g., Kandel et al., 2011; Afonso, Alvarez, & Kandel, 2015).

Finally, it is important to note that this study was limited to upper-case letters. This is the format that produces less variability because the writing style is more constrained than in cursive writing for example. Future studies should examine variability in other writing styles and lower case writing.

Acknowledgements

We acknowledge funding from the Agence Nationale de la Recherche (ANR ECRIRE-14-CE30–0013) attributed to Sonia Kandel.

References

Afonso, O., Alvarez, C., & Kandel, S. (2015). Effects of Grapheme-to-Phoneme probability on writing durations. *Memory & Cognition*, 43, 579–492.

Berninger, V.W., Winn, W.D. (2006). Implications of advancements in brain research and technology for writing development, writing instruction, and educational evolution. In C. MacArthur, S. Graham, & J. Fitzgerald (Eds.), *Handbook of Writing Research.* (pp. 96–114) New York: Guilford.

Bourdin, B., & Fayol, M. (1994). Is written language production more difficult than oral language production? A working memory approach. *International Journal of Psychology, 29,* 591–620.

Chartrel, E., & Vinter, A. (2004). L'écriture: une activité longue et complexe à acquérir. *Approche Neuropsychologique de l'Apprentissage chez l'Enfant, 78,* 174–180.

Christensen, R.H.B. (2015). Regression Models for Ordinal Data. R package version 2015.6–28. https://cran.r-project.org/web/packages/ordinal/index.html.

Goodnow, J.J., & Levine, R.A. (1973). "The grammar of action": Sequence and syntax in children's copying. *Cognitive psychology, 4,* 82–98.

Graham, S., Harris, K.R., & Fink, B. (2000). Is handwriting causally related to learning to write? Treatment of handwriting problems in beginning writers. *Journal of Educational Psychology, 92,* 620–633.

Guinet, E., & Kandel, S. (2010). Ductus: A software package for the study of handwriting production. *Behavior Research Methods, 42,* 326–332.

Hayes, J.R. (2012). Modeling and remodeling writing. *Written Communication, 29,* 369–388.

Kandel, S., Peereman, R., Grosjacques, G. & Fayol, M. (2011). For a psycholinguistic model of handwriting production: Testing the syllable-bigram controversy. *Journal of Experimental Psychology: Human Perception and Performance, 37,* 1310–1322.

Meulenbroek, R.G., & Van Galen, G.P. (1990). Perceptual-motor complexity of printed and cursive letters. *The Journal of experimental education, 58,* 95–110.

Mojet, J.W. (1991). Characteristics of the developing handwriting skill in elementary education. In J. Wann, A. Wing, & N. Sovik (Eds.), *Development of graphic skills: Research, perspectives and educational implications* (pp. 53–75). London: Academic Press

Olive, T., & Kellogg, R.T. (2002). Concurrent activation of high-and low-level production processes in written composition. *Memory & Cognition, 30,* 594–600.

R Core Team (2014). R: A language and environment for statistical computing. *R Foundation for Statistical Computing,* Vienna, Austria. http://www.R-project.org/.

Russell V. Lenth (2016). Least-Squares Means: The R Package lsmeans. Journal of Statistical Software, 69(1), 1–33.

Spinelli, E., Kandel, S., Guerassimovitch, H., & Ferrand, L. (2012). Graphemic cohesion effect in reading and writing complex graphemes. *Language and Cognitive Processes, 27,* 770–791.

Teulings, H.L. (1996). Handwriting movement control. *Handbook of perception and action, 2,* 561–613.

Thomassen, A.J.W.M., Tibosch, H.J.C.M., & Maarse, F.J. (1989). The effect of context on stroke direction and stroke order in handwriting. In R. Plamondon, C.Y. Suen, & M. Simner (Eds.), *Computer recognition and human production of handwriting* (pp. 213–230). Singapore: World Scientific.

Tutz, G. & Hennevogl, W. (1996). Random effects in ordinal regression models. Computational Statistics & Data Analysis 22, 537–557.

Van Sommers, P. (1984). *Drawing and cognition: descriptive and experimental studies of graphic production processes.* Cambridge: Cambridge University Press.

CHAPTER 10

EEG Methods of Exploring Written Word Production

Cyril Perret and Qingqing Qu

Writing down words in a syntactically correct order on a sheet of paper in order to convey meaningful information—in other words, handwriting—is an activity to which adults devote a significant part of their time. In the last few years, the use of Short Message Systems (SMS) and / or social networks such as Facebook® or Twitter® have greatly increased the time spent using writing as a communication tool. This frequent use can give the impression that written production is relatively simple. The last twenty-five years of research into psycholinguistics show that this is not the case (see all the chapters in this volume). Understanding the cognitive mechanisms involved in the "simple" handwritten production of an isolated word is a significant challenge.

Beyond the conceptual aspects, the development of an adequate methodology to explore issues related to handwritten production is in itself a difficulty. Indeed, if the object of study concerns the cognitive mechanisms involved in text production, some of the tools will be different from those used to explore subject-verb agreement or the cognitive processes involved in the handwritten production of isolated words. However, whatever the level of research, two main approaches can be listed. Some studies have focused on error analysis, with the aim of exploring the characteristics of what the participants have written. For example, Fayol, Huppet, and Largy (1999) explored developmental changes in subject-verb agreement in written French by observing the number and type of agreement errors (e.g., *les* enfant*s* chant*ent*; The children are singing). In a sentence-transcription task, they presented sentences orally and the participants were asked to write down each sentence after its presentation and, in some cases, perform a secondary task (e.g., click detection). The sentences had an "N1 of N2 + Verb" structure in which the number of the nouns was varied. The behavioral variable was the number of errors as a function of the experimental conditions. The error analysis approach has also been used to explore the written production of isolated words. For example, Berg (2002) collected and analyzed production errors made by participants while typing.

Although it provides information about the cognitive representation involved in handwritten production, error analysis does not make it possible

© KONINKLIJKE BRILL NV, LEIDEN, 2019 | DOI:10.1163/9789004394988_011

to explore issues relating to dynamics. Drawing on the tradition of studies of mental chronometry in cognitive psychology (Donders, 1868), studies of written production generally use two kinds of chronometric measures. On the one hand, reaction time makes it possible to track the cognitive processes that take place between the presentation of a target (i.e., auditory or visual information) and the responses (i.e., the Reaction Times, or RTS hereafter). Reaction times (the intervals between picture onset and initial contact of the pen with the tablet) are widely used in studies of the production of isolated words. They can also serve as a measure during text production in a secondary task. For example, Olive, Kellogg & Piolat (2002) asked their participants to perform a task to detect a stimulus during the writing of a text. The participants had to press a button as soon as possible when a sound was presented. According to Olive et al. (2002), reaction times provide information on the processes involved in text production. At the same time, writing movement times and writing speed can also be collected. These measures have, for example, made it possible to show that linguistic information such as word regularity (e.g., see Bonin & Méot and Damian, this volume) can have an impact on the characteristics of writing. Several recent studies have used this measure (e.g., Kandel & Perret, 2015, Roux, McKeef, Grosjacques, Afonso, & Kandel, 2013).

These two measures of mental chronometry are based on the same assumption: the increase in the complexity of cognitive activities is time-consuming. This results in an increase in the time required to perform a complex activity compared to that of a simple activity. For example, two of the most robust effects in the language production literature are those of word frequency and age-of-acquisition. Because low-frequency words or late-acquired words are more complex than high-frequency words or early acquired words, reaction times on the former are longer than on the latter. However, like error analysis, these chronometric measures are not without their limitations. Comparing reaction times in several experimental conditions is tantamount to establishing an order based on the overall processing speed, without considering the duration of each individual process. In other words, latencies are a consequence of the output produced by a large number of individual cognitive processes. The increase / decrease in the reaction times is then difficult to attribute to variations in any specific cognitive process. If we again take the influence of the age of acquisition or word frequency as examples, it is possible to identify a global change in the latencies without being able to indicate the level or levels of processing directly affected by these factors.

In this chapter, we propose to show how electroencephalographic recordings can partially compensate for the limitations of mental timing measurements. First, we will describe the characteristics of the EEG measurements.

We will focus on two possible analytical approaches: the so-called ERP analysis and spatio-temporal segmentation.[1] In our second section, two examples are developed to illustrate this issue. In both cases, the main aim was to specify the time period of two linguistic effects and thus to make an assumption about the level or levels of processing influenced by these variables. The study by Qu, Zhang and Damian (2016) was aimed at specifying the temporal effect of lexical frequency in Chinese Mandarin, while Perret, Bonin and Laganaro (2014) attempted to test the hypothesis of multiple loci for the effects of age of acquisition.

1   Electrophysiological Brain Activity, Recordings and Processing Operations

The aim of EEG recordings is to collect the electrophysiological activity of the pyramidal neurons in the cerebral cortex. The neurons use neuromediators, i.e., a set of various chemical molecules liberated in the synapse slot, to communicate. This chemical inter-neural communication produces electrical micro-currents of a few nanovolts. These post-synaptic potentials (PSP) are too small to be detected. During a cognitive activity, a set of several thousand neurons are synchronized, i.e., they concomitantly release neuromediators. Several PSPs are then produced at the same time. An equivalent current dipole (ECD) is obtained by summing the PSPs. The intensity of the ECD is sufficient for an EEG system installed on a participant's scalp to be able to record it. It should be noted that, due to a phenomenon of diffusion through the cerebral matter, it is not possible to connect the recording position of an electrophysiological activity directly to the scalp and the cerebral area immediately below it.

The aim of the EEG recording is to collect the electrophysiological activity of groups of neurons that are synchronized in order to perform a cognitive activity. A system (e.g., Biosemi° or Neuroscan°) is placed on the surface of the participant's scalp. The number of electrodes is variable. Berger's initial work (1929) used less than a dozen, and the current systems vary from 64 to 256 electrodes. Each of them makes it possible to measure an electric current between active electrodes and a reference electrode. Because of methodological difficulties (e.g., positioning the reference electrode correctly, Dien, 1998), the current

---

1   It should be noted that other approaches to EEG experimentation may be as good or even better, but the two approaches described here have been used in the field of written production to date. Moreover, rhythm analyses (alpha, beta, gamma waves) or time-frequency analyses are beyond the scope of this chapter.

strategies use a double reference or an average reference (see Dien, 1998; Luck, 2005). Finally, the electrical current is measured at a frequency ranging from 512 to 2048 Hz.

EEG recording is a quasi-continuous measurement of the electrical activity of the brain. However, only certain parts of the recorded signal are of interest and these correspond to the Event-Related Potentials (ERPs). These correspond to the modification of EEG activity in response to the presentation of a stimulus. The researcher then has to define the precise period corresponding to the ERPs. In the majority of studies of handwritten word production, the targeted activity is the latency. It is interesting to note that depending on the analytical methods used (see below), constraints appear regarding the choice of these periods of time, which are referred to as epochs (Laganaro & Perret, 2011). Moreover, the EEG measure has the great disadvantage of combining both the signal (1%) and the noise (99%). The latter has two major sources. All the neurons not involved in the cognitive activity studied are, unfortunately, not without activity. They produce electrical activity, which is in turn recorded by the system. The advantage of this type of noise is that it corresponds to a random phenomenon. The average of all the ERPs extracted from the experiment is generally calculated. The influence of the noise then tends towards zero, while that of the signal remains constant. It is therefore necessary in an experiment that uses EEGs to have enough epochs (i.e., items in each experimental condition) to make this mathematical procedure reliable. The other source of noise consists of a set of artefacts such as potential skin, blinking or eye movements. Many methods are available to clean the signal of these sources of influence before being processed (e.g., Luck, 2005). The baseline correction method is widely used (see, however, Michel et al., 2009 for a discussion of problems relating to the use of baseline correction).

After eliminating the noise in the EEG signal, the researcher obtains a raw wave of evoked potentials for each experimental condition and for each participant. The objective is then to compare the activity between the experimental conditions in order to test for the presence of possible changes in the electrical activity of the brain. The reasoning is based on the idea that any modification of the cognitive processes between two experimental conditions has an impact on the characteristics (intensity, localization) of the ECDs generated in the cerebral cortex. In what follows, two types of analyses are described: waveform and spatio-temporal segmentation.

To undertake waveform analysis, one first needs to average the single-trial waveforms (ERPs) for each subject for each experimental condition, and then to average the averaged waveforms of the individual subjects in order to create grand average ERP waveforms. Three approaches have commonly been used to analyze the amplitudes of grand average ERP in language production. The most common way is to define time windows of interest and regions of interest (ROIs), and then to calculate the mean voltage of the waveforms for each time window at each ROI. This is the so-called mean amplitude. The time windows of interests and ROIs can be identified on the basis of a visual inspection of the waveforms or from previous research. This type of time window analysis enables us to probe the time course of ERP differences across conditions, and ROI analysis enables us to identify the scalp distribution of ERP differences. Mean amplitudes from each time window are entered into ANOVAs with experimental conditions and regions as factors.

The second common method is to perform onset latency analysis by comparing ERPs in different experimental conditions. This is done by running t-tests at each sampling point in order to identify the latency at which the ERPs in the experimental conditions start to diverge significantly from each other. To protect against problems associated with multiple comparisons (Type I error increase), researchers perform onset latency analyses using a method developed by Guthrie and Buchwald (1991) (see e.g., Costa, Strijkers, Martin, & Thierry, 2009; Strijkers, Costa, Thierry, 2010; Thierry, Cardebat, & Démonet, 2003; Qu et al., 2016 for use of this method in recent studies). This method assumes that difference potential waveforms possess a first-order autoregressive structure with statistically dependent sampling points and uses this assumption to generate "the critical run length for determining statistical significance" by means of computer simulations. If the observed number of consecutive significant time points is larger than the critical run length, this would indicate a statistically significant interval. The onset point of a sequence of consecutive significant points can be identified as the onset of a particular effect. One could plot a figure (see Figure 10.1, derived from Qu et al., 2016) presenting significant p-values resulting from the t-tests at each sampling point across all electrodes, thus presenting the spatial and temporal distribution of a particular effect.

The third common method is to perform correlation analyses which help us understand the relationship between ERPs and behavioral data (e.g., response latencies). Correlation analyses can be performed on the onset latency of effects with response latencies, the peak latencies of a particular component with response latencies, or on the mean amplitude differences between conditions in the time window of interest in which there are differences in response latencies between conditions (see Strijkers et al., 2010 for details).

Although widely used, waveform analyses can be criticized in at least two respects. On the one hand, the measures used are dependent on the reference electrode (e.g., Brunet, Murray, & Michel, 2011; Koenig, Stein, Gieder, & Kottlow,

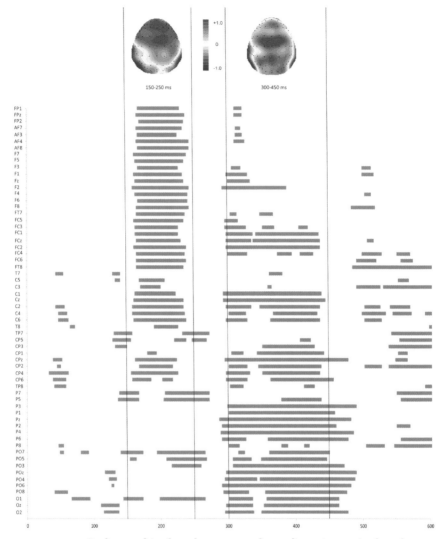

FIGURE 10.1   P-values resulting from the t-test at each sampling point starting from the
picture presentation across all 62 channels. Gray points correspond to those
p-values below 0.05. Topographic maps correspond to the difference waves
between low- and high-frequency conditions in the 150–250 ms and 300–450
ms time windows. The vertical lines depict the time windows used for mean
amplitude analyses.

2014; Michel, Koenig, Brandeis, Gianotti, & Wackermann, 2009; Murray, Brunet,
& Michel, 2008). Koenig & Gianotti (2009) showed that certain changes occur
depending on the specifically chosen position for the reference electrode. On
the other hand, the association between the effects observed through the wave-

form analyses and the interpretation in terms of cognitive processes is also open to criticism. Such processing makes it possible to indicate precisely the time period(s) and the spatial period(s) of difference(s) in electrophysiological activity. However, there is no indication of what is at the origin of this divergence across the experimental conditions. A modulation of the field strength produced by one and the same neural source or a change in this source may equally well account for the amplitude variation. From a cognitive point of view, the consequences are not the same. A modulation of the strength of the field produced by one and the same source suggests a modulation in the same processing operation (e.g., the more or less complex resolution of a competition between different representations), whereas the change in neural source suggests a change in cognitive processing (e.g., transition from one processing level to another).

Researchers have proposed a different way of analyzing ERPs (Lehmann, 1987; Lehmann & Skrandies, 1980, 1984; Brunet et al., 2011; Koenig et al., 2014; Michel et al., 2009; Murray et al., 2008). Spatio-temporal segmentation analysis is based on two main facts. Even if the neural source cannot be specified directly from the ERP recording at the scalp, the observation of different topographies indicates a change in cognitive processing (Lehmann, 1987). Moreover, a direct observation of ERPs suggests periods of stability of the electrophysiological field interrupted by brief changes. It therefore seems possible to segment the ERP wave into a series of stable spatial configurations of electric fields, separated by sudden transitions (Brunet et al., 2011; Koenig et al., 2014; Michel et al., 2009; Murray et al., 2008). The identification of the topography of the electric fields on the scalp at each recording time point is the first step in this approach. A hierarchical clustering procedure is used on the grand average for each experimental condition (see Murray et al., 2008). Each map corresponds to a modeling of electrophysiological activity in terms of relative field intensity (Koening & Gianotti, 2009). It should be noted that a minimum number of 64 electrodes is required to perform this analysis. It is also necessary to use interpolations for electrodes whose recording reliability is doubtful (Koening & Gianotti, 2009). Figure 10.2 presents an example (Perret & Laganaro, 2012) of segmentation in a task requiring the production of handwriting from pictures. A series of six stable spatial configurations is obtained. Perret & Laganaro (2012) have compared this segmentation with that of oral production (Inderfreys, 2011) and made corresponding proposals regarding the temporal course of access to the various representations in handwritten production.

It is worth noting that this type of analysis can answer the criticisms described above. First, it is independent of the choice of reference electrode because this analysis is based on a modeling of the spatial distribution of the

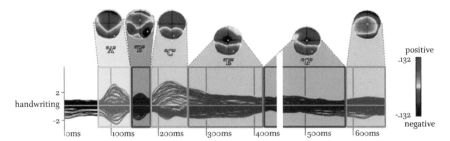

FIGURE 10.2   Spatio-temporal segmentation of electrophysiological activity recorded during
a spoken picture naming task

electrophysiological activity. Unlike waveform analyses, for which the absolute electrophysiological activity is recorded by a specific electrode, spatio-
temporal analysis is based on the relative distribution of activity across all electrodes (see Murray et al., 2008). Moreover, the spatio-temporal analysis makes
it possible to specify whether the ERP differences between the experimental
conditions arise from a change of source or a modulation of the strength of
one and the same source. Indeed, the latter case assumes a modulation of the
characteristics of one and the same topography, whereas a change of neural
source assumes a change of map configurations. Finally, it has been reported
that the results of the different types of analyses converge. Indeed, when waveform analyses and spatio-temporal segmentation are compared (e.g., Laganaro
& Perret, 2011, Perret & Laganaro, 2012), the periods of change of activity in
the waveform analyses appear at the same time as the changes of topography. Other differences observed with regard to waveform analyses appear to
be due to statistical problems associated with multiple comparisons (Michel
et al., 2009).

    Once the various topographic maps have been identified in the grand aver-
ages, analyses are carried out in order to test the hypotheses. First, the consistency of the maps for given periods is tested (Koenig, & Melie-Garcia, 2010).
Next, a so-called "Fitting" procedure (e.g., Koenig et al., 2014; Michel et al.,
2009; Murray et al., 2008) is applied in order to look for various indicators of
the presence of functional micro-states within the average ERP waves of each
participant for each experimental condition. It is thus possible to create statistical series comparing the presence or absence of a map or the percentage
of variance explained by the latter between conditions. The duration of a specific micro-state can also be collected for each participant and then used for
comparisons (see the study of AoA effects described below).

2   The Temporal Properties of Frequency Effects in Handwritten
     Word Production

Frequency effects have been widely documented in the psychology of language (e.g., Forster & Chambers, 1973; Morton, 1969). Frequency effects also emerge consistently in picture naming tasks. It has been demonstrated that pictures whose names occur more frequently are named faster than pictures whose names occur less frequently (e.g., Alario, Ferrand, Laganaro, New, Frauenfelder, & Segui, 2004; Jescheniak & Levelt, 1994; Oldfield & Wingfield, 1965). However, the exact locus of such frequency effects remains controversial: 1) Word frequency effects may arise in recognition processes (Bates et al., 2003; Johnson, Paivio, & Clark, 1996). This idea that has received support from the finding that frequency effects emerge in tasks that do not necessarily require lexical access, such as picture recognition and picture-word matching tasks (e.g., Kroll & Potter, 1984; but see Jescheniak & Levelt, 1994, Experiment 2 which fails to show such effects in a picture-word matching task); 2) Word frequency exclusively affects the stage of phonological encoding in speaking (e.g., Jescheniak & Levelt, 1994; Jescheniak, Meyer, & Levelt, 2003); 3) Word frequency effects arise both during lexical-semantic ("lemma") access and during phonological processing in speech production (e.g., Navarrete, Basagni, Alario, & Costa, 2006).

In recent years, frequency effects in spoken word production have been investigated using EEG and overt speaking tasks. Existing studies have found that high-frequency ERPs start to diverge from low-frequency ERPs within 200 ms after picture onset, and that differences between low-frequency and high-frequency ERPs are present in the early P2 (approx. 160–240 ms) and later N3 (approx. 240–320 ms) time windows, during which lexical access and phonological encoding are thought to take place (Strijkers, Baus, Runnqvist, Fitzpatrick, & Costa, 2013; Strijkers et al., 2010; Strijkers, Holcomb, & Costa, 2011; see Strijkers & Costa, 2011 for a review). These ERP studies have provided evidence in support of the idea that frequency effects arise at the stage of both lexical-semantic access and phonological processing during speech production.

In written (rather than spoken) word production, frequency effects also appear to emerge consistently in behavioral measures such as response latencies (e.g., Bonin & Fayol, 2000; Bonin, Fayol, & Chalard, 2001). However, to date there have been very few EEG-based studies of written production (e.g., Perret & Laganaro, 2012; Perret et al., 2014; Pinet, Hamamé, Longcamp, Vidal, & Alario, 2015), and little research has been devoted to the source of frequency effects in written production. In a recent study, Qu et al. (2016) manipulated word frequency in a picture naming task with written responses, and explored the electrophysiological correlates of frequency effects, thereby providing important insights into the onsets of frequency effects and the locus of such effects. It should be noted that age-of-acquisition (AoA), as a major determinant of latencies in language production tasks (e.g., Barry, Morrison, & Ellis, 1997; Bonin et al., 2001, see above in this chapter), is correlated with frequency, with high-frequency words tending to be learned earlier. In order to better investigate the independent effects of frequency, Qu et al. controlled AoA and other relevant variables (e.g., word length in number of characters; stroke number of first character, second character, and two-character words; image variability; image agreement; concept familiarity; visual complexity; name agreement as a percentage; concept agreement, and rated age of acquisition).

The behavioral results showed a classical word frequency effect, with shorter response latencies for pictures with high-frequency names than for those with low-frequency names (Bonin & Fayol, 2002; Jescheniak & Levelt, 1994; Oldfield &Wingfield, 1965). More critically, the ERP results revealed a word frequency effect in the time windows of 150–250 and 300–450 ms, starting at 168 ms after picture onset, with low-frequency words eliciting more positive amplitudes than high-frequency words (see Figure 10.3). The two time windows observed in Qu et al. are roughly consistent with the time windows for lexical selection (200–275 ms) and phonological encoding (275–455 ms) in spoken production as estimated by a meta-analysis conducted by Indefrey and Levelt (2004; Indefrey, 2011), and are also consistent with the findings of previous electrophysiological studies in the spoken modality (e.g., Costa et al., 2009; Maess, Friederici, Damian, Meyer, & Levelt, 2002). Based on these findings, Qu et al. proposed that frequency effects affect both lexical selection and word-form encoding in written word production, which is consistent with the temporal properties of frequency effects observed in spoken word production (see Strijkers et al., 2010). These findings support the idea that the same underlying mechanisms are involved in frequency effects in spoken and written picture naming.

3   One Locus for the Age-of-Acquisition Effect?

Together with the effect of lexical frequency (Qu et al., 2016, see below), the influence of the age at which a word was learned (AoA effect) is systematically reported in studies of single written word production. Words learned early in childhood are produced more quickly (with shorter reaction times) and with a higher degree of accuracy than those learned later. For instance, shorter latencies and lower error rates have been systematically reported for words like *Pixie* than for words such as *platypus*. Even though the influence of the AoA in handwritten picture naming is well-established (e.g., Bonin et al.,

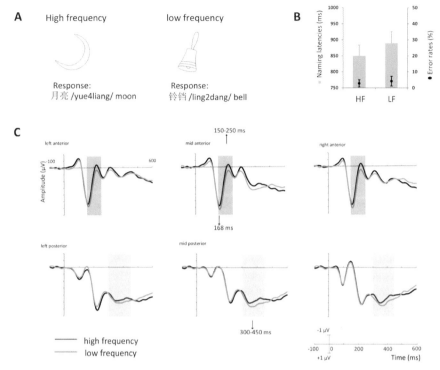

FIGURE 10.3   (A) Twenty-two participants were asked to write down the names of one hun-
dred fifty pictures, half of which had high-frequency and the other half low-
frequency names. (B) Behavioral data show a classical word frequency effect
on naming latencies (gray bars, left axis) or error rates (right axis). Error bars
represent 95% confidence intervals. Lf stands for low-frequency items and
HF for high-frequency items. (C) Grand average ERPs from 22 native Chinese
speakers for the high-frequency (black line) and low-frequency (gray line)
conditions at six ROIs: left-anterior (electrodes: F7, F5, FT7, FC5, FC3), mid-
anterior (F1, FZ, F2, FCZ, FC2, C1, CZ, C2), right-anterior (F4, F6, F8, FC4, FT8),
left-posterior (CP5, CP3, P5, P3, PO7, PO5), mid-posterior (CP1, CPZ, CP2, P1, PZ,
P2, PO3, POZ, PO4, O1, OZ, O2), and right-posterior (CP4, CP6, P4, P6, PO6, PO8).
Picture onset occurs at 0 ms. Low-frequency ERPs were significantly more
positive than high-frequency ERPs in two time windows (150–250 ms, purple
shading and 300–450 ms, blue shading). Low-frequency and high-frequency
ERPs diverged from each other as of 168ms after picture onset, indicating early
lexical access during written production.

2001; Chalard, Bonin, Méot, Boyer, & Fayol, 2003) the locus(i) impacted by this
factor has (have) been the object of intense debate for more than two decades.

It is widely accepted that conceptually driven written word production (sim-
ulated using a picture naming paradigm) involves three major levels of processing. Production begins with a communicative intention based on seman-

tic / conceptual processing. In picture naming, a processing level processes the visual characteristics of the picture, thus permitting access to a semantic / conceptual representation. This is the input for lexical access. It is generally accepted that lexical access involves two main steps: 1) access to lexical-semantic and syntactic information (lemma) and 2) retrieval of the wordform (lexeme) in the mental lexicon. A final processing level takes the form of the translation of the abstract (phonological or orthographical) surface codes into a set of commands that can be used directly by the neuromuscular system. The results reported by the studies that have attempted to identify the locus of influence of the AoA (see Juhasz, 2005, for an extensive review) tend toward the idea that each of the levels of processing—process of visual perception; semantic processing; lexical selection and the retrieval of the wordform—can be influenced by the age at which a word was learned.

Even if the hypothesis of multiple loci cannot be rejected a priori, it seems that the debate on the locus of AoA effects is due in part to the methodology used to explore the question. The majority of studies have been based on a task comparison strategy. The principle is to test the presence and / or absence of an influence of AoA in different tasks that have certain levels of processing in common. If an effect is reported for two tasks, then it is possible to assume that AoA impacts the common areas of processing. For example, authors (e.g., Johnston & Barry, 2005) have observed that the latencies in picture naming and semantic categorization tasks are influenced by the age at which a word is learned. It is generally accepted that the processes of visual perception and semantic processing are common to both tasks. Lexical access and motor programming are only present for picture naming, whereas the selection process is involved only in semantic categorization. An influence of AoA on processing times in the two tasks suggests that this factor affects common processing levels, i.e., visual processing and semantic processing.

However, this strategy raises both theoretical and methodological problems. First, it seems theoretically difficult to reject a priori the idea that certain processing levels are not involved in a task. Indeed, there are currently no empirical arguments in support of the idea that lexical access is never performed during a semantic decision task and therefore does not influence processing times. Secondly, this strategy relies in part on null hypothesis tests. Indeed, in order to exclude certain levels of processing, it is necessary to search for the absence of an effect. For example, to test whether AoA influences motor programming processes, participants can be asked to perform a delayed naming task. In this context, a picture is presented as a stimulus. Unlike the classic conditions of picture naming, the participants do not have to initiate their answers as quickly as possible but instead have to wait until a signal tells them that they can respond. If a non-significant effect is reported, this does not in any way exclude the level of motor preparation as the locus of AoA effects. It only makes it possible to indicate a statistical non-significance, the origin of which it is impossible to determine, e.g., due to inadequate statistical power, a real absence of effects, etc. Finally, the approach based on a comparison between tasks requires a high level of overall control of the variables. Indeed, it is necessary for all the factors that can influence the response latencies of each task to be properly controlled. This is a major difficulty for a variable such as AoA because it is quite highly correlated with many other variables (e.g., Chalard et al., 2003).

Recordings of electroencephalographic activity can be a tool that can be used to obtain additional evidence in support of this type of exploration of the locus of effects. The major problem that we have described above can be summarized as follows: the reaction time cannot be reliably divided into a time period that can be associated with the different processing levels. Consequently, alternative strategies have been developed. As described in the first part of this chapter, EEG methods make it possible to analyze activity during this period of time. Based on the timeframe proposals of Indefreys (2011), Perret et al. (2014) explored the issue of the locus of the AoA effect. These authors asked their participants to write down labels for 120 images. 60 of these had a name acquired early in childhood and the rest had a label acquired late. (e.g., Name Agreement, Image Agreement, Lexical Frequency, Number of letters, etc.). EEG activity was recorded during the participants' handwritten production.

Analyses were performed using the spatio-temporal segmentation described above. Using the concatenation procedure proposed by Laganaro and Perret (2011), the ERPs were segmented for the entire period from stimulus presentation through to time of response. A series of six stable electrophysiological configurations was observed for both types of words (Figure 10.4). This suggests that the same types of processing are involved in both experimental conditions. In addition, the segmentation was very similar to that reported by Perret & Laganaro (2012, see Figure 10.2). These authors showed that the EEG activity diverged between the two types of production approximately 260 ms after the presentation of the picture. According to Perret & Laganaro (2012), this suggests that the processes become specific as of the retrieval of the wordform in the mental lexicon. This proposal is based on the time period estimates made by Indefrey (2011) for spoken word production. The processes of visual perception (0–150 ms), semantic processing (150–180 ms) and access to lemmas (180–300 ms) are common to both production modalities, while access to lexemes (300–450 ms) and peripheral processing (450 ms—RT) is specific to each modality. Perret et al. (2014) observed that the duration of the period of sta-

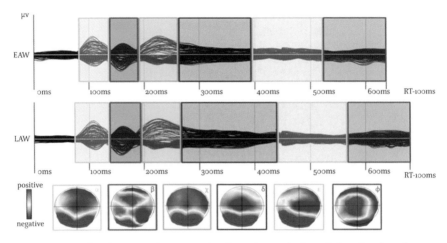

FIGURE 10.4   Spatio-temporal segmentation for early acquired words (EAW) and words
acquired late (LAW) in handwritten production from images

ble electrophysiological activity between 260 and 450 ms (map δ, Figure 10.4)
was directly impacted by AoA. Indeed, the difference in duration was found to
be about 40 ms. The increase in this time period also brings about a shift in
the following periods, albeit not of the same duration. This shift is reflected in
the classical analyses by the differences observed around 400 ms and 520 ms,
when the cerebral generators change in one condition (Early acquired words)
but not in the other (Late acquired words). In summary, thanks to the use of
EEG recordings and spatio-temporal segmentation, Perret et al. (2014) showed
that the recovery of the orthographic wordform is the only level of processing
directly impacted by the age at which a word was learned.

4   Conclusion

The aim of this chapter was to briefly present how EEG recordings can be used
to explore certain issues involved in the handwritten production of isolated
words. We hope to have convinced the reader of the value of EEG measurement, despite the difficulties inherent in it. As shown in the two examples
(Perret et al., 2014; Qu et al., 2016), the main advantage of this measure is
that it makes it possible to analyze with precision (of the order of a millisec-
ond) the time course of the cognitive processing operations and not only the
consequences—the reaction times or the errors—of the output produced by
the latter. However, just as latencies have never replaced error analysis (e.g.,
Goldrick & Larson, 2008), EEG recordings should be seen as an additional

source of information when exploring hypotheses. They are not a panacea for experimental psycholinguistics and have limitations. There are some areas where EEG recordings do not appear to be the most appropriate exploratory tool. For instance, this method cannot help us to explore the question of the transmission of the activation flow between processing levels. It seems difficult to explore the characteristics of the cascaded transmission of activation using EEG recordings (e.g., Kandel & Perret, 2015). Finally, it seems that this type of measure can be used to explore questions relating to linguistic units larger than the isolated word. For example, the different steps involved in the production of text (Olive, 2014) could be explored using a so-called long-term record (Michel et al., 2009) and analyses of spatio-temporal segmentation.

Acknowledgements

We acknowledge funding from the French Agence Nationale de la Recherche (ANR ECRIRE-14-CE30–0013) awarded to Cyril Perret and the National Natural Science Foundation of China (31400967) to Qingqing Qu.

References

Alario, F.-X., Ferrand, L. Laganaro, M., New, B., Frauenfelder, U.H., & Segui, J. (2004). Predictors of picture naming speed. *Behavior Research Methods, Instruments, and Computers, 36,* 140–155.

Alario, F.-X., Costa, A., & Caramazza, A. (2002). Frequency effects in noun phrase production: Implications for models of lexical access. *Language and Cognitive Processes, 17,* 299–319.

Barry, C., Morrison, C.M., & Ellis, A.W. (1997). Naming the Snodgrass and Vanderwart pictures: Effects of age of acquisition, frequency, and name agreement. *The Quarterly Journal of Experimental Psychology: Human Experimental Psychology, 50A,* 560–585.

Bates, E., D'Amico, S., Jacobsen, T., Szekely, A., Andonova, E., Devescovi, A., et al. (2003). Timed picture naming in seven languages. *Psychonomic Bulletin & Review, 10,* 344–380.

Berg, T. (2002). Slips of the typewriter key. *Applied Psycholinguistics, 23,* 185–207.

Berger, H. (1929). Uber das Elektrenkephalogramm des Menschen. *Arch. Psychiatrie Nerv. 87,* 527–570.

Bonin, P., & Fayol, M. (2000). Writing words from pictures: What representations are activated, and when? *Memory & Cognition, 28,* 677–689.

Bonin, P., Fayol, M., & Chalard, M. (2001). Age of acquisition and word frequency in written picture naming. *The Quarterly Journal of Experimental Psychology, 54A*, 469–489.

Brunet, D., Murray, M.M., & Michel, C.M. (2011). Spatiotemporal analysis of multichannel EEG: CARTOOL. *Computational Intelligence and Neuroscience, doi: 10.1155/2011/813870*

Chalard, M., Bonin, P., Méot, A., Boyer, B., & Fayol, M. (2003). Objective age-ofacquisition (AoA) norms for a set of 230 objects names in French: Relationships with psycholinguistic variables, the English data from Morrison et al. (1997), and naming latencies. *European Journal of Cognitive Psychology, 15*, 209–245.

Costa, A., Strijkers, K., Martin, C., & Thierry, G. (2009). The time course of word retrieval revealed by event related brain potentials during overt speech. *Proceedings of the National Academy of Sciences of the United States of America, 106*, 21442–21446.

Dien, J. (1998). Issues in the application of the average reference: Review, critiques, and recommendations. *Behavior Research Methods, Instruments & Computers, 30*, 34–43.

Donders, F.C. (1868). Die Schnelligkeit psychischer Prozesse. *Archiv für Anatomie und Physiologie und wissenschaftliche Medizin*, 657–681

Fayol, M., Hupet, M., & Largy, P. (1999). The acquisition of subject-verb agreement in written French: From novices to experts' errors. *Reading and Writing: An Interdisciplinary Journal, 11*, 153–174.

Forster, K.I., & Chambers, S.M. (1973). Lexical access and naming time. *Journal of Verbal Learning and Verbal Behavior, 12*, 627–635.

Goldrick, M., & Larson, M. (2008). Phonotactic probability influences speech production. *Cognition, 107*, 1155–1164.

Guthrie, D., & Buchwald, J.S. (1991). Significance testing of difference potentials. *Psychophysiology, 28*, 240–244.

Indefrey, P. (2011). The Spatial and Temporal Signatures of Word Production Components: A Critical Update. *Frontiers in Psychology, 2, 1–16. doi:10.3389/fpsyg.2011.00255*

Indefrey, P. & Levelt, W.J.M. (2004). The spatial and temporal signatures of word production components. *Cognition, 92*, 101–144.

Jescheniak, J.D., & Levelt, W.J.M. (1994). Word frequency effects in speech production: Retrieval of syntactic information and of phonological form. *Journal of Experimental Psychology: Learning, Memory, and Cognition, 20*, 824–843.

Jescheniak, J.D., Meyer, A.S., & Levelt, W.J.M. (2003). Specific-word frequency is not all that counts in speech production: Comments on Caramazza, Costa, et al. (2001) and new experimental data. *Journal of Experimental Psychology: Learning, Memory, and Cognition, 29*, 432–438.

Johnson, C.J., Paivio, A., & Clark, J.M. (1996). Cognitive components of picture naming. *Psychological Bulletin, 120*, 113–139.

Johnston, R.A., & Barry, C. (2005). Age of acquisition effects in the semantic processing of pictures. *Memory and Cognition, 33*, 905–912.

Juhasz, B.J. (2005) Age-of-acquisition effects in word and picture identification, *Psychological Bulletin, 131*, 684–712.

Kandel, S., & Perret, C. (2015). How does the interaction between spelling and motor processes build up during writing acquisition? *Cognition, 136*, 325–336.

Koenig, T., & Gianotti, L.R.R. (2009). Scalp field maps and their characterization. In C.M. Michel, T. Koening, D. Brandeis, L.R.R. Gianotti, & J. Wackermann (Eds.). *Electrical Neuroimaging* (pp. 25–47). Cambridge: Cambridge University Press.

Koenig, T., & Melie-Garcia, L. (2010). A method to determine the presence of averaged event-related fields using randomization tests. *Brain Topography, 23*, 233–242.

Koenig, T., Stein, M., Gieder, M., & Kottlow, M. (2014). A tutorial on data-driven methods for statistically assessing ERP topographies. *Brain Topography, 27*, 72–93.

Kroll, J.F., & Potter, M.C. (1984). Recognizing words, pictures, and concepts: A comparison of lexical, object, and reality decisions. *Journal of Verbal Learning and Verbal Behavior, 23*, 39–66.

Laganaro, M., & Perret, C. (2011). Comparing electrophysiological correlates of word production in immediate and delayed naming through the analysis of word age of acquisition effects. *Brain Topography, 24*, 19–29.

Lehmann, D. (1987). Principles of spatial analysis. In A.S. Gevins & A. Remond (Eds.). *Handbook of electroencephalography and clinical neurophysiology vol. 1: methods of analysis of brain electrical and magnetic signals* (pp. 309–354). Elsevier: Amsterdam.

Lehmann, D., & Skrandies, W. (1980). Reference-free identification of components of checkerboard-evoke multichannel potential fields. *Electroencephalography and Clinical Neurophysiology, 48*, 609–621.

Lehmann, D., & Skrandies, W. (1984). Spatial analysis of evoked potentials in man—a review. Progress in Neurobiology, 23, 227–250.

Luck, S.J. (2005). *An introduction to the event-related potential technique*, Cambridge, MIT Press.

Maess, B., Friederici, A., Damian, M.F., Meyer, A.S., & Levelt, W.J.M. (2002). Semantic category interference in overt picture naming: Sharpening current density localization by PCA. *Journal of Cognitive Neuroscience, 14*, 455–462.

Michel, C.M., Koenig, T., Brandeis, D. Gianotti, L.R.R., & Wackermann, J. (2009). *Electric neuroimaging*. Cambridge University Press: Cambridge.

Morton, J. (1969). Interaction of information in word recognition. *Psychological Review, 76*, 165–178.

Murray, M.M., Brunet, D., & Michel, C.M. (2008). Topographic ERP analyses: A step by-step tutorial review. *Brain Topography, 20*, 249–264.

Navarrete, E., Basagni, B., Alario, F.-X., Costa, A. (2006). Does word frequency affect lexical selection in speech production? *The Quarterly Journal of Experimental Psychology, 59*, 1681–1690.

Oldfield, R.C., & Wingfield, A. (1965). Response latencies in naming objects. *Quarterly Journal of Experimental Psychology, 17*, 273–281.

Olive, T. (2014). Toward a parallel and cascading model of the writing system: A review of research on writing processes coordination. *Journal of Writing Research, 6*, 173–194.

Olive, T., Kellogg, R.T., & Piolat, A. (2002). Studying text production with the triple task technique: Why and how? In T. Olive & C.M. Levy, C.M. (Eds.), *Contemporary tools and techniques for studying writing* (pp. 31–58). Dordrecht: Kluwer Academic Press.

Perret, C. & Laganaro, M. (2012). Comparison of electrophysiological correlates of writing and speaking: A topographic ERP analysis. *Brain Topography, 25*, 64–72.

Perret, C., Bonin, P., & Laganaro, M. (2014) Exploring the multiple-level hypothesis of AoA effects in spoken and written picture naming using a topographic ERP analysis. *Brain and Language, 135*, 20–31.

Pinet, S., Hamamé, C.M., Longcamp, M., Vidal, F., & Alario, F. (2015). Response planning in word typing: Evidence for inhibition. *Psychophysiology, 52*, 524–531.

Qu, Q., Zhang, Q., & Damian, M. (2016). Tracking the time course of lexical access in orthographic production: An event-related potential study of word frequency effects in written picture naming. *Brain & Language, 159*, 118–126.

Roux, J.-S., McKeeff, T.J., Grosjacques, G., Afonso, O., & Kandel, S. (2013). The interaction between central and peripheral processes in handwriting production. *Cognition, 127*, 235–241.

Strijkers, K., & Costa, A. (2011). Riding the lexical speedway: a critical review on the time course of lexical selection in speech production. *Frontiers in Psychology, 2*, 356. doi: 10.3389/fpsyg.2011.00356

Strijkers, K., Baus, C., Runnqvist, E., Fitzpatrick, I., & Costa, A. (2013). The temporal dynamics of first versus second language production. *Brain & Language, 127*, 6–11.

Strijkers, K., Costa, A., & Thierry, G. (2010). Tracking lexical access in speech production: electrophysiological correlates of word frequency and cognate effects. *Cerebral Cortex, 20*, 913–928.

Strijkers, K., Holcomb, P.J., & Costa, A. (2011). Conscious intention to speak proactively facilitates lexical access during overt object naming. *Journal of Memory and Language, 65*, 345–362.

Thierry, G., Cardebat, D., Demonet, J.F. (2003). Electrophysiological comparison of grammatical processing and semantic processing of single spoken nouns. *Brain Research, 17*, 535–547

PART 3

Conclusion

..

CHAPTER 11

Research on Written Word Production and Writing Research

Michel Fayol

1   Words, Still Words

In 1994, Balota wrote that "the word is as central to the psycholinguist as the cell is to biologist", and we could add as the atom to physicists. Ten years later (2004), Bonin edited a whole book devoted to the mental lexicon, extending the study of words in order to deal with the many types of representations associated with them: phonological, morphological, and orthographic representations. In 2017, words are again at the forefront of research in psycholinguistics, and both new data and new theoretical approaches are available. Why is this?

Over the last 20 years, researchers have investigated the production of isolated words, mainly nouns, in the oral modality, and more recently in writing. They have explored both the different levels of representations and the timing of their activations, using different tasks (e.g. picture naming, spelling to dictation, copying) and different procedures (e.g. SOA variations, EEG recording). The dominant theories of word production distinguish several, generally four, main levels of processing: conceptual preparation, formulation (i.e., grammatical encoding and phonological/orthographic encoding), and articulation. There is also general agreement that lexical access in speaking or writing can be subdivided into a phase that is concerned with the retrieval of semantic and syntactic characteristics (i.e., lemma) and a phase that involves access to the phonological and/or orthographic properties of the intended word (i.e., lexemes) (Bonin & Fayol, 2000; Levelt, Roelofs, & Meyer, 1999). In such models, words are the natural output of the production system. In picture naming, as well as in spelling to dictation, researchers have found a reliable frequency effect located at the orthographic level. By contrast, in the written modality, the consistency effect only appears in spelling-to-dictation tasks. More recently, the course of word production was explored using EEG (see Perret & Qu, this volume). The results confirmed that speaking and writing share the conceptual and lemma representations and start to diverge at around 260 ms (Indefrey, 2011), at the time of word-form encoding (see Bonin & Meot, this volume), and then at articulation. However, this is only the beginning of the story.

2   A Series of Questions

2.1   *The Phonological Mediation Hypothesis*

Most researchers have assumed that phonological mediation is systematic. However, some results from neuropsychology and from experimental studies that have focused on the production of isolated words have contradicted this assumption. As set out in Damian's chapter (this volume), a number of experiments suggest that phonological mediation is almost always involved, even in non-alphabetic systems. However, recent results based on the behaviour of baboons are worth considering here. These monkeys are able to learn isolated "words", and even orthographic regularities (i.e. sublexical sequences of letters; Pacton et al., this volume) without any phonological help (Grainger, Dufau, Montant, Ziegler, & Fagot, 2012). Most probably, human beings have inherited the same capacity, and can keep true words in temporary memory (i.e. graphemic buffer) while transcribing them without reference to the phonological forms of the same words. Another argument comes from developmental studies: When children start to use writing for the very first time, they use written forms and even written combinations of forms without any corresponding phonological forms (Gombert & Fayol, 1992; Pacton & Fayol, 2000; Treiman, 2017). The question is therefore: Is there a length limit for these words and letter combinations? What about series of words? Interestingly, to justify the mandatory character of phonological mediation, Damian refers to an argument that we will return to later: in habitual production activities, we rarely write isolated words. We generally produce clauses or sentences containing several words and this necessitates the phonological buffering of several lexical constituents while the slow process of written transcription takes place.

2.2   *The Relations between Central and Peripheral Processes*

The previous observation leads to a second question regarding the relations between central (e.g. orthographic representations) and peripheral (e.g. handwriting or typing) processes in written production. Spelling-to-dictation tasks provide evidence that two routes could be concurrently involved in written word production (Tainturier & Rapp, 2001). The first one, the lexical (or direct) route, directly retrieves lexical forms from memory and transcribes them: The more frequent the form, the faster the retrieval, and the shorter the latency before the beginning of writing is. The second starts with a phonological form, segments it into sublexical components of varying granularity (depending on expertise in reading and spelling), and maps the phonological segments with graphemic segments, the number of which depends on the written orthographic systems available to the writer (see Tainturier's BAST model, this volume). Written words correspond not simply to linear sequences of letters but to multidimensional structures. The impact of several different potential sublexical processing units has been studied in word reading: graphemes (Rey, Ziegler, & Jacobs, 2000), letter identities and positions (Grainger, Dufau, & Ziegler, 2016), and so on. Fewer studies are available on the impact of letter identities and word positions (Roux, McKeef, Grosjacques, Afonso, & Kandel, 2013) or sublexical units in written production: syllables and graphosyllables (Kandel, Herault, Grosjacques, Lambert, & Fayol, 2009; Kandel, Grosjacques, Peereman, & Fayol, 2011), bigrams and trigrams, geminates (Pacton et al., 2000; this volume), strokes (Kandel et al., 2009), etc. Most experiments report that the impact of central processes (e.g. consistency) cascades over the entire word.

The two routes are activated concurrently and compete at the level of the graphemic buffer (Delattre, Bonin, & Barry, 2006). Bonin and Meot (this volume) report that this competition only happens in spelling to dictation. When longer messages have to be written down from their phonological buffered format, their production very much seems to take the form of a (self-) spelling-to-dictation task (see Damian, this volume). As a consequence, it seems plausible that the two competing routes are involved in the production of habitual messages (e.g. emails). The spelling-to-dictation processing model might plausibly complement the picture of the naming/writing processing model of production in cases where the message contains multiple words and is too long to be temporarily stored in the written format in the graphemic buffer.

2.3   *The Limited Capacity of the Graphemic Buffer*

A third question has to do with the limited capacity of the graphemic buffer (or orthographic working memory: OWM) and the consequences that this limitation has for the peripheral processing of written production. Alfonso and Alvarez (this volume) claim that "central and peripheral processes influence each other" as they are engaged in parallel in written production. In order to make fluent production possible, people must distribute resources either automatically (e.g. handwriting) or strategically (e.g. processing of agreements) depending on the levels of representation that they are dealing with. Different signatures of this resource attribution can be seen in adult productions, from stroke durations to within-word pauses and pre-writing latencies. Alfonso and Alvarez (this volume) are right to question the comparability of these different measures and their relevance for studying any given situation. However, most studies deal with the impact of the limited OWM on the **management** of written production (Fayol, 1999). As far as we know, little research has explored the possible impact of this limited output capacity on higher-order processes: does this bottleneck have any negative effects on the management of agreement processes, syntactic planning, lexical choices, or even the conceptual organization of texts? Some years ago, Bourdin and Fayol (1994, 2002) provided evidence that children, and even adults, are sensitive to such limitations: e.g. word recall, sentence production, and text composition are negatively impacted by the use of unusual transcriptions tools (e.g. capital letters). Handwriting difficulties go at least some way to explaining the poor quality and the restricted length of children's texts in grades 1 to 3 (Fayol, 2012; Fayol, Foulin, Maggio, & Lété, 2011). This possible bottom-up effect of peripheral conditions on more central processes could help us understand and analyse the data reported in the various disorders described by Alfonso, Connelly, and Barrett (this volume).

3   Two Main Questions to Explore Further

3.1   *From Isolated Words to Sentence Production*
The first question relates to the fact that, most often, neither speakers nor writers produce single words. Instead, they combine words into larger utterances. For example, in French, even simple noun production involves one determinant followed by a noun (e.g. le chat; the cat) and only exceptionally a bare noun (e.g. cat) (Alario & Caramazza, 2002). It is thus necessary to study noun production in more realistic situations. Maggio et al. (2015) asked French adults to name pictures of objects with or without using determiners. They compared the time-course of the written production of bare nouns with that of noun phrases and measured pauses and writing rates in relation with reference to word-orthographic frequency, syllabic length and phoneme-to-grapheme consistency at the end of words. The results provide evidence that the noun production process begins as soon as production of the determiner is initiated (word frequency effect on latencies, length and consistency effects on determiner writing rate) and continues during the course of noun transcription. Some form of parallel processing occurs in written word production.

There are two ways in which researchers move from the study of single-word production to that of the production of multiword utterances. The more traditional approach investigates the production of sequences of two or three words, and so on, while manipulating the relationships between the successive stimuli: associative versus categorical relations, phonological versus orthographic overlap, etc. (Roux & Bonin, 2012). Currently, most results come from the study of the oral or written production of multi-word juxtapositions. The main question relates to the simultaneity versus sequentiality of activation of the representations of the different words (Bonin, Mallardier, Meot, & Fayol, 2006). An integrative model suggests that in such cases, all lemmas are selected before speech onset but only the initial lexeme of the series is activated (Bürki, Sadat, Dubarry, & Alario, 2016). Considerable caution must be exercised before attempting to extend this conclusion to longer messages.

The second approach tries to integrate two dimensions of language production, namely lexical and syntactic. When people produce a message, they decide what they want to say and how they want to say it; they then have to map conceptual representations onto language (Konopka & Meyer, 2014). This mapping has two aspects: the mapping from concepts to lemmas for content words, on the one hand, and the mapping of thematic roles (agent and patient) onto function assignment, thus leading to the linearization of sentence structures (e.g. active versus passive forms), on the other. Using a lexical priming paradigm that opposed easy and hard-to-code items (Experiment 1) and a syntactic priming paradigm (Experiment 2: active versus passive structures; Bock, Dell, Chang, & Onishi, 2007), Konopka and Meyer studied the on-line linearization of messages describing two interacting characters (e.g. The dog is chasing the mailman). They reported flexibility in planning, e.g. the patient prime was stronger in events with harder-to-name agents, with a general trend for participants to complete easier processes before harder ones (i.e. the minimal load principle evoked by Levelt, 1989). These results and a series of others provide evidence for independent and interacting contributions of lexical and syntactic dimensions in sentence planning, leading to increased efficiency (i.e. speed and fluency) in sentence production. Interestingly, these two dimensions should sometimes compete, and this competition likely entails observable traces: errors, re-initialization, hesitations. Combining priming and SOA variations could help index this phenomenon.

3.2 A Step Further: from Word Production to Text Production

Online studies of written text composition have analysed temporal parameters, and pause durations in particular, under the assumption that pause durations reflect the planning cost of the next segments. Writing rates have rarely been considered. In addition, the lexical and sublexical levels have been almost systematically ignored in text production models despite the fact that it is impossible to ignore them in any model of language perception and production (Alamargot & Chanquoy, 2001). Because working memory demands imposed by text-production processes are different from those imposed by single-word production processes, different effects are expected when writers produce more than a single word at a time. In addition, in written composition, it seems highly plausible that parallel processing occurs, for example planning during writing (for a review, see Olive, 2014). Indeed, handwriting is far slower than speaking, potentially leaving room for modulations of the production rhythm, and making it possible to re-read and control the forms that have already been produced (Chanquoy, Foulin, & Fayol, 1990; Schilperoord, 2002). Pause duration and speed of writing could thus be modulated by the load imposed by the processing of what has already been written (e.g. revising) or what is to be transcribed (e.g. accessing the lexeme of the next word) (Roux et al., 2013).

Following Kliegl, Nuthmann and Engbert's (2006) study of the dynamics of reading, Maggio, Lété, Chenu, Jisa and Fayol (2012) tried to "track the mind" during text composition. They measured pause durations between words, pause durations within words, and word writing rates (the variations of which were weakly correlated, suggesting that they were sensitive to different variables). They predicted the variations of these parameters using regression analyses which took account of attested lexical and sublexical variables (frequency, consistency, neighbourhood, word length, word rank, etc.; Fayol & Lété, 2012). They then tracked the dynamics of composing by searching for delayed, anticipatory and immediate effects. This was done by introducing the characteristics of words n, n-1 and $n+1$. To our knowledge, this was the first attempt to bring together data from word studies and issues from text production. The question was: how do people manage the word production processes (i.e. moving from a word to the following word) while they are composing meaningful texts.

The data show that, when composing texts, the mind usually processes several words in parallel together with various dimensions of these words, with the impact being observed at the level of between-word pauses, intra-word pauses, and writing rate. In addition, processes are characterized by a cognitive lag between the cognitive and linguistic operations related to the word and its graphic production, contrary to the assumptions of the immediacy-of-processing models. Some results are worth noting because they are discrepant from the data. First, the between-word pauses are associated only with the characteristics of the previous word: The simpler the word that has just been transcribed—the shorter and the more embedded within a large neighbourhood it is—the shorter the pause, as if either the control and/or the subsequent cognitive effort were reduced. The fact that writing rates and internal word pauses are sensitive to the characteristics of both the current and the next word suggests that these two words are at least partially processed in parallel. The more frequent and the longer the current word is, the faster the writing rate; the more consistent and frequent the word form, the shorter the internal word pause. Overall, the data show the complexity of the dynamics of written production and the difficulty of unambiguously revealing the nature of the cognitive processes thought to be captured in our three chronometric measures.

4   A Few Words to Conclude

To quote Eleanor Rosch, the word is, so to speak, a "natural category" worthy of exploration. This exploration can take two different directions.

On the one hand, it is possible to analyse the components of written words (things are not so clear and simple with regard to the status of words in the oral modality, especially in French, due to the fuzzy boundaries between words; e.g. /lezarbrabaty/ corresponding to the written "les arbres abattus" [the felled trees]). Written words correspond not simply to linear sequences of letters but to multidimensional structures: they are complex structures embedding several potential processing units: strokes, graphemes, syllables, graphotactic regularities, morphemes, and so on. Most of them have been identified and their "behaviour" has been studied in isolated word production. However, a range of studies are still required in order to determine whether and how they contribute, either independently or concurrently, to variations in the production of isolated words. Most probably, variations in pauses, rates, etc. are highly correlated, but how are they distributed as a function of letters and their positions in words (e.g. see Kandel et al 2011 regarding the control of bigram frequencies in order to study the impact of syllables)? Another set of questions must be addressed concerning the way in which these subunits are processed when larger segments are to be produced (e.g. clauses, sentences, texts) (see Maggio et al., 2012, for example). Are some of them specifically affected when people concurrently write a word *n* and plan the transcription of the orthographic form of the following word *n* + *1*? Is there any flexibility in this type of resource allocation? Does this change when children's graphic activities become automated? And what happens in the case of language disorders (e.g. dysgraphia, SLI)?

At the same time, words are processing units. A number of results suggest that concepts are mapped onto lemmas, which are selected first before the activation of lexemes, i.e. phonological and/or orthographic forms (Levelt et al., 1999). This conception works well with clauses and isolated sentences. Things are not so simple at the level of text production. For example, in narratives, the hero is the main character and his/her name (i.e. lexeme) is repeatedly used or replaced by pronouns. How do writers manage situations such as this on line? Chanquoy et al. (1990) and Fayol et al. (2011) have started to explore this question, although the vast majority of the work remains to be done, while Maggio et al. (2012) have developed a paradigm to deal with this question.

It goes without saying that words will be necessary in the future for the production of texts as well as in order to describe how people act when doing this.

References

Afonso, O. & Alvarez, J.C. (this volume). Measuring writing durations in handwriting research: What do they tell us about the spelling process?

Afonso, O., Connelly, V., & Barnett, A. (this volume). Struggling with writing: An examination of writing difficulties in Specific Languag Impairment, Developmental Dyslexia and Developmental Coordination Disorder.

Alamargot, D., & Chanquoy, L. (2001). *Through the models of writing*. Dordrecht: The Netherlands: Kluwer Academic Publishers.

Alario, F.-X., & Caramazza, A. (2002). The production of determiners: Evidence from French. *Cognition, 82* (3), 179–223.

Bock, K., Dell, G.S., Chang, F., & Onishi, K.H. (2007). Persistent structural priming from language comprehension to language production. *Cognition, 104*, 437–458.

Balota, D.A. (1994). Visual word recognition: The journey from features to meaning. In M.A. Gernsbacher (Ed.), *Handbook of psycholinguistics* (pp. 303–348). San Diego, CA: Academic Press.

Bonin, P. (2004). *Mental lexicon*. New York: Nova Science Publishers.

Bonin, P., & Fayol, M. (2000). Writing words from pictures: What representations are activated and when? *Memory and Cognition, 28*, 677–689.

Bonin, P., & Méot, A. (this volume). Task differences and individual differences in skilled spelling.

Bonin, P., Mallardier, N., Méot, A., & Fayol, M. (2006). The scope of advance planning in written picture naming. *Language and Cognitive Processes, 21*, 205–237.

Bourdin, B. & Fayol, M. (1994). Is written language production really more difficult than oral language production? *International Journal of Psychology, 29*, 591–620.

Bourdin, B. & Fayol, M. (2002). Even in adults, written production is still more costly than oral production. *International Journal of Psychology, 37*, 219–227.

Bürki, A., Sadat, J., Dubarry, A.-S., & Alario, F.-X. (2016). Sequential processing during noun phrase production. *Cognition, 146*, 90–99.

Chanquoy, L., Foulin, J.-N., & Fayol, M. (1990). The temporal management of short text writing by children and adults. *European Bulletin of Cognitive Psychology, 10*, 513–540.

Damian, M. (this volume). A role of phonology in orthographic production? A historical prespective and some rencent new evidence.

Delattre, M., Bonin, P., & Barry, C. (2006). Written spelling to dictation: Sound-to spelling regularity affects both writing latencies and durations. *Journal of Experimental Psychology: Learning, Memory, and Cognition, 32*, 1330–1340.

Fayol, M. (1999). From on-line management problems to strategies in written composition. In M. Torrance & G. Jeffery (Ed.), *The cognitive demands of writing*. Amsterdam: Amsterdam University Press.

Fayol, M. (2012). Cognitive processes of children and adults in translating thoughts into written language in real time. In V.W. Berninger (Ed.), *Past, present, and future contributions of cognitive writing research to cognitive psychology* (pp. 27–39). New York: Psychology Press.

Fayol, M., Foulin, J.-N., Maggio, S., & Lété, B. (2011). Towards a dynamic approach of how children and adults manage text production. In Grigorenko, E., Mambrino, E. & Preiss, D.D. (Eds.). *Handbook of writing: a mosaic of perspectives.* (pp. 141–158) New York: Psychology Press.

Fayol, M. & Lété, B. (2012). Contributions of online studies to understanding translation from ideas to written text. In M. Fayol, D. Alamargot, & V. Berninger, V. (2012). *Translation of thoughts to written text while composing: Advancing theory, knowledge, methods, and applications (pp. 289–313).* New York: Psychology Press.

Gombert, J.-E. & Fayol, M. (1992). Writing in preliterate children. *Learning and Instruction, 2,* 23–41

Grainger, J., Dufau, S., Montant, M., Ziegler, J.C., & Fagot, J. (2012). Orthographic processing in baboons (Papio papio). *Science, 336,* 245–248.

Grainger, J., Dufau, S., & Ziegler, J.C. (2016). A vision of reading. *Trends in Cognitive Science, 20,* 171–179.

Indefrey, P. (2011). The spatial and temporal signatures of word production components: A critical update. *Frontiers in Psychology, 2, 1–16. doi:10.3389/fpsyg.2011 .00255.*

Kandel, S., Herault, L., Grosjacques, G., Lambert, E., & Fayol, M. (2009). Orthographic vs. phonologic syllables in handwriting production. *Cognition, 110,3,* 440–444.

Kandel, S., Grosjacques, G., Peereman, R., & Fayol, M. (2011). The syllable-bigram controversy in handwriting production. *Journal of Experimental Psychology: Human Perception and Performance, 37 (4),* 1310–1322.

Kliegl, R., Nuthmann, A., & Engbert, R. (2006). Tracking the mind during reading: The influence of past, present, and future words on fixation duration. *Journal of Experimental Psychology: General, 135,* 12–35.

Konopka, A.E., & Meyer, A.S. (2014). Priming sentence planning. *Cognitive Psychology, 73,* 1–40.

Levelt, W.J.M. (1989). *Speaking: From intention to articulation.* Cambridge, MA: MIT Press.

Levelt, W.J.M., Roelofs, A., & Meyer, A.S. (1999). A theory of lexical access in speech production. *Brain and Behavioral Sciences, 22,* 1–75.

Maggio, S., Lété, B., Chenu, F., Jisa, H., & Fayol, M. (2012). Tracking the mind during writing: Immediacy, Delayed, and Anticipatory Effects on Pauses and Writing Rate. *Reading and Writing, 25,* 2131–2151

Maggio, S., Chenu, F., Bes De Bec, G., Pesci, B., Lété, B., Jisa, H., & Fayol, M. (2015). Producing written noun phrases in French. *Written Language and Literacy, 18,* 1–24.

Olive, T. (2014). Toward a parallel and cascading model of the writing system. *Journal of Writing Research, 6,* 173–194.

Pacton, S. & Fayol, M. (2000). The impact of phonological cues on children's judgments of nonwords plausibility: the case of double letters. *Current Psychological Letter, 1,* 39–54.

Pacton, S., Fayol, M., Nys, M., & Peereman, R. (this volume). Implicit statistical learning of graphotactic knowledge and lexical orthographic acquisition.

Perret, C. & Qu, Q. (this volume). EEG methods of exploring handwriting.

Rey, A., Ziegler, J.C., & Jacobs, A.M. (2000). Graphemes as perceptual reading units. *Cognition, 74,* 1–12.

Roux, S., & Bonin, P. (2012). Cascaded processing in written naming: Evidence from the picture-picture interference paradigm. *Language and Cognitive Processes, 27,* 734–769

Roux, S., McKeef, T.J., Grosjacques, G., Alfonso, O., & Kandel, S. (2013). The interaction between central and peripheral processes in handwriting production. *Cognition, 127,* 235–241.

Schilperoord, J. (2002). On the cognitive status of pauses in discourse production. In T. Olive & C.M. Levy (Eds.), *Contemporary tools and techniques for studying writing* (pp. 61–90). Dordrecht, The Netherlands: Kluwer Academic Publisher.

Tainturier, M.-J. & Rapp, B. (2001). The spelling process. In B. Rapp (Ed.), *The handbook of cognitive neuropsychology* (pp. 263–289). Hove, UK: Psychology Press.

Treiman, R. (2017). Learning to spell: Phonology and beyond. *Cognitive Neuropsychology, 22,* 83–93.

CHAPTER 12

Writing Research in the 21st Century

Brenda Rapp

Written language is considered among the greatest of human inventions, both for the impact it has had on the advancement of human civilization and, arguably, for what it reveals about the evolution of the human mind.

With regard to the progress of human civilization, written language allowed for the communication of human knowledge across space and time, independently of the individuals who generated the information and ideas. The written word could be transported across cities and countries, allowing for the spread of information and ideas and, furthermore, it could be preserved indefinitely, well beyond the lifespan of the individuals who were the source of the information. This allowed for the accumulation of knowledge that was needed for the development commerce, literature and science, the cornerstones of civilization as we know it.

With regard to the evolution of the human mind, the invention of written language constitutes a leap in human symbolic capacities. Spoken language most certainly represents the single greatest advance in human cognition, allowing for abstraction over the myriad tokens of human experience. It does so with the representation of concepts and ideas via generative systems for words and sentences that allow for the uniquely human capacity for nuanced thinking and communication. Written language represents a second order abstraction over the abstraction of spoken language. It does so, because written codes provide an abstraction over the sounds, morphemes, and words of spoken language. For example, letters are abstract symbols unifying sometimes mutually unintelligible sound differences across dialects and even, in some cases, providing for a common representation of the morphological structure of words, invariant to sound differences (e.g., the English plural /dogz/ and /kats/ → dogS and catS; Haley & Chomsky, 1968). Written language may well correspond to our most abstract, symbolic code, a representational system that is in a non-analog relation with the perceptual-motor experiences that written language is able to represent.

Having briefly summarized the very significant place that written language holds in human experience, in this chapter I will first review why it is that research on writing is important and then I will go on to discuss how writing research can make progress as we move forward into the 21st century.

1   Why Writing Research Matters

1.1   *Increasing Use of Written Language in the Age of E-communication*
Despite the clear importance of written language in the development of modern civilization it is fair to ask if written language continues to be important in the current age of e-communication with the increasing sophistication and availability of voice recognition systems. However, if we look around us we see people focused on their phones and other electronic devices, busily writing and sending messages and information. This suggests that, quite possibly, people are producing written language more than ever before.

To examine the issue of human communication modalities, we recently carried out a study (Rapp, Shea & Wiley, in preparation) which involved a language use survey using Mechanical Turk. We asked participants to carry out pairwise rankings of different types of communication: electronic and non-electronic, spoken and written language. Spoken-non-electronic communication is listening or talking in person, while spoken-electronic communication includes device-based spoken language (phone, TV, radio, movie, online videos, podcasts, Skype, etc.). Written-non-electronic includes reading or writing on paper (books, magazines, letters, etc.) whereas written-electronic includes reading or typing in electronic media (texting, e-mail, websites, online chatting, word processing, etc.). Results, as can be seen in Figure 12.1, reveal a shift from older to younger individuals in the use of written-electronic communication. In the older, 36+ age group, it is less used than spoken-non-electronic and is comparable to spoken-electronic. However, in the younger 18–25 year old group, written-electronic constitutes the most common communication modality, surpassing even in-person listening and talking. These results indicate that younger individuals are shifting to increasing written language use because of increasing use of electronic media.

These results are among the first to quantify the growing importance of written language communication in the current communication environment. Clearly, written language is increasingly vital in everyday life, both for professional success and also as a primary means of communication with friends and family. Given this, research on writing will be increasingly important in order to better understand the writing process so as to optimize how we teach writing and remediate writing in cases of developmental and acquired impairments.

1.2   *Written Language: a Window into Foundational Issues in Mind and
         Brain*
In addition to the important pragmatic importance of writing research, there are also the important opportunities that writing provides as a window onto

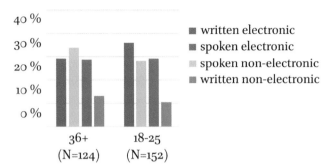

FIGURE 12.1   Distribution of language use of electronic and non-
electronic written and spoken communication in
daily life, for an older (age 36+) and younger group
of participants ages (18–25). The results show a shift
to increasing use of written electronic communication over face-to-face spoken and spoken electronic
communication. See text for details

long-standing issues for our understanding of the human mind/brain. Here
I briefly summarize three foundational issues that are illustrated by writing
research described in this volume.

1.2.1   Interactivity and Modularity

Since the beginning of modern neuroscience, debate has raged regarding
whether representation and processing are carried out in the human brain/
mind in a holistic (interactive) manner or whether there is specialization of
function (modularity) (Finger, 2001). This debate regarding the fundamental
character of cognitive computation has continued over the past two centuries,
with the focus shifting depending on the data and scientific methods of each
period. Writing provides a domain that is rich with important opportunities
to examine and shed light on this issue. In the context of the writing process,
this issue can be considered in terms of understanding the degree of interactiv-
ity/modularity *across* writing and other cognitive systems, as well as in terms
of the interactivity/modularity *within* the writing system itself.

   Writing provides an opportunity to understand the extent to which different
cognitive systems interact. The question is: Can we understand writing without reference to other cognitive systems, such as speech, reading, motor and
visual perception? The answer to this question illuminates the degree to which
cognitive functions are fundamentally interactive and integrated. This issue is
considered by Afonso, et al. (Chapter 6, this volume) who evaluate the extent to
which difficulties in the acquisition of writing necessarily co-occur with developmental deficits in other cognitive domains: spoken language, reading and

motor functions. These authors review evidence regarding the co-occurrence of developmental dysgraphia with Specific Language Impairment, developmental dyslexia and developmental coordination disorder. Turning to the question of interactivity and modularity in the adult system, Wamain (Chapter 5, this volume) considers the degree and nature of the of interaction between perceptual (reading) and motor (writing) systems, specifically evaluating the extent to which letter recognition and reading are influenced by information regarding the motor characteristics of letters. Damian (Chapter 2, this volume) examines evidence regarding the interaction between spoken and written language in word production.

Considerable research has also been directed at understanding the interactivity/ modularity of the subcomponents of the writing system. This work has attempted to determine the extent to which the different writing processes/subcomponents interact with one another via mechanisms such as feedback or cascading activation. For example, Afonso & Alvarez (Chapter 8, this volume) focus on the interaction between central spelling and peripheral writing processes. Central processes include such things as lexical and sublexical processes while peripheral ones include the multiple processes involved in producing letter shapes. On the modular view, peripheral writing processes commence only once central spelling processes are completed, operating independently of one another. In contrast, on an interactive view, peripheral and central processes interact with one another via cascading activation and/or feedback. In a quite different context, Tainturier (Chapter 4, this volume) considers the interactivity vs. modularity of spelling processes in bilingual individuals. On the one hand, bilingual individuals are able to write without words intruding from one language to the other, indicating functional specialization and modularity. On the other hand, there are various findings indicating that spelling knowledge is shared and interacts across scripts, especially those that share similar words (cognates) and similar scripts. Understanding the bilingual spelling system requires accounting for and reconciling these findings.

1.2.2   Neuroplasticity and Neuronal Recycling

Written language is a relatively recent human invention, with its roots approximately 6,000 years ago, and it is a skill that has been mastered by large segments of the human population only in the last 50 years. In this regard it differs from other cognitive skills such as speaking, visual object recognition, navigation, spatial attention that have been part of the human repertoire for tens of thousands of years. As a consequence, unlike evolutionarily older skills, written language has not had the opportunity to influence the human genome and its neuronal circuitry is not dictated by our genetic blueprint. This raises the important question of how the human brain incorporates recently acquired cognitive skills, namely: Do evolutionarily recent skills have dedicated neural substrates, or are they parasitic on the substrates of evolutionarily older skills? One view, referred to by Dehaene (2009) as "neuronal recycling" posits that written language is instantiated in neural substrates originally designed by the genetic blueprint for other cognitive skills but which has been repurposed for written language. Specifically in the context of writing, this issue has been examined by considered the extent to which written language production is parasitic on spoken language production. Damian (Chapter 2, this volume) reviews findings from psycholinguistics and cognitive neuropsychology that specifically relate to this question. One hypothesis is that production of a written word requires prior retrieval of its spoken form, while another hypothesis—Orthographic Autonomy—posits that written and spoken word production can occur independently of one another (Rapp, Benzing, & Caramazza, 1997). While the neuropsychological and psycholinguistic data provide strong evidence indicating that the modalities can act independently of one another, Damian considers conditions under which interactions between the modalities may occur. In other words, modularity and interactivity may coexist, influenced by factors such as the time point during production, the characteristics of scripts (e.g., English vs. Chinese), or in multi-word writing.

1.2.3   Embodied Cognition and the Question of Abstraction
A foundational issue in cognitive and brain sciences concerns the extent to which human cognition can be understood as the reactivation of sensory and motor brain states encoded during previous experiences. In this context, two opposing hypotheses correspond to the embodied cognition and abstractionist positions. According to the embodied cognition hypothesis, a concept consists only of the reactivation of sensory, emotional motor experiences associated with the concept, whereas abstractionist views hold that at least some aspects of human knowledge involve abstract (amodal) representations that are distinct from sensory-motor memories. Writing provides significant opportunities to contribute to this issue because letters have been posited to have multiple modalities of representation: visual, phonological, motor and abstract. Cognitive neuropsychological evidence from individuals with acquired dysgraphia (e.g., Rapp & Caramazza, 1997) and neuroimaging data (e.g., Rapp & Dufor, 2011) have provided strong support for the view that our knowledge of spellings of words is encoded in abstract, symbolic letter representations that lack form, sound or motor information. Nonetheless, it is still important to understand the extent to which sensory-motor information can contribute to letter processing.

Wamain (Chapter 5, this volume) specifically considers methods and findings relevant to addressing the question of whether—as would be predicted by the embodied cognition position—memories of the movements involved in writing a letter play a necessary role in the visual perception and recognition of letters.

This section has provided examples of how writing research is not only important for practical reasons, but also provides an extraordinarily rich domain within which to address fundamental issues of human cognition. The findings reviewed and discussed in the chapters of this volume reveal that the answers are unlikely to be simple. In other words, although dichotomous, opposing views have dominated these debates, the findings indicate a more complex picture. In all likelihood, modularity and interactivity coexist, as do abstract representations and sensori-motor interactions and while the neuroplastic capacities of the brain are striking, they operate within the constraints of a genetically-based brain design. Writing research can continue to contribute to our more detailed understanding of these and other key issues.

2   The Way Forward: Multiple Methods, Multiple Constraints

The way forward undoubtedly involves the use of multiple experimental methods to generate multiple constraints on our understanding of the writing process. It is abundantly clear from the chapters in this volume that cognitive, behavioral research is leading the way. It has provided an extraordinarily rich source of experimental paradigms and empirical findings about written language production. These have transformed our understanding of writing from what could be gained from superficial observation to a highly detailed understanding based on sophisticated experimentation. Paradigms include picture word interference approaches in which the timing of interference is manipulated to examine the time-course of writing, Stroop, cross-modal priming and even visual world paradigms in which eye movements to different written words are tracked. Dependent variables have expanded to include not only writing response times and errors, but also writing duration, inter-letter intervals, mean stroke durations and letter durations. These have allowed an understanding of writing that extends from an understanding of "architectural" aspects of the writing process—the subcomponents of the writing and their relations with one another and with other cognitive processes—to an understanding of the detailed nature of our knowledge of the statistical regularities of letter strings and how this changes across development (Pacton et al., Chapter 3, this volume) and even how our knowledge of letter shapes and our application of a grammar of action allow us to produce letters which are both recognizable to most readers and yet also distinctive for each writer (Séraphin-Thibon, et al., Chapter 9, this volume).

In the following sections I briefly discuss the role in writing research of other methods such as neuroimaging, study of acquired and developmental deficits and computational modeling.

2.1   *The Neural Bases of Writing and the Role of Neuroimaging Data*

Written language production is the least researched of the language modalities. Until recently it was largely neglected compared to spoken language comprehension and production and written language comprehension (reading). This has been especially true in terms of neuroimaging research.

Nonetheless, there have been two relatively recent meta-analyses of neuroimaging studies of spelling that summarize the existing neuroimaging studies of spelling (Purcell, Turkeltaub, Eden, & Rapp, 2011 and Planton, Jucla, Roux, & Démonet, 2013). Figure 12.2 depicts results from the Purcell et al. meta-analysis of 11 studies regarding the central processes of spelling. This meta-analysis identifies areas that are likely to correspond to activation peaks across studies, yielding the following 6 key nodes of the spelling network: left inferior frontal gyrus (IFG), left anterior cingulate, left superior parietal lobule/intraparietal sulcus, left and right superior temporal gyrus and the left fusiform/inferior temporal gyrus. The Planton, et al. (2013) meta-analysis of 18 studies had the additional goal of identifying the neural substrates of handwriting. In addition to the areas that Purcell et al. (2011) associated with central spelling processes, Planton et al. (2013) found activation likelihood peaks associated with written production processes in: left sensori-motor cortex, right cerebellum, thalamus, putamen as well as in bilateral superior frontal sulci and left SMA and pre-SMA.

In addition to identifying the brain bases of spelling, what can we learn from findings such as those depicted in Figure 12.2? From a cognitive perspective, the identification of neuro-topographically distinct brain areas indicates (not surprisingly) that spelling is a complex process likely composed of multiple sub-processes supported by different neural substrates. In addition, based on the neural locations of the activation clusters we may gain additional information regarding the nature of the cognitive operations carried out by the sub-processes. With fMRI data,this will be possible only to the extent to which we have independent evidence and confidence regarding the cognitive functions of the specific regions in which the nodes of the spelling network are located. For example, the fact that there is a node in the left superior parietal lobule/intraparietal sulcus indicates the involvement of spatial attention and/or working memory, while the left fusiform suggests high-level visual or visual

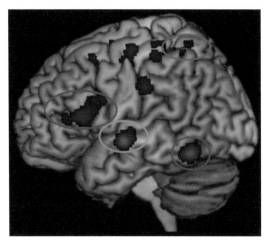

FIGURE 12.2   Key nodes of the central components
of the spelling process (adapted from
the Purcell et al. (2011) meta-analysis of
neuroimaging studies of spelling). Red
circles indicate nodes most closely associated with frequency but not length
effects and the blue circle indicates
the node most closely associated with
word length but not frequency effects
as reported in Rapp & Lipka (2011) and
Rapp & Dufor (2011). The green circle
marks the node most closely associated
with sound-to-spelling conversion as
reported in Ludersdorfer, et al. (2015).

word form representations (Cohen, et al., 2002). Although informative, additional more specifically targeted investigations are needed to further our understanding of the nature of the processes supported by the nodes of the spelling
network. One source of additional evidence comes from neuroimaging studies
of spelling that are specifically designed to identify the possible neural substrates of the multiple cognitive components of spelling such as those depicted
in Figure 12.3 (see also, Bonin and Meot, this volume). In this regard, there have
been only a handful of fMRI studies that have investigated the neural substrates
of specific sub-processes of spelling, including: orthographic long-term memory (Orthographic Lexicon), orthographic working memory (graphemic buffer)
and the phonology-orthography conversion (sound-to-spelling conversion process).

Rapp & Lipka (2011) and Rapp & Dufor (2011) attempted to identify the neural substrates supporting orthographic LTM and orthographic WM by manip-

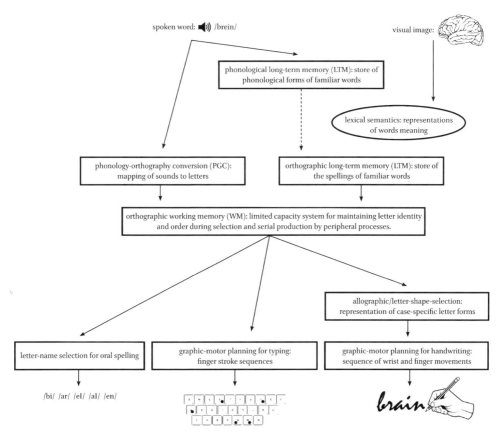

FIGURE 12.3   Schematic depiction of the functional architecture of the spelling process, including sub-components and their relationships (from Rapp & Damian, 2018)

ulating the variables that these processes are known to be most sensitive to. Orthographic LTM, as the system responsible for the LTM storage and retrieval of word spellings, is sensitive to the frequency of usage of different words although relatively insensitive to their length (in terms of number of letters). In contrast, Orthographic WM is sensitive to the length of words and relatively insensitive to their frequency (see Buchwald & Rapp 2009, for empirical support for these distinctions). Rapp and colleagues examined the brain responses of participants performing spelling tasks during fMRI scanning while varying the length and frequency of the word stimuli, in order to determine if there are brain regions sensitive to one of these variables but not the other. In fact, they identified regions that have a strong correspondence to specific areas that were identified in the meta-analysis of the spelling network. Figure 12.2, indicates (in red) areas sensitive to word frequency but not length and (in blue) areas sensitive to length but not frequency. In this way, the neural data provide convergence with the behaviorally based evidence indicating distinct orthographic LTM and WM sub-components within the cognitive system for spelling.

The sound-to-spelling conversion process generates possible spelling for speech sounds based on knowledge of the systematic relationships between speech sounds and letters that is acquired while learning how to spell words of one's language. For unfamiliar words, or words whose spellings may not have been previously encountered, this process generates spellings which would be plausible although they may not necessarily correspond to the spelling designated by the language. For example, for the sounds /yot/ the system may generate spelling such as YOT, YAT, YAUGHT, but would be very unlikely to generate the actual spelling YACHT. Different languages vary in terms of the degree to which the spellings of words can be correctly predicted or generated from sound to spelling conversion processing. Some languages, such as Finnish, have highly predictable spellings and are considered to be "transparent scripts", while others have intermediate transparency such as English and yet others are highly opaque such as Chinese. Interestingly, research has shown that spelling systems include both Orthographic LTM and sound-to-spelling conversion processes, despite dramatic differences in the transparency/opacity of their scripts (for a review, see Rapp & Damian, 2018). Ludersdorfer, Kronbichler, & Wimmer (2015) attempted to identify the neural substrates of sound-to-spelling conversion through fMRI scanning during word and pseudoword spelling tasks in German (a highly transparent language). The key activation sites they identified were quite consistent with the nodes of the spelling network (in green) in the Figure 12.2 (but see DeMarco, Wilson, Rising, Rapcsak, & Beeson, 2017).

The spatial precision of fMRI allows for neurotopographical dissociations and associations of brain responses according to task and stimulus parameters that, in turn, provide important information regarding the content and organization of the cognitive operations supported by specific brain areas. Another type of evidence is provided by techniques with high temporal resolution, such as EEG and MEG. Perret & Qu (Chapter 10, this volume) cogently argue that an important limitation of reaction time approaches is that they have access only to the "consequences" of processing and that task and stimulus comparisons are required to elucidate the multiple processes that contributed to a set of RTS. In contrast, approaches such as EEG and MEG (despite their own limitations) allow for the examination of the time-course of processing as it unfolds. This provides a powerful method for examining the multiple processes of spelling that may be initiated at different (and possible overlapping) time points. These can be identified by, among other things, determining the point in time at which different stimulus dimensions produce divergent brain responses. For example, in Figure 10.4 C Perret & Qu (this volume) depict the divergence of the brain response to low and high frequency words. In a manner analogous to the role of the spatial location of activity in fMRI, the time window in which an effect occurs in EEG contributes to the interpretation of the effect. This is possible only to the extent to which we have independent evidence and confidence regarding the cognitive functions that occur within specific time windows. For example, in the case described by Perret & Qu, the divergence of high and low frequency word responses starting at 168 ms after stimulus presentation is consistent with previous findings indicating that this time window corresponds to lexical selection and segmental encoding in spoken production, contributing to the interpretation of results from spelling. It is well known that these methods do not provide reliable information regarding the specific source of neural signals. However, Perret & Qu point out that it is still the case that different cognitive processes do produce different and stable spatial patterns of activity on the scalp and that, therefore, changes in these spatial patterns over time can be exploited to determine the time points at which different cognitive processes come on line (see Figure 10.3, Perret & Qu, this volume). From this premise, spatio-temporal segmentation analysis can address specific cognitive issues. For example, Perret & Qu provide evidence that it is specifically the orthographic word form retrieval process (orthographic LTM) that gives rise to age of acquisition effects in spelling.

   This section has provided a brief overview of the neural substrates of the spelling processes while also summarizing the empirical logic by which neuroimaging methods with spatial or temporal specificity can be used to contribute to our understanding of the cognitive processes involved in producing written language.

2.2   *Testing Causality: Acquired, Developmental and Reversible Deficits*
As has often been pointed out, neuroimaging studies reveal brain areas that are active during tasks but that this activity does not indicate that these are *necessary* for specific cognitive functions. This is because areas that are not strictly necessary may nevertheless be active. A stronger test for the causal, necessary involvement of a specific brain area or a specific cognitive process comes from deficits. Deficits prove the opportunity to test whether or not a given cognitive process can be performed when a specific brain area or cognitive function is not available due to an acquired, developmental or reversible deficit (or lesion) affecting the brain area or process of interest. Quite simply, the causal role of a function is tested by removing the function from the equation and observing the consequences.

For example, we could ask whether the brain areas identified in the meta-analyses, although they are clearly reliably active during spelling, are actually necessary for spelling. We can do so by considering the consequences of damage to these areas. Figure 12.4 depicts the results of the Rapp, Purcell, Hillis, Capasso, & Miceli (2016) investigation of the neural substrates uniquely associated with acquired deficits subsequent to strokes affecting either orthographic LTM or WM. The figure indicates left posterior, superior parietal areas (in blue/pink) that were specifically associated with orthographic WM deficits, while two loci of damage (in red/orange)—left IFG and mid-fusiform/inferior temporal gyrus—were associated with orthographic LTM deficits. We can relate these findings to the activation peaks of the spelling network depicted in Figure 12.2. A comparison indicates that the areas of the spelling network associated with orthographic LTM in healthy participants (frequency but not length effects) are precisely the areas which, when damaged, result in orthographic LTM deficits. Similarly, areas of the spelling network associated with orthographic WM (length but not frequency effects) are associated with orthographic WM deficits when damaged. This correspondence between neuroimaging data from healthy controls and brain lesion data subsequent to stroke provides strong evidence regarding the causal role of these brain areas in the spelling process.

Establishing the causal role of specific cognitive processes can also be critical for understanding certain issues. For example, Waiman (Chapter 5, this volume) argues for the importance of testing for the causal role of motor processes in letter perception. While considerable evidence has been reported that motor information is recollected and active during perception, as Waiman explains, this could be merely epiphenomenal and not causal. This can been tested in a variety of ways, such as via motor interference paradigms that make sensorimotor networks unavailable allowing the experimenter to observe the consequences for visual perception, with the study of individuals with motor deficits or through temporary, reversible deficits caused by electrical stimulation approaches such as TMS (transcranial magnetic stimulation). Based on generally similar logic, the study of individuals with developmental deficits as described by Afonso et al. (Chapter 4, this volume) also allows for causal testing. A key question for understanding the acquisition of writing skills concerns the relationship between writing and other cognitive skills. Specifically, for example, one may want to know whether intact spoken language, reading or motor skills are necessary for successful writing acquisition. The study of individuals with primary deficits in spoken language, reading or motor coordination, as reported by Afonso et al., allows for testing of the causal role of spoken reading and motor skills in writing acquisition.

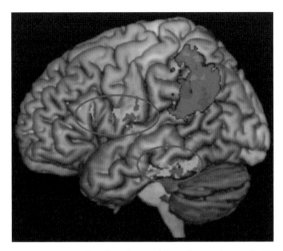

FIGURE 12.4   Results of a voxel-based mapping analysis
               of 27 individuals with acquired dys-
               graphia, adapted from Rapp et al. (2016).
               Red/yellow indicates voxels uniquely
               associated with orthographic LTM deficits
               (n=17) and blue/pink indicates voxels
               uniquely associated with orthographic
               WM deficits (n=10).

This brief review provides just a few examples illustrating the critical role to be played by studies of acquired, developmental and reversible deficits in testing hypotheses and furthering our understanding of spelling.

2.3   *Towards a Computational Theory of Writing*

The work described in this volume exemplifies the diversity of experimental methods and empirical approaches that have been successfully deployed to yield an impressive set of findings that have advanced our understanding of the writing process.

One way of evaluating our understanding is through the development and testing of computational models. Computational models instantiate our understanding while also allowing us to test our theories and generate new hypotheses. Some computational modelling of the writing process has been carried out, including work by Houghton, Glasspool, & Shallice (1994), Houghton & Zorzi (2003) and Goldberg & Rapp (2008) but this is still a relatively underdeveloped aspect of writing research. However, as our knowledge base becomes increasingly more detailed and complex and our measurements more fine-grained, this type of work will become increasingly useful. In the age of big data and powerful algorithmic approaches, computational models and the theoretical developments that they can generate will become increasingly relevant. Several chapters in this volume provide examples of types of data which may be especially well-suited for computational modelling. Examples include questions of individual differences such as those identified by Bonin and Méot (Chapter 7, this volume), the detailed sensitivities to graphotactic patterns reported by Pacton et al., (Chapter 3, this volume) and the variability in stroke patterns documented by Séraphin-Thibon et al. (Chapter 9, this volume).

What is the goal for 21st century research on writing? It must be to develop detailed theories of the writing process that explain and predict individual human performance and also serve as the basis of optimized, personalized intervention in cases of impairment. It should be clear from this volume that it is through the continued deployment of these highly productive empirical methods, their increased integration and the development of computationally explicit models that progress towards this goal will continue to be made.

Acknowledgements

Support for this work was provided by the generous support of grant 006740 from the NIDCD.

References

Afonso, O., & Alvarez, C.J. (this volume). Measuring writing durations in handwriting research: What do they tell us about the spelling process?

Afonso, O., Connelly, V., & Barnett, A. (this volume). Struggling with writing: An examination of writing difficulties in Specific Languag Impairment, Developmental Dyslexia and Developmental Coordination Disorder

Bonin, P., & Méot, A. (this volume). Individual differences and task differences in skilled spelling.

Buchwald, A., & Rapp, B. (2009). Distinctions between orthographic long-term memory and working memory. *Cognitive Neuropsychology, 26,* 724–751

Chomsky, N., & Halle, M. (1968). The Sound Pattern of English. Chicago: The University of Chicago Press.

Cohen, L., Lehéricy, S. Chochon, F., Lemer, C., Rivaud, S., & Dehaene, S. (2002). Language-specific tuning of visual cortex? Functional properties of the Visual Word Form Area. *Brain, 125,* 1054–1069.

Damian, M. (this volume). A role of phonology in orthographic production? A historical perspective and some recent new evidence.

Dehaene, S. (2009). Reading in the Brain: The New Science of How we Read. Penguin.

DeMarco, A. R., Wilson, S.M., Rising, K., Rapcsak, S.Z. & Beeson, P.M. (2017). Neural substrates of sublexical processing for spelling. *Brain & Language, 164*, 118–128.

Rapp, B., & Dufor, O. (2011). The neurotopography of written word production: An fMRI investigation of the distribution of sensitivity to length and frequency. *Journal Cognitive Neuroscience, 12*, 4067–4081.

Finger, S. (2001). Origins of Neuroscience: A History of explorations into Brain Function. Oxford: Oxford University Press.

Goldberg, A., & Rapp, B. (2008). Is compound chaining the serial order mechanism of spelling? A simple recurrent network investigation. *Cognitive Neuropsychology, 25*(2), 218–255.

Houghton, G., & Zorzi, M. (2003) Normal and impaired spelling in a connectionist dual-route architecture. Cognitive Neuropsychology, 20, 115–162.

Houghton, G., Glasspool, D.W., & Shallice, T. (1994). Spelling and serial recall: Insights from a competitive queueing model. In G.D.A. Brown & N.C. Ellis (Eds.), Handbook of spelling: Theory, process and intervention (pp. 365–404). Chichester, UK: John Wiley & Sons.

Ludersdorfer, P., Kronbichler, M., & Wimmer, H. (2015). Accessing orthographic representations from speech: The role of the left ventral occipitotemporal cortex in spelling. *Human Brain Mapping, 36*, 1393–1406.

Pacton, S. Fayol, M., Nys, M., & Peereman, R. (this volume). Implicit statistical learning of graphotactic knowledge and lexical orthographic acquisition.

Perret, C. & Qu, Q. (this volume). EEG methods of exploring handwritten production.

Planton, S., Jucla, M., Roux, F.-E., & Démonet, J.-F. (2013). The "handwriting brain": A meta-analysis of neuroimaging studies of motor versus orthographic processes. *Cortex, 49*, 2772–2787.

Purcell, J.J., Turkeltaub, P.E., Eden, G.F., & Rapp, B. (2011). Examining the central and peripheral processes of written word production through meta-analysis. *Frontiers in psychology, 2:1, doi:10.3389/fpsyg.2011.00239.*

Rapp, B., Benzing, L., & Caramazza, A. (1997). The autonomy of lexical orthography. *Cognitive Neuropsychology, 14*, 71–104.

Rapp, B., & Caramazza, A. (1997). From graphemes to abstract letter shapes: Levels of representation in written spelling. Journal of Experimental Psychology: *Human Perception and Performance, 23*, 1130–1152.

Rapp, B., & Damian, M. (2018). From thought to action: Producing written language. In, Rueschemeyer, S.A. & Gaskell, G. (Eds.) Oxford Handbook of Psycholinguistics. (pp. 398–431) Oxford University Press.

Rapp, B., & Dufor, O. (2011). The neurotopography of written word production: An fMRI investigation of the distribution of sensitivity to length and frequency. *Journal of Cognitive Neuroscience, 23*, 4067–4081.

Rapp, B., & Lipka, K. (2011). The literate brain: The relationship between reading and spelling. *Journal of Cognitive Neuroscience, 23, 5*, 1180–1197.

Rapp, B., Purcell, J., Hillis, A.B., Capasso, R., & Miceli, G. (2016). Neural bases of orthographic long-term memory and working memory in dysgraphia. *Brain, 139*, 588–604.

Rapp, B., Shea, J., & Wiley, R. (in preparation). Communication in the digital age: The increasing use of written language in daily life.

Séraphin-Thibon, L., Gerber, S., & Kandel, S. (this volume). Analyzing variability in upper-case letter production in adults: A methodological contribution.

Tainturier, M.-J. (this volume). BAST: A theory of bilingual spelling in alphabetic systems.

Wamain, Y. (this volume). The role of handwriting in reading: Behavioral and neurophysiological evidence of motor involvement in letter recognition.

Index